Gramsci on Tahrir

Reading Gramsci

General Editors:

Peter Ives, Professor of Politics, University of Winnipeg
and
Adam David Morton, Professor of Political Economy,
University of Sydney

Also available

Gramsci, Culture and Anthropology
An Introductory Text
Kate Crehan

Language and Hegemony in Gramsci
Peter Ives

Unravelling Gramsci:
Hegemony and Passive Revolution in the Global Political Economy
Adam David Morton

Subalternity, Antagonism, Autonomy:
Constructing the Political Subject
Massimo Modonesi
Translated by Adriana V. Rendón Garrido and Philip Roberts

Solidarity without Borders
Gramscian Perspectives on Migration and Civil Society Alliances
Edited by Óscar García Agustín and Martin Bak Jørgensen

Gramsci on Tahrir

Revolution and Counter-Revolution in Egypt

Brecht De Smet

PlutoPress
www.plutobooks.com

First published 2016 by Pluto Press
345 Archway Road, London N6 5AA

www.plutobooks.com

British Library Cataloguing in Publication Data
A catalogue record for this book is available from the British Library

ISBN   978 0 7453 3558 2   Hardback
ISBN   978 0 7453 3557 5   Paperback
ISBN   978 1 7837 1345 5   PDF eBook
ISBN   978 1 7837 1347 9   Kindle eBook
ISBN   978 1 7837 1346 2   EPUB eBook

This book is printed on paper suitable for recycling and made from fully managed
and sustained forest sources. Logging, pulping and manufacturing processes are
expected to conform to the environmental standards of the country of origin.

Typeset by Stanford DTP Services, Northampton, England
Simultaneously printed in the European Union and the United States of America

Contents

Series Preface

Antonio Gramsci (1891–1937) is one of the most frequently referenced political theorists and cultural critics of the twentieth century. His pre-disciplinary ideas and especially his articulation of hegemony are commonly referred to in international relations, social and political theory, political economy, historical sociology, critical geography, postcolonial studies, cultural studies, literary criticism, feminism, new social movements, critical anthropology, education studies, media studies and a host of other fields. And yet, his actual writings are steeped in the complex details of history, politics, philosophy, and culture that shaped Italy's formation as a nation-state as well as in the wider turmoil of twentieth-century world history.

Gramsci began his practical and intellectual odyssey when he moved to Turin University (1911). This move to mainland industrial Italy raised cultural and political contradictions for the young Sardinian, whose identity had been deeply formed by the conditions of uneven development in the 'South'. These issues were pursued by Gramsci whilst he devoted his energy to journalism (between 1914 and 1918) in the newspapers *Il Grido del Popolo, Avanti!* and *La Città Futura*. His activity centred on the Factory Council movement in Turin – a radical labour mobilisation – and editorship of the journal *L'Ordine Nuovo* (1919–20). Exasperated by the Italian Socialist Party's lack of leadership and effective action during the *Biennio Rosso*, Gramsci turned his attention to the founding and eventual leadership of the Italian Communist Party (PCd'I) as well as the organisation of the workers' newspaper *L'Unità* until 1926. Gramsci spent from May 1922 to December 1923 in the Soviet Union actively involved in organisational issues within the Communist International (Comintern). This included functioning on the Executive Committee of the Comintern in Moscow as the representative of the PCd'I and as a member of various commissions examining organisational, political, and procedural problems that linked the various national communist parties. During this period, Gramsci had direct contact with Leon Trotsky and led discussions on the 'Italian Question', including the united front tactics to tackle Fascism, the trade union relationship, and the limits of party centralism. These issues were developed by Gramsci through the work of ideological hegemony carried out by the PCd'I and, following his Moscow period, as a central author and architect of 'The Lyon Theses' –

a collection of positional statements on the tactics and strategies needed in response to Fascism. The theses are regarded as a major survey of the conditions of uneven development confronting social forces within Italy and the European states-system at the time.

By 1926, after drafting his famous essay 'Some Aspects of the Southern Question', Gramsci was arrested as a Communist Party deputy by the Fascist authorities and was incarcerated until a few days before his death in 1937. Gramsci wrote almost 500 letters in prison; over half were to his sister-in-law, Tatiana Schucht, who was living in Rome and became his key supporter and his most frequent visitor. She also conveyed Gramsci's ideas to another significant patron, Piero Sraffa, the Italian economist then at Cambridge. These letters constitute a rich mixture of intellectual, cultural, and political analysis as well as representing the daily struggle of prison life including Gramsci's increasingly severe health problems. But the most enduring and influential component of his legacy is the 33 notebooks penned between 1929 and 1936 that together constitute the *Quaderni del carcere* (*Prison Notebooks*). Tatiana Schucht hid these notebooks in a vault at the *Banca Commerciale Italiana* while she arranged for their transportation to Moscow. Publication of the *Prison Notebooks* in Italian ensued from the late 1940s onwards and has continued in various languages ever since.

The breadth of the above political and intellectual journey is perhaps matched by the depth of detail and coverage contained within Gramsci's pre-prison and prison writings. The study of intellectuals in Italy, their origins and grouping according to cultural currents; his engagement with, and critique of, Italy's most important intellectual of the time, Benedetto Croce; the study of comparative linguistics and the Italian language question; analysis of the Sicilian writer Luigi Pirandello and the potential his plays offered for transforming Italian culture and society; and discussion of the role of the serialised novel and popular taste in literature would be later expanded into a wider plan. This chiefly focused on Italian history in the nineteenth century, with special attention being directed to Italy's faltering entrance into capitalist modernity under conditions of 'passive revolution', including the imposition of a 'standard' Italian language; the theory of history and historiography; and the expansion of the capitalist labour process through assembly plant production techniques beyond the United States under the rubric of 'Americanism and Fordism'. In summary, issues of hegemony, consciousness, and the revolutionary process are at the centre of Gramsci's attention. It is for such reasons that Antonio Gramsci can be regarded as one of the most significant Marxists of the twentieth century, who merits inclusion in any register of classical social theorists.

Reading Gramsci, however, is no easy task. He plunges into the complexities of debates of his time that are now obscure to many readers and engages in an enormous range of topics that at first seem unrelated. Moreover, the prison conditions and his own method yield a set of open-ended, fragmented, and intricately layered *Prison Notebooks* whose connections and argumentation do not lead linearly from one note to the next, but seem to ripple and weave in many directions. This has sometimes led to aggravation on the part of Gramsci scholars when they see how often his name is invoked by those with quite partial or superficial understanding of these complexities. It has also generated frustration on the part of those who want to use Gramsci's ideas to illuminate their own studies, analyses, and political acumen. After all, while Gramsci himself was a meticulous researcher with a rigorous philological method, he was deeply committed to people understanding their own political and cultural contexts in order to engage and change them. These points, about the necessity of deploying an openness of reading Gramsci to capture the branching out of his thought *and* the necessity of deploying a practical interest in understanding the here and now of contemporary events, were central to Joseph Buttigieg's original idea for initiating this 'Reading Gramsci' series. Buttigieg's contributions to Gramscian scholarship extend also to his monumental and superbly edited and translated English critical edition of the *Prison Notebooks* (Columbia University Press), the final volumes of which are still in process. In keeping with Buttigieg's initial goals, this series aims to provide expert guides to key features and themes in Gramsci's writings in combination with the pressing political, social, and cultural struggles of our time. Rather than 'applying' Gramsci, the point of the series is to provide monographs that think through and internalise Gramsci's method of thinking about alternative historical and contemporary social conditions. Given that no single study can encapsulate the above political and intellectual depth and breadth, each volume in the 'Reading Gramsci' series is focused in such a way as to open readers to specific aspects of his work as well as raise new questions about our contemporary history.

Peter Ives
Adam David Morton

Acknowledgments

This book develops the argument I first presented in my article 'Revolution and Counter-Revolution in Egypt' (2014a), which became the subject of a stimulating debate with Joel Beinin in *Jadaliyya* (Beinin 2014a, 2014b; De Smet 2014b, 2014c). This exchange has helped me to clarify my position on passive revolution, rendering the concept more precise and my understanding more sophisticated. Hence any theoretical inconsistency between this book and the original article should be resolved to the advantage of the text at hand.

The content that follows also draws on my dissertation about the pedagogic relation between Egyptian political activists and the workers' movement, which has been published as *A Dialectical Pedagogy of Revolt: Gramsci, Vygotsky, and the Egyptian Revolution* (2015). This monograph was the fruit of a Ph.D. grant from the Special Research Fund at Ghent University. I thank my supervisor and now colleague Sami Zemni for the support and confidence he has shown me throughout the years at Ghent University. I would also like to thank the members of my examination committee, Maha Abdelrahman, Gilbert Achcar, Colin Barker, and Jo Van Steenbergen, who continued to give me valuable advice and assistance long after my Ph.D. defence in 2012.

The text also incorporates material from other publications (De Smet 2012, 2014b, 2014d; Versieren and De Smet 2014, 2015; Zemni, De Smet, and Bogaert 2013). I am very grateful for the cooperation with Koen Bogaert, Sami Zemni, and Jelle Versieren on these occasions and I acknowledge their influence on my own work.

Although the responsibility for the content of this book is fully mine, I am indebted to Jamie Allinson, Matthias Lievens, Seppe Malfait, Adam Morton, Sara Salem, Mathijs van de Sande and Jelle Versieren for their insightful comments on draft versions of the manuscript. Conversations, offline and online discussions, and collaborations that inspired parts of the content were held with Andy Blunden, Gennaro Gervasio, Neil Ketchley, Vivienne Matthies-Boon, and Andrea Teti. My gratitude also goes to David Castle of Pluto Press and Hesham Sallam of *Jadaliyya* for their correct and engaged editorial management of my work. I thank the editorial board of the 'Reading Gramsci' series, and especially Adam Morton, for their enthusiasm and support for my book project. Finally, I would like to thank Rudolf De Jong and Tilly Mulder of the

Netherlands–Flemish Institute in Cairo for allowing me to organize the summer school on 'Bread, Freedom, and Social Justice' in 2015, which was a great opportunity to discuss some of the topics of this book with Egyptian and foreign students.

Between 2008 and 2012 I interviewed Egyptian activists and trade unionists, listening to their stories, observing some of their meetings and actions, talking and discussing with them about politics and life in Egypt. Few of these precious conversations have become an explicit part of this book. Nonetheless, they are ever present below the surface, pushing the argument forward. Unfortunately I cannot list here the more than 100 labour, youth, and political activists without whom my work wouldn't have been possible. Nevertheless, for a variety of reasons, I would like to mention Haisam Hassan, Fatma Ramadan, and Wael Tawfiq, each of whom has played a key role in my research.

Whereas most of my previous work has focused on the agency of the workers' movement and the persistent possibility of emancipation, this book explores the theme of their continuous negation. Although the situation in Egypt and elsewhere in the Arab world may seem bleak at the moment, my central message is one of hope, not despair. The history of Egypt shows many instances of strong, emancipatory movements from below. We may wish to turn Gramsci's aphorism that he's 'a pessimist because of intelligence, but an optimist because of will' on its head; with the popular 'will to power' currently waning, what remains is our rational understanding that in the past things have changed for the better and in the future they will inevitably change again.

Abbreviations

ADNP	Arab Democratic Nasserist Party
ASU	Arab Socialist Union
CPE	Communist Party of Egypt
CSF	Central Security Forces
DMNL	Democratic Movement for National Liberation
ECP	Egyptian Communist Party
EDLC	Egyptian Democratic Labour Congress
EFITU	Egyptian Federation of Independent Trade Unions
EMNL	Egyptian Movement for National Liberation
EPCSPI	Egyptian Popular Committee in Solidarity with the Palestinian Intifada
ERSAP	Economic Reform and Structural Adjustment Programme
FIS	Front Islamique du Salut
GATT	General Agreement on Tariffs and Trade
GFETU	General Federation of Egyptian Trade Unions
GFLU	General Federation of Labour Unions
GFLUKE	General Federation of Labour Unions in the Kingdom of Egypt
GID	General Investigations Department
HMLC	Hisham Mubarak Law Centre
ISI	Import Substitution Industrialization
MTWU	Manual Trades Workers' Union
NAC	National Association for Change
NCWS	National Committee for Workers and Students
NDF	National Democratic Front
NDP	National Democratic Party
NFTUE	National Federation of Trade Unions in Egypt
NSF	National Salvation Front
OWS	Occupy Wall Street
RCC	Revolutionary Command Council
RETAU	Real Estate Tax Authority Union
RS	Revolutionary Socialists (Tendency)
SCAF	Supreme Council of Armed Forces
SSIS	State Security Investigations Sector
WCNL	Workers' Committee for National Liberation

1. Introduction

Egypt 2011. A small group of activists from a variety of leftist organizations, youth movements, opposition parties, human rights centres, and football clubs has called for a demonstration in Midan Tahrir (Liberation Square) on Tuesday 25 January. The protesters demand 'the sacking of the country's interior minister, the cancelling of Egypt's perpetual emergency law, which suspends basic civil liberties, and a new term limit on the presidency that would bring to an end the 30-year rule of president Hosni Mubarak' (Shenker 2011a). Neither the activists nor the security apparatus really expect the demonstration to attract tens of thousands of ordinary Egyptians, let alone be the herald of a mass uprising (Sowers 2012: 4). After their initial bewilderment, the Central Security Forces (CSF) try to repress the peaceful protests with water cannons, sound bombs, batons, rubber bullets, and tear gas. Demonstrators retaliate with rocks and bricks. Cairo becomes an urban battlefield with unremitting street fights between police forces and thousands of protesters. The protests in Egypt's capital spark off similar demonstrations in Alexandria and in cities in the Delta, the Canal Zone, and Upper Egypt. Throughout the '18 Days' of popular uprising, mass gatherings and violent countermeasures up the ante, transforming the original, tame demands into the revolutionary slogan *al-sha'b yurid isqat al-nizam* (the people want the fall of the regime).[1] Protesters occupy Tahrir Square, workers strike, and ordinary citizens burn down hated police stations and party offices of the ruling National Democratic Party (NDP). Suddenly people realize they are making a revolution – there is no way back. Pressured by Egypt's panicking elites, Mubarak, Egypt's president since 1981, steps down.

The revolutionary events, first in Tunisia and then in regional heavyweight Egypt, reinvigorated mass emancipatory politics throughout the Middle East and the world at large. Protest movements such as Indignados and Occupy Wall Street (OWS) were directly inspired by the apparent success of the Tahrir occupation. Through Al Jazeera and other (social) media outlets the uprising was literally projected into the living rooms of the global community, offering a powerful, contemporary example of a genuine popular revolution. Whereas alter-globalization and anti-war mobilizations in the decade before 2011 had reinvigorated a critique of capitalism and imperialism, the revolutionary movements in the Middle East functioned as a salient reminder of the possibility of a spontaneous popular mass movement in the twenty-first century. Moreover, the interpenetration of the political and the social struggle, expressed in the slogan *aysh, horreya, adala egtemaʿeya* (bread, freedom, social justice) and the material conjunction of political protests and economic strikes underlined the continued validity of Marx's and Trotsky's concept of *permanent revolution* (see Choonara 2011). The workers' movement played a crucial role, not only in disorganizing state power during the final days of Mubarak's rule, but also in the decade-long preparation of the uprising. The insurrection fertilized the organizational seeds of independent trade unionism that were already planted before 2011. New syndicalist formations popped up at the local and national level and every section of the Egyptian working class became involved in strikes and collective actions to defend material livelihoods and the right to organize. Permanent revolution, in its core meaning of a transition from political to social emancipation, was not an empty slogan or wishful thinking, but a real possibility. Additionally, the wave of international protests inspired by Tahrir illustrated the geographic dimension of the 'uninterrupted' revolution. Tahrir came to represent the potential for a global rupture of what Antonio Gramsci called the *duration* of capitalism – the 'empty time' of a social formation that had outlived itself (see Thomas 2009: 152). Duration is history twiddling its thumbs, not in the sense that nothing is going on, but that individual events progress linearly and sequentially, without really becoming entwined and capable of unleashing a transformative dynamic. Conversely, an *epoch* is a 'historical break, in the sense that a whole series of questions which piled up individually ... have precisely formed a "mound", modifying the general structure of the previous process' (Gramsci 1971: 106, Q15§59). Could the events of the 'Arab Spring' – an orientalist misnomer – constitute a new epoch?

Yet by 2015 the outcomes of the Egyptian uprising were all but revolutionary. The military, bureaucratic, and civil security elites from the Mubarak era had reasserted their full control over the state apparatus. The economic structure, based on a neoliberal strategy of accumulation, remained unchanged. After four years the popular movement was, at least momentarily, smothered by a triumphant counter-revolution. However, the most peculiar feature of the ongoing counter-revolution was not its success, but the fact that it had been accomplished on the waves of mass mobilization. The current military strongman, Abdel Fattah al-Sisi, who was elected president in 2014, came to power through a clever and agile appropriation of the Tamarod (Rebel) campaign, which rallied hundreds of thousands, if not millions of ordinary Egyptians in the streets. The

Egyptian experience raises important questions about the *agency* of counter-revolution, the protagonists of which are able to dislodge the dynamic of permanent revolution and gain popular legitimacy despite the enduring crisis of state and economy.

Reading (with) Gramsci

Just a few months after the uprising, Bassem Hassan claimed that 'the way things have been unfolding since last January resembles more Gramsci's notion of caesarism than the scenario of a victorious popular revolution' (Hassan 2011: 4). In this book I hope to shed light on the dynamic of revolution and restoration, not only by 'reading Gramsci' to unearth the meaning of central concepts such as hegemony, passive revolution, and Caesarism, but mainly by reading the Egyptian Revolution *with* Gramsci to understand the processes at hand. Conversely, through a discussion of the Egyptian case, I aim to contribute to the field of Gramsci studies and especially to the discussion of his notion of Caesarism, which has not yet been the object of much scholarly debate (see Fontana 2004). Nevertheless, my goal is not to investigate Gramsci's thought in a genealogical or philological way, but to *deploy* his concepts in order to construct new forms of understanding appropriate to the present. I admit that this approach runs the risk of turning into what Hal Draper (2011a: 21) called 'quotation-mongering' and Roccu (2012: 20) 'a *prêt-à-porter* version of Gramsci': using decontextualized fragments of the *Prison Notebooks* as sources of authority to 'prove' one's own point. However, such fragments can also be deployed in a less apologetic and a more dialogical way, as conceptual threads that weave together a new narrative, which engages with problems relevant to our time and place. Moreover, as Gramsci himself appears to indicate (Q4§1), there is a coherent leitmotiv or 'rhythm of thought' operating throughout the *Prison Notebooks* that transcends its atomistic character. But how are the ideas of a Sardinian Marxist who was politically active almost a century ago relevant for our current day and age?

Antonio Gramsci (1891–1937), born into a Sardinian middle-class family, joined the Italian Socialist Party in 1913, becoming an editor and journalist. His political views were influenced by socialist and nationalist circles and by the industrialization of Turin, which attracted proletarianized[2] farmers from the Italian South. Building on thinkers such as Antonio Labriola (1843–1904) and Benedetto Croce (1866–1952), Gramsci complemented the 'vulgar' Marxism that circulated in the party with a more sophisticated Hegelian outlook. During the First World War Gramsci was active in the organization and education of Turin workers.

After the war, he set up the revolutionary socialist weekly *L'Ordine Nuovo* (The New Order) which became the voice of Bolshevik politics in Italy. In 1920, the group around *L'Ordine Nuovo* played a crucial role in assisting the workers' councils that emerged spontaneously during the general strike and factory occupations in Turin in 1919 and 1920. The compromise negotiated between moderate trade union leaders, the Socialist Party, and the state representing the interests of landholders and factory owners not only stabilized the capitalist system for a brief period, but it also blocked the self-emancipatory movement of the Italian working class (Le Blanc 1996: 281). Disillusioned with the reformist policies of the Socialist Party, Gramsci and many other Italian socialists founded the Italian Communist Party in 1921.

Until 1924, the leadership of the party was in the hands of Amadeo Bordiga (1889–1970), who was criticized by Lenin in 'Left-Wing Communism: an Infantile Disorder' (1920) for his ultra-left politics. Whereas Gramsci advocated a united front against the rise of Fascism, Bordiga insisted on shielding the party from 'bourgeois' influences such as the Socialist Party. In 1924 Gramsci was elected into parliament. In the same year Bordiga was arrested and Gramsci took over the leadership of the Italian Communist Party until he was himself imprisoned in 1926, despite his parliamentary immunity. He remained in prison until 1937, when he died following a deterioration in his already weak health. While imprisoned, he wrote 34 notebooks, which dealt with diverse topics, ranging from political theory, through philosophy, to Italian history.

Only after the Second World War, when the Italian Communist Party published select sections of the *Prison Notebooks*, did Gramsci's ideas begin to circulate. Gramsci's thought was appropriated by the Italian 'Eurocommunist' movement, which sought to anchor its reformist politics in the works of the respected Marxist. In 'The Antinomies of Antonio Gramsci' (1976) Perry Anderson famously criticized this reformist instrumentalization of Gramsci's ideas. While defending Gramsci's revolutionary project, Anderson rejected the coherence of his thought, which, due to Fascist censorship, the use of obscure terminology, and its fragmented form, appeared contradictory and multi-interpretable. Recent scholarship, however, has affirmed the internal consistency of Gramsci's concepts (see Thomas 2009).

Gramsci clearly positioned his thought in the debates about the development of capitalism and revolutionary strategy after the First World War. Consequently, he should not be read as a cultural or political 'theorist', but as a *Marxist* concerned with developing a philosophy of praxis: theory as a necessary tool in the emancipatory struggles of subaltern[3] groups. In this regard, Gramsci should be read along with other Marxists – in the first place Marx, Engels, and Lenin, but also Trotsky, who functions in many ways as a complementary thinker (see Burawoy 1989: 793; Thomas 2015). The starting text for such a reading is Marx's 'Preface to a Contribution to the Critique of Political Economy' (1859), as Gramsci himself indicated: 'It would seem that the theory of the passive revolution is a necessary critical corollary to the Introduction to the Critique of Political Economy' (Gramsci 1971: 114; Q15§62; see also Gramsci 1971: 106–7; Q15§7). In the 'Preface' Marx famously claimed that:

> In the social production of their existence, men inevitably enter into definite relations, which are independent of their will, namely relations of production appropriate to a given stage in the development of their material forces of production. The totality of these relations of production constitutes the economic structure of society, the real foundation, on which arises a legal and political superstructure and to which correspond definite forms of social consciousness.[4] The mode of production of material life conditions the general process of social, political and intellectual life. It is not the consciousness of men that determines their existence, but their social existence that determines their consciousness. At a certain stage of development, the material productive forces of society come into conflict with the existing relations of production or – this merely expresses the same thing in legal terms – with the property relations within the framework of which they have operated hitherto. From forms of development of the productive forces these relations turn into their fetters. Then begins an era of social revolution. The changes in the economic foundation lead sooner or later to the transformation of the whole immense super-structure....
>
> No social formation is ever destroyed before all the productive forces for which it is sufficient have been developed, and new superior relations of production never replace older ones before the material conditions for their existence have matured within the framework of the old society.
>
> Mankind thus inevitably sets itself only such tasks as it is able to solve, since closer examination will always show that the problem itself arises only when the material conditions for its solution are already present or at least in the course of formation. (Marx 1987: 263)

Gramsci's concept of passive revolution directly addressed Marx's general remarks regarding societal *crisis*, *revolution*, and *transformation*. These three concepts serve as threads that tie this book together.

Discarding millenarian interpretations of the First World War and the rise of Fascism, Gramsci transcended the eschatological binary of 'socialism or barbarism'. Instead of taking capitalist crisis as his main problematic, he tried to comprehend capitalism's historical stubbornness and agility in the face of its recurring crises. His insights are important to our understanding of the persistence of capitalism today, despite the ongoing political and economic crisis of its current, neoliberal form. Arguably, his concept of passive revolution stands at the centre of such an analysis, functioning as the conceptual antipode of permanent revolution (see Thomas 2015).

Outline

After this introductory first chapter I have organized the book into two parts. Readers are warned that Gramsci arrives in Egypt only in the second part of the book. Part I, 'On the Subject of Revolution', offers a theoretical discussion of Gramsci's concepts of passive revolution and Caesarism, whereas Part II, 'Gramsci in Egypt', engages with the specific case of the Egyptian revolution. When I was writing 'On the Subject of Revolution' I chose not to present Gramsci's 'theory' in a schematic, 'logical' manner, but instead to let the concepts emerge organically as part of a historical narrative about the constitution of the capitalist mode of production and bourgeois society. The goal here is not to present the past, but to evoke the rich, historical concreteness from which Gramsci distilled his concepts. Chapter 2, 'From Bourgeois to Permanent Revolution', kicks off the story by discussing the English and French trajectories of 'bourgeois revolution'. Concepts such as 'hegemony' and 'intellectuals' are, for example, explained by bringing them into the orbit of Jacobinism. The chapter ends with a comment on Marx's notion of the revolution 'in permanence', which delivers a historical promise that remained unfulfilled. This sets the stage for the next chapter, 'A Criterion for Interpretation', which is devoted entirely to the concept of passive revolution. I closely follow Gramsci's narration of the 'Risorgimento', the unification of Italy, in order to arrive at his passive-revolutionary interpretation of the process of Italian state formation. I continue with his extension of the concept to the domain of the constitution of European capitalism in general. Subsequently, I illuminate Gramsci's application of the interpretive criterion of passive revolution to the process of the *reconstitution* of capitalism as a means of understanding its stubborn survival. Attention is paid to imperialism, Fascism, and Fordism/Americanism as global reconfigurations of existing historical blocs that temporarily displace both the fettering of productive forces and the threat of social revolution. At this point Gramsci's understanding of passive revolution as a critical corollary to Marx's 'Preface' shows its true significance. Finally, I pose the question of whether neoliberalism can be interpreted from the perspective of passive revolution, critically engaging with scholars who suggest that neoliberal counter-reform is of a different order. I suggest that we should take seriously Gramsci's own definition of passive revolution as *a criterion of interpretation*, and deploy it accordingly.

Chapter 4, 'Caesarism', returns to the question of revolution. I explore the meaning of revolution and conclude that the Marxist tradition contains both an objectivist and subjectivist perspective, which respectively focus on the external outcomes and internal dynamics of the process. I use the subjectivist angle to re-approach the concept of permanent revolution as the development of social emancipation from the conditions of political emancipation. The difference between political and social emancipation also brings us back to the problem of the state. With a brief sidetrack into Hegel, which is interpellated by Gramsci's use of the terms 'mechanical' and 'organic', I differentiate between a mechanical, chemical, and organic relation between state and class. This distinction will prove crucial in my discussion of bourgeois hegemony and Caesarism in particular. Before I can move to Gramsci's concept of Caesarism, I address Marx's notion of Bonapartism, concentrating on the rule of Napoleon III. This clears the way for Gramsci's treatment of the topic, which expands on Marx's understanding by discerning qualitative and quantitative, progressive and reactionary, classic and modern, military and civil variants. I finish the chapter by reflecting on the possibility and desirability of 'progressive' Caesarism. This concludes the first part of the book.

At this point the reader might wonder about the relevancy of the European historical trajectory and the universal applicability of Gramsci's 'Western' concepts to the particular Egyptian case. This is a healthy critical reflex, seeing that liberal, conservative, and socialistic Eurocentrist modernization narratives have functioned as ideological means to subordinate, discipline, and control non-Western societies. The Western modern experience has served as an ideal typical standard that other nations have to follow in order to become 'civilized' and 'developed'. Here, however, a concern for Eurocentrism is misplaced. Before I continue with the structure of the book, I address this issue in a few cursory remarks.

Firstly, with the rise of capitalism and the forceful integration of different parts of the world into the emerging global market economy separate histories became for the first time a shared world history. The universalist concepts that are deployed by Marx and Gramsci to criticize capitalism are not transcendental categories or products of free-floating thought, but they express the material generalization of capital, both in a spatial and social sense. In other words, their critique does not presume some universalist human essence, modelled on Western premises, but the violent construction of the universal life world of capitalism. This process of universalization does not necessarily encompass a tendency towards cultural and economic homogenization and identity – on the contrary, as explained in Chapter 5, the expansion of capitalism is fundamentally characterized by unevenness, which turns external differences into internal contradictions. Analysing the relation between the Italian North and the South, Gramsci shows his strength as a thinker of unevenness and difference *within* capitalist totality (see Rosengarten 2009). Permanent revolution as a general strategy is only true for capitalism in general; its concrete form as proletarian hegemony has to be developed for each particular form of capitalism. The task of deconstructing orientalism and knowing the 'Other' is primarily *political*, practically achieved by forging alliances, organizing solidarity, and struggling together. Consequently, instead of belonging to a culturalist category of reified 'Western' thought, Gramsci's concepts operate as subaltern weapons of emancipation from capital, which have to be *translated* to different struggles. As I point out in Chapter 3, this idea of 'translation' was very important to Gramsci.

Secondly, a clear distinction should be made between the normative thesis that capitalist modernity is intrinsically Western and should be emulated by non-Western nations, and the analytical argument that the capitalist mode of production originated in the West. The first statement is Eurocentrist; the second one not necessarily so. Some critical authors, especially from the dependency school or operating in a world-system analysis framework, find the idea that 'capitalism' originated historically in Western Europe (or, more specifically, England) and 'diffused' from there already Eurocentric and a form of colonizing thought (for example Blaut 1993; 1999). They understand the 'Western origin thesis' as a colonial view of Europe's civilizational superiority and exceptionalism. Often their rejection of this thesis includes a – correct – acknowledgment of the role of pre-industrial colonialism and global developments in the rise of capitalism, and/or a – less correct – assertion that other countries were well on their way to developing a capitalism of their own until this autonomous movement was blocked by colonialism. However, from a Marxian perspective, such a comprehension of capitalism is problematic as it equates commercialization, the amassing of wealth, the expansion of the world market, and the presence of money capital to the capitalist mode of production, not distinguishing between the conditions, obstacles, and stimulants for the emergence of capitalism and the process of the actual becoming and subsequent development of this new social form (see Wood 2007). I return to this point in the next chapter. Moreover, the final chapters of Marx's *Capital* make the point that capitalism's originating in England was nothing to be proud of and did not reflect any civilizational superiority – quite the contrary. In any case, despite our normative rejection of the colonial and imperialist expansion of capitalism, we cannot deny the very fact of its historical 'diffusion' – and the diffusion or translation of many concepts and practices of struggle of Western subaltern groups by non-Western actors. For example, the French Revolution is important to Egyptian history because it has become an integral part of its own trajectory (and vice versa), shaping both elite and subaltern goals, methods, and discourses.

Returning to the book, the second section, 'Gramsci in Egypt', looks at the 25 January Revolution from a long-duration perspective, working its way upwards from the nineteenth century to 2015. Gramsci's concepts are deployed to gain an insight into Egypt's historical trajectory and, conversely, the story of Egypt's past and present is told in order to render his theory concrete and enter into dialogue with other Marxists. Chapter 5, 'Passive Revolution and Imperialism', begins with an overview of Egypt's gradual subordination to British imperialism. I take a moment to explain Trotsky's theory of uneven and combined development and permanent revolution, which show an emancipatory way out of the Scylla and Charybdis of 'too much' and 'too little' capitalist development. Yet, the survival of a reconfigured colonial historical bloc after Egypt's 1919 revolution also necessitates the interpretative criterion of passive revolution for understanding this episode. The phase of national capitalism between the 1920s and 1940s is found wanting, incapable of solving the tasks of the 'bourgeois revolution'. A new organic crisis is building up, coming to the surface after the Second World War in the form of an explosion of protests and strikes. I close the chapter with a few general remarks on the relation between passive revolution and imperialism. The following chapter, 'Lineages of Egyptian Caesarism', opens with a flash forward to February 2011 and the 'soft coup' of the Supreme Council of Armed Forces (SCAF). The capacity of the Egyptian military to displace popular initiative is retraced to the historical lineage of Nasserism. The debate about the character of Nasserism leads me to the concepts of 'deflected permanent revolution' and 'proletarian Bonapartism'. Then I return to the Egyptian case, discussing the limits of the Nasserist project and its subsequent demise in the late 1960s and 1970s. I conclude with a reflection on the various 'shades' of passive revolution.

I start Chapter 7, 'The 25 January Revolution', with a detailed account of the form that the global neoliberal offensive took in Egypt. I return to the discussion in Chapter 4 about the character of revolution and I briefly describe the political and social movements that prepared the way for the 25 January uprising. Next I give a description of the flow of events during the 18 Days, which is followed by an analysis of 'The Republic of Tahrir' from a subjectivist perspective. I end the chapter with a discussion of the unfulfilled potential of the Egyptian revolution to become permanent. Chapter 8, 'Revolution and Restoration', functions as the negative of Chapter 7, drawing a sober picture of the success of the counter-revolution and highlighting its bourgeois–democratic and Caesarist forms. I return to Gramsci's point that hegemony is the concrete form of permanent revolution by glimpsing the actors and methods of struggle that are able to turn the tide. In the final chapter I summarize the main argument of the book and look at revolution, restoration, and Caesarism beyond Tahrir.

Practical Remarks

Arabic words, names, and places have been transcribed in a simplified system that reflects their Egyptian colloquial variants and that conforms to their popular appearance in non-specialist sources (such as the media).

References to Gramsci's *Quaderni del Carceri* (*Prison Notebooks*) follow the format of Valentino Gerratana's 1975 critical edition, of which Notebooks 1–5 have been translated by Joseph A. Buttigieg. For instance, 'Q3§2' means *quaderno* (notebook) 3, section 2. Whenever possible the concordant fragment in the *Selection from the Prison Notebooks* (1971), edited and translated by Quintin Hoare and Geoffrey Nowell-Smith, has been indicated in the reference.

Part I

On the Subject of Revolution

2. From Bourgeois to Permanent Revolution

The Constitution of Capitalism

Marx finished 'A Contribution to the Critique of Political Economy' (1859) in London surrounded by the salient facts of societal transformation. Eight years earlier, the 'Great Exhibition of the Works of Industry of All Nations', the first world fair, had displayed Europe's and especially Great Britain's remarkable progress in science, technology, and industry. The glamour of the development of productive forces contrasted sharply with the poverty and appalling living conditions of millions of ordinary Londoners. The English proletariat, employed in the new industries, was joined by immigrants, such as political activists who had fled the continent after the repression of the 1848 revolutions and Irish farmers fleeing the nation's 'Great Famine' (1845–52). Of all places in the mid-nineteenth century, London epitomized 'bourgeois society' most profoundly, reflecting both the disintegration of the old, precapitalist order, and the contradictions inherent in the newly emerging social formation: industrial productive forces fettered by capitalist relations of production.

With regard to the crisis and collapse of the feudal Ancien Régime, England had anticipated developments on the continent by more than a century. Unlike the French absolute monarch, the English king was directly dependent on the ability of the petty landed aristocracy to raise taxes at the local level. Conversely, when Parliament was summoned, the gentry used their economic class power to put political pressure on the king. Tensions between the anti-royalist gentry, the 'Roundheads', who wished to expand the powers of Parliament and make it a permanent representative organ, and the 'Cavaliers', supporters of Charles I, led to the English Civil War (1642–51). Leading the forces of Parliament, Oliver Cromwell defeated the monarchy, but he quickly replaced the new parliamentarian republic by a military dictatorship under his personal rule.

After the death of Cromwell the monarchy was reinstated under James II, but it could not return to its position of supremacy as it faced a more confident Parliament. On the Continent the political struggle between absolutism and republicanism was articulated along religious and national lines, represented in their most archetypical forms by the Catholic French kingdom of Louis XIV and the Protestant Dutch Republic ruled by William of Orange, grandson of Charles I. Invited by discontented English nobles and keen to forge an English–Dutch alliance against France, William invaded England, expelling the king and ushering in the 'Glorious Revolution' of 1688. The 'Bill of Rights' (1689), the primary legal product of the revolution, subjected the rule of the new monarchs William and his wife Mary to the laws of Parliament.

The new constitutional monarchy did not simply abolish the feudal order by decree, but it offered the 'nobility of birth' and the growing 'money aristocracy' – that is, the bourgeois[1] class – a political compromise, creating the institutional framework for a transition towards what the young Engels called 'modern feudalism ... the division of society into owners of property and non-owners' (Engels 1975a: 478). Note that Engels did not equate the Glorious Revolution with a capitalist revolution. Although the first historical shape of capital is *money* – 'in the form of monetary wealth, merchants' capital and usurers' capital' (Marx 1990: 249) – capital accumulation requires 'the confrontation of, and the contact between ... on the one hand, the owners of money, means of production, means of subsistence ... [and] on the other hand, free workers, the sellers of their own labour-power' (Marx 1990: 874). The mere existence of trade, money, markets, and commodities in society was an insufficient factor to kick-start the process of capital accumulation. Capital had existed as loan and merchant capital since the Middle Ages, but this money capital did not develop into the self-propelling engine of a capitalist *mode of production*. It remained largely peripheral to the production process. At the very core of capitalism as a mode of production is the 'economic' relation of power – and therefore the class struggle – between the owners of the means of production and those who have only their labour power to sell. Capitalism, as a proper mode of production based on the separation of producers from their means of production and generalized commodity production for anonymous markets (see Dobb 1976: 7), emerged from a process of 'primitive accumulation', which Marx, unlike Adam Smith, understood not simply as the amassing of wealth, but as the constitution of an exploitative social relation.[2] With hindsight, English 'modern feudal' commercial society functioned as an embryonic capitalist social formation first and foremost because of its institution of new property relations, which became 'forms of development of the productive forces'.[3] In other words, the marvels of technology and science of England's world fair were the result of a violent process of dispossession of producers from their means of production.

Marx located moments of primitive or original accumulation in the historical trajectories of Spain, Portugal, Holland, and France – represented by such diverse forms as colonization, public debt, modern taxation, protectionism, and commercial wars – but observed that these moments only came together as a single process in England at the end of the seventeenth century (Marx 1990: 915). In England, the 'classic form' (Marx 1990: 876) of primitive accumulation consisted, in chronological order, of the expropriation of the agricultural population from the land and the formation of industrial labour relations. The end of serfdom opened up the privatization and commercialization of landed property. Feudal privileges were changed into private property rights and taxation. Whereas in France landed property was parcelized to a great extent, English lords owned large estates, which they leased to an intermediate group of farmers (Engels 1975a: 477; Wood 2012: 135). From the sixteenth century onwards, the flow of precious metals from the colonies stimulated the money economy, leading to an accumulation and concentration of wealth among this agricultural class (Marx 1990: 906–7).

The rise of a rich money-capitalist class of farmers went hand in hand with the demise of small-scale independent peasants (Engels 1975a: 477). The gradual process of dispossession created a rural and urban proletariat, an increasing mass of wage labourers who were employed, at first, in capitalist farms and non-corporatist 'manufactures'. This phase represented a *formal subsumption of labour under capital*, in the sense that labour, in its form as wage labour, was subjugated to the control of (money) capital, without the production process itself being fundamentally transformed by the new relations of production (Marx 1990: 900). Although the formal subsumption of labour under capital is a precondition for capitalist relations of production, it 'can be found in the absence of the specifically capitalist mode of production' (Marx 1990: 1019). The relation between labour and capital remains external: capital 'takes over *an existing labour process*' (Marx 1990: 1021), which is subjugated to its direction and interests.

In the countryside the formal subsumption of labour under capital stimulated a higher labour productivity along with 'improved methods of cultivation, greater co-operation, a higher concentration of the means of production' (Marx 1990: 908). In the proto-industrial 'manufactures', capital became concentrated, divorcing the social organization of agricultural production from manufacturing proper. The separation of producers from their means of production also involved the creation of a new 'home market' for commodity production, as a former peasant family could no longer produce and consume its own means of subsistence (Marx 1990: 910–11). Trade, slavery, and the colonial system created worldwide markets, modern banking, and rapid means for accumulating money capital. However, these important developments still represented capitalism in its infancy: a commercial society of which manufacturing was an epiphenomenon, not the motor. Money, wage labour, and the production and circulation of commodities constituted necessary, but by themselves insufficient preconditions of the capitalist mode of production (Marx 1990: 949). As a system of *generalized* commodity production, capitalism required large-scale production – that is, industrialization. The 'simple' commodity of precapitalist society then becomes the 'mass' product of capitalism (Marx 1990: 953).

Commercialization and marketization established new property relations governed by 'the *imperatives* of competition and profit-maximisation, a *compulsion* to reinvest surpluses, and a systemic and relentless *need* to improve labour-productivity and develop the forces of production' (Wood 2012: 43). In this manner relations of production became, in the language of the 'Preface', 'forms of development of the productive forces', stimulating the rise of industry, technology, science, education, labour discipline, the factory system, etc. Cotton manufacturing became the spearhead of a rapidly developing English industry. Soon the industrial revolution penetrated all sectors of the economy and transformed commercial society. Whereas capital had subjugated already existing forms of the labour process as part of the formal subsumption of labour under capital, now the labour process itself became revolutionized 'through co-operation, division of labour within the workshop, the use of *machinery*, and in general the transformation of production by the conscious use of the sciences ... through the enormous increase of *scale*' (Marx 1990: 1024). This transformation of the social and technical process of production is the *real subsumption of labour under capital*. It is only at this moment that '*capitalist production* ... establishes itself as a mode of production *sui generis* and brings into being a new mode of material production' (Marx 1990: 1035). Marx's remark that this process of real subsumption is 'constantly repeated' (Marx 1990: 1035) will prove important for the discussion of passive revolution as capitalist reconstitution in the next chapter.

The Integral State

The rapid process of real subsumption in the nineteenth century – put simply: capitalist industrialization – had been anticipated by gradual economic changes in the relations of production – that is, the rise of money capital and the expansion of wage labour. These changes in the 'base' of feudal society were reinforced and stimulated by transformations in the 'superstructure(s)': the material, social, and ideal forms of the economic content (see Thomas 2009: 172; Williams 1991: 410). In other words, the emergence of new dominant and subaltern classes went hand in hand with the formation of new forms of state and ideology, which mediated the class rule of the dominant groups. Referring to Marx's 'Preface', Gramsci observed that in any stable social formation '[s]tructures and superstructures form an "historical bloc". That is to say the complex, contradictory and discordant *ensemble* of the super-structures is the reflection of the *ensemble* of the social relations of production' (Gramsci 1971: 366; Q8§182). A historical bloc represents the moment of unity of a society, pointing to the integration of a diversity of economic relations and forces of production, accumulation strategies,[4] political state forms and class alliances, and cultural practices and signs (see Hesketh 2010: 391–2; Morton 2007: 96). Whereas Marx's concept of 'mode of production' is an analytical abstraction of the 'economic structure' of a social formation that conceptually determines those parts of the production process that are in a *logical* unity, Gramsci's synthetic notion of 'historical bloc' encompasses the *historically developed* forms of society, which function as a concrete whole. As a methodological instrument the concept of the 'capitalist mode of production' reveals the universal and static character of capitalism as a system, while 'historical bloc' discloses the specific and dynamic ensemble of social relations and forms of a society (see Roccu 2012: 56).

The event of the Glorious Revolution marked the consolidation of a new historical bloc – 'modern feudalism' or 'commercial society' – in seventeenth-century England, structured around a class compromise between the 'nobility of birth' and the new 'money aristocracy'. Whereas in France modern state formation had been the result of the supremacy of one feudal power over the rest, in England 'the crown developed in close conjunction with the self-centralisation of the feudal class as a whole' (Wood 2012: 136). The English political settlement was expressed in the formula of a constitutional, parliamentary monarchy, which assembled the nobility into a 'House of Lords' and the feudal structures of the medieval boroughs into a 'House of Commons'. This arrangement safeguarded the rule of the existing dominant class while supporting the rise of money capital. Although the essentially feudal organization of the House of Commons enabled the aristocracy to continue its domination through the election of its deputies from rural areas and small townships, the real base for its power had shifted from 'sacral' privilege to 'secular' property. The nobility was 'commercialized', while the upper layers of the 'monied' class were 'aristocratized'. In other words, by protecting its class interests against the bourgeoisie, the English nobility was already acting as a bourgeois class (see Engels 1975b: 497–8; Draper 2011a: 329–32). Gramsci remarked that '[t]he old aristocracy remained as a governing stratum, with certain privileges, and it too became the intellectual stratum of the English bourgeoisie' (Gramsci 1971: 83; Q18§24; see Gramsci 1971: 18; Q12§1).

Not only the form of the state – a constitutional, parliamentary monarchy – but also its content was qualitatively transformed. Wood highlighted the point that the history of class society is characterized by the growing differentiation between *class* and *state* power: 'The long historical process that ultimately issued in capitalism could be seen as an increasing – and uniquely well-developed – differentiation of class-power as something distinct from state-power, a power of surplus-extraction not directly grounded in the coercive apparatus of the state' (Wood 2012: 22). In brief, the organization of production and human community required a protopolitical (Draper 2011a: 240) 'administration of things and men'. From this amorphous decision-making process the 'political rule over men' (Engels 1989b: 292) was differentiated as a distinct function and entity: the *state*. In its most general sense as a body of governance, the state emerged as a structure that mediated and subsumed the increasingly complex activity of society under its coercive control. The formation of the state went hand in hand with the creation of specialized military, security, bureaucratic, and ideological personnel, which detached themselves as special bodies from society. The production of an economic surplus led to the development of a systemic social division of labour (beyond the 'natural' sex-based division of labour), which stimulated the differentiation of society into *classes* – social groups that were defined 'in relation to control over the appropriation of the surplus product' (Draper 2011a: 14). The primordial state became a *class state*, which appropriated the surplus for the dominant class.

With the arrival of bourgeois society, the precapitalist subsumption of the 'economic' under the 'political' – the direct appropriation of surplus by state power – is seemingly reversed: the system of wage labour embeds the process of surplus extraction in the sphere of production itself, letting the 'silent compulsion of capitalist relations' (Marx 1990: 899) do its work. In contrast to the feudal lord, the capitalist appropriator relinquishes his *direct* political power over the workforce, which he can only control *indirectly* through the state (Wood 2012: 26–27). The emancipation of money capital from the shackles of feudal privilege created the framework for modern politics. Developing Hegel's concept of the modern state, Marx observed that bourgeois political emancipation eliminated the direct political character of feudal society, abolishing the particularist nature of Ancien Régime politics by differentiating the individual as a private person, a *bourgeois*, with particular interests in *civil society* from the individual as a *citoyen*, a citizen of the universal community expressed by *political society*. Whereas the feudal social formation had erected insurmountable barriers between the different estates, commercial society flattened the social distinctions on the basis of birth and rank. The bourgeoisie appeared as a class able to absorb the whole of society:

> No class of civil society can play this role without awakening a moment of enthusiasm in itself and in the masses; a moment in which this class fraternizes and fuses with society in general, becomes identified with it and is experienced and acknowledged as *its universal representative*; a moment in which its claims and rights are truly the rights and claims of society itself and in which it is in reality the heart and head of society. Only in the name of the universal rights of society can a particular class lay claim to universal domination. (Marx 1992a: 254)

Advancing Marx's argument, Gramsci claimed that the bourgeoisie was able to become (or pose as) a 'universal class', because its rule differed qualitatively from the Ancien Régime ruling groups:

> The previous ruling classes were essentially conservative in the sense that they did not tend to construct an organic passage from the other classes into their own, i.e. to enlarge their class sphere 'technically' and ideologically: their conception was that of a closed class. The bourgeois class poses itself as an organism in continuous movement, capable of absorbing the entire society, assimilating it to its own cultural and economic level. The entire function of the State has been transformed; the State has become an 'educator' (Gramsci 1971: 260; Q8§2).

Whereas the dominant classes of the Ancien Régime ruled society almost 'from the outside', the bourgeoisie ruled by *becoming* society and reshaping it in its own image (see Thomas 2009: 143).[5] Instead of creating a new state, external to the dominated classes, bourgeois class rule aimed to absorb and transform 'the people' into a bourgeois subject. This 'organic passage' from society to the bourgeoisie was formally realized in the political community, where every citizen was equal before the law, and in the civil community, where '[t]hose social elements which were most highly endowed with energy and spirit of enterprise rose from the lower classes to the ruling classes' (Gramsci 1971: 80n49; see Q5§48) – at least in theory. Moreover, through universal suffrage and the abolishment of property qualification for voting *the state itself* was legally emancipated from private property and, conversely, private interests were liberated from their direct feudal fusion with politics (Draper 2011a: 119). Marx observed that the equality of citizens in political society strengthened the real, property-based inequalities between individuals in civil society: 'Far from abolishing these factual distinctions, the state presupposes them in order to exist, it only experiences itself as a political state and asserts its universality in opposition to these elements' (Marx 1992a: 219).

Gramsci elaborated Marx's concept of bourgeois society[6] and the state and claimed that the division between civil and political society disguised their concrete unity as an 'integral' or 'extended' state: 'the entire complex of practical and theoretical activities with which the ruling class not only justifies and maintains its dominance, but manages to win the active consent of those over whom it rules' (Gramsci 1971: 244; Q15§10). The process of differentiation between civil and political society takes place *within* the class state. Apart from the reconstitution of society as a *national* space, the formation of the modern state represented a qualitative development of the already existing class state: 'an increasingly more sophisticated internal articulation and condensation of social relations within a given state-form' (Thomas 2009: 140). Although united, civil and political society are not in a relation of perpetual equilibrium: they follow an alternating historical chain wherein one moment is subsumed under the other (see Thomas 2009: 192–3). Modern political society emerged from a primordial, amorphous civil society within the womb of the Ancien Régime. Once it became dominant, it reshaped this fluid civil society in its own image. The modern state, however, in its narrow sense as political society, is not the ideal image of a universal human community, but of *bourgeois* society. The bourgeoisie had emancipated the whole of society from feudalism, but from its particular perspective as a bourgeois class. Its particular condition – as a possessor of wealth but not of noble birth or privilege – was raised as the universal measure for all classes.

Whereas the Continent was ablaze with revolutionary uprisings throughout the nineteenth century, England had already experienced its moment of 'political emancipation' with the Glorious Revolution in the seventeenth century, which had removed the institutional obstacles for money capital without dethroning the aristocratic classes. The gradual shift in the balance of power from the nobility to the bourgeoisie, based on the rapid expansion of industrial capital, became legally articulated in the Reform Bills of 1832, 1867, and 1884, which turned the House of Commons into a representative chamber. These reforms were enforced by the bourgeois Whigs and, later, by the Liberals, under popular pressure of movements such as the Chartists. Whereas the English Glorious

Revolution of 1688 cleared the path for the dominance of money capital, the French Revolution of 1789 expressed the political rationale of bourgeois, commercial society in its most radical and 'complete' terms.

Bourgeois Revolution in France

In England the crisis of feudalism had led to a class compromise between nobility and bourgeoisie in the form of a constitutional, parliamentary monarchy. Class power was disentangled from direct state power. The commercialization of society and the process of primitive accumulation supplanted the traditional, feudal mode of surplus extraction by extra-economic means with the purely economic compulsion of the labour market. Without means of subsistence, proletarians had to sell their labour power in order to survive. The dispossession of producers from their means of production opened the way for the formal and real subsumption of labour under capital – that is, the development of the capitalist mode of production.

Conversely, in France feudal production relations which, in the jargon of Marx's 'Preface', 'fettered' the expansion of money capital were overcome not by the constitution of new property relations, but by a *centralization of surplus appropriation*. Agricultural producers were not divorced from their means of production: their surplus was appropriated through state taxation instead of feudal rent. Class power was directly subsumed under state power: 'Office became a major means of extracting surplus-labour from direct producers, in the form of tax; and the state, which became a source of great private wealth, co-opted and incorporated growing numbers of appropriators from among the old nobility as well as newer "bourgeois" office-holders' (Wood 2012: 47). The surplus extraction of the French absolutist 'tax-office state' constituted a variant of 'modern feudalism' that differed fundamentally from the process of primitive accumulation in the English countryside, illustrating that the crisis of feudalism and the expansion of money capital did not automatically and inevitably lead to the capitalist mode of production.

Because of its political and economic primacy as an organizer of class rule and extractor and distributor of surplus, the French state did not become differentiated in civil and political society as did its English counterpart, nor did its centralization negate the corporatism and particularism of the feudal era (Wood 2012: 134–6). As long as the absolutist state was able to generate sufficient income for the upper layers of the bourgeoisie and as long as the interests of money capital were successfully aligned with that of the ruling House of Bourbon and the nobility, the bourgeois class remained in what Gramsci called a *corporate* state, 'in the traditional sense, of the immediate and narrowly selfish interests of a particular category' (Gramsci 1971: 77; Q19§24). There were, of course, clashes of interests between the monarchy, the nobility, and the bourgeoisie, but these were successfully absorbed by the mechanism of the 'tax-office' state. Absolutism continued the 'mechanical' character of the feudal historical bloc in which the different social groups functioned as disconnected parts, each remaining focused on its own position within the whole (see Chapter 4).

However, the 'steady-state' political economy of absolutism was undermined from within, as its mode of surplus appropriation was fundamentally a contradictory process. The state was not only a *source* of income for the aristocracy and upper layers of the bourgeoisie, but also their main *competitor* in the taxation of the peasantry, which was, after all, the foundation of state revenues. Independent peasants had to be squeezed financially by the state in order to redistribute surplus to the rural and urban elites, but their dispossession and proletarianization had to be evaded at all costs, for this would bereave the state of its main tax resource. Unproductive agricultural production and costly wars plunged the French state into debt, since the population would not have tolerated any further tax increases. Hence the tax code, which exempted the nobility from paying taxes, had to be reformed, along with privileges and corporatist restrictions on production and trade, those other lingering remains of the classical feudal era. In the eyes of the aristocracy, this threatened the equilibrium of the absolutist historical bloc.

When in 1789 attempts by Louis XVII of the House of Bourbon to change the tax code were thwarted by the nobility, he decided to convene the Estates-General, the elected organ of the old feudal estates of 1614: clergy, nobility, and tax-paying 'common people'. The *sans-culottes*[7] – the popular classes of workers and peasants – were not represented. Whereas the clergy and the aristocracy were opposed to any reform that undermined their feudal privileges, the third estate or *Communes* (Commons) desired a more equal distribution of taxation. The king probably hoped to scare the nobility into a tax compromise, playing off the first and second estates against the third. The *Communes* then convoked their own meeting, the National Assembly, a single popular congress, which the majority of the clergy and some members of the aristocracy joined. While the assembly began the process of drafting a constitution, a popular uprising broke out in the streets of Paris in support of the newly named Constituent Assembly. On 14 July the *sans-culottes* stormed the hated Bastille prison, which represented the power of the absolutist state. This signalled the entry of the masses into the process. A conflict over taxation had become a popular revolution, which swept away the legal remnants of feudalism.

Any historical bloc expresses an equilibrium that contains internal class contradictions by material concessions and ideological justifications for the limits of its economic structure. When internal or external dynamics disturb the fundaments of the equilibrium, centrifugal forces become stronger than the centripetal power and a crisis ensues. Gramsci made a methodological distinction between *conjunctural* and *organic* crises. A conjunctural crisis appears 'as occasional, immediate, almost accidental' and does 'not have any very far-reaching historical significance' (Gramsci 1971: 177; Q13§17). Conversely, an organic crisis means that the systemic contradictions inherent to the historical bloc come to the surface and that the bloc *as a whole* – that is, in all its political, economic, and cultural dimensions – suffers a crisis, ushering in a long period of societal instability. As organic crises always first appear in a conjunctural form, it is difficult to assess their impact until *post factum*. In this regard, France's 'conjunctural' fiscal crisis was directly connected with the structural limitations of the 'tax-office' state and the contradictions of absolutist appropriation, leading to an organic crisis of the whole historical bloc.

Due to the direct and centralized role of the French state in appropriating the surplus in the form of taxes, *economic* exploitation immediately appeared as *political* oppression, which easily turned any social struggle into a political one, and vice versa (Wood 2012: 137). Unsurprisingly, the uprising in Paris was quickly joined by peasant insurrections in the countryside. Moreover, the open subordination of civil society to political society, of the community to the state, radicalized the political critique of monarchical sovereignty beyond liberal notions of representative democracy. In the political thought of ideological forerunner Jean-Jacques Rousseau (1712–78), for example, sovereignty is not a power external to the people that has to be kept 'in check' by a constitution and intermediate bodies such as parliament, but it is the *volonté générale*, the collective will of the community itself. In contradistinction to the concept of the *volonté de tous* (will of everyone), the *volonté générale* (general will) directly expresses the people as a whole political entity.[8]

The concept of popular sovereignty manifested itself in the French Revolution not only through the formal gathering of the National Constituent Assembly or its 'Declaration of the Rights of Man and of the Citizen' (1791), but also through spontaneous signs and practices such as the rallying cry of *Vive le Nation*, the wearing of the tricolor cockade, the spontaneous occupation of the Parisian Hôtel de Ville (city council), and the formation of a popular municipal government (the first Paris

Commune); or the interpellation of one's revolutionary companion as *citoyen* (citizen). These social forms articulated a collective national-popular will, which was tightly connected to the formation of a new state.

As Marx observed in 'On the Jewish Question' (1844), the revolutionary distinction between the 'Rights of Man' and the 'Rights of the Citizen' expressed an advanced differentiation between civil and political society. Whereas in England the early development of bourgeois civil society – that is, property rights, parliamentarism, constitutionalism, etc. – impeded a radical transformation of the political sphere, in France it was the revolutionary constitution of a bourgeois *political* community that liberated its primordial civil society from absolutism. France's social conditions of 'modern feudalism' did not stimulate the formation of a strong agricultural capitalism (let alone 'proper' industrial capitalism), but fragmented its bourgeois class into various money-capitalist fractions, such as buyers and sellers of state offices, lands, and titles, master craftsmen and merchants who had commercialized the feudal guild system, etc. (Versieren and De Smet 2015: 115). The most archetypical of all 'bourgeois revolutions' was not at all led by industrial capitalists; even wealthy commercial capitalists played a minor role compared to the petty bourgeoisie and especially its 'professional' fractions, such as doctors, lawyers, professors, journalists, artisans, small shopkeepers, etc. As Wood observed: 'In England, there was capitalism, but it was not called into being by the bourgeoisie. In France, there was a (more-or-less) triumphant bourgeoisie, but its revolutionary project had little to do with capitalism' (Wood 2012: 33).

Marx, Engels, and Gramsci always considered the histories of England, France, and Germany as closely entwined, for each nation represented, in ideal typical terms, one moment of a shared trajectory – respectively: social, political, and philosophical transformation (see Marx 1977: 161; Gramsci 1971: 82–4; Q19§24). In order to 'catch up' with England in the social or civil domain, France took a political detour by radicalizing and advancing the achievements of the English and American (1765–83) revolutions. Thus it was a completely *rational* contradiction that the politically most complete bourgeois transformation took place in a country that was economically less capitalist than England. Although the French bourgeoisie – in the sense of a class which exercises its rule through private property rights and the separation of class power from state power – was economically less developed than its English counterpart, it compensated its relative economic backwardness with the salient expression of a 'collective will'. As Countinho (2012) observes, the theme of collective will – 'will as operative awareness of historical necessity, as protagonist of a real and effective historical drama' (Gramsci

1971: 130; Q13§1) – returns in Gramsci's writings as the problem of the formation of collective subjects, in which *hegemony* plays a key part.[9]

Hegemony and Jacobinism

The radical separation of political from civil society not only represented the transition of the French bourgeoisie from a corporate collection of actors (a class in itself) to a political force (a class for itself) (see Thomas 2009: 190), it also entailed the birth of modern politics in the sense that bourgeois class power became grounded in both 'domination' and 'hegemony'. *Domination* (or 'dictatorship', see Gramsci 1971: 107; Q15§59) is simply 'naked' and 'top-down' class rule, whereby the ruled are the passive object of state power. *Hegemony*, on the other hand, is the active acceptance of the bourgeoisie's class power because of its political leadership, its prestige, its directive capacities, its cultural aura, and its technical ability to 'manage' society and resolve societal problems. Bourgeois domination and hegemony are achieved by a combination of force (violence, or coercion), fraud (or corruption), and consent-generating policies (Q1§48).[10] The difference between bourgeois domination and hegemony is not so much the quantitative *proportion* between coercion and consent, but the degree to which force is successfully *grounded* in popular consent (see Thomas 2009: 162–5).[11] The hegemonic rule of the dominant class can very well rely on a disproportionate use of force (war, occupation, state violence), as long as this is accepted as necessary and in the interest of the common good by its allies. In France, for example, after the 1789 uprising the swift justice handed out by the guillotine, the sequestration of Church properties, and the general violence of the Terror came to represent, for a while, revolutionary coercion embedded within the popular consent of the *sans-culottes*.

Domination and hegemony not only express different *forms* of class power, they also denote different *relations* between classes and class fractions. Gramsci remarked that '[a] social group dominates the antagonistic groups, which it tends to "liquidate", or to subjugate perhaps even by armed force; it leads kindred and allied groups' (Gramsci 1971: 57; Q1§44). Domination describes the relation between the dominant class and subordinate groups that do *not* accept its leadership. Conversely, hegemony defines the hierarchical alliance between the ruling class and those groups (both elite and subaltern) that accept its leadership. Finally, hegemony and domination refer to the relation of a dominant class to society as a whole. In other words, a ruling class can be hegemonic within a restricted coalition of class forces that is not accepted by the majority of social groups.

When bourgeois hegemonic policies are deeply rooted in consent-generating policies, the ruling class has to take into account the 'interests and the tendencies of the groups over which hegemony is to be exercised, and [the fact] that a certain compromise equilibrium should be formed' (Gramsci 1971: 161; Q13§18). Even though this equilibrium requires concessions on the part of the directive class, 'there is also no doubt that such sacrifices and such a compromise cannot touch the essential; for though hegemony is ethical–political, it must also be economic, must necessarily be based on the decisive function exercised by the leading group in the decisive nucleus of economic activity' (Gramsci 1971: 161; Q13§18). In other words, only those social and political concessions are allowed which do not undermine the foundations of class rule.

Apart from ideas, sentiments, and conceptions, the material form of hegemony in civil and political society is the ruling class's *hegemonic apparatus*: 'the material organization meant to preserve, defend, and develop the theoretical or ideological "front"' (Q3§49) – which Peter Thomas summarizes as 'the wide-ranging series of articulated institutions (understood in the broadest sense) and practices – from newspapers to educational organisations to political parties – by means of which a class and its allies engage their opponents in a struggle for political power' (Thomas 2009: 226). Hegemony is concentrated in the hegemonic apparatus of the *party*, which, for Gramsci, does not necessarily mean a clearly delineated, electoral organization: different formal parties may represent the same class, or a single party can contain multiple class projects. Alluding to Niccolò Machiavelli's (1469–1527) concept of *Il Principe* (The Prince), which articulated a modern notion of politics through the ideal type of an individual political ruler, Gramsci likened the party to a collective 'modern prince': 'an organism, a complex element of society in which a collective will, which has already been recognized and has to some extent asserted itself in action, begins to take concrete form' (Gramsci 1971: 129; Q13§1).

In France, bourgeois hegemony gained its concentrated form chiefly through the political clubs that were established in the course of the revolution (see Gramsci 1971: 259; Q1§47). These clubs organized what Gramsci called the *organic intellectuals* of the bourgeoisie.[12] Gramsci distinguished between organic and traditional intellectuals. The constitution of *organic* intellectuals is entwined with the historical formation of the class they represent:

> Every social group, coming into existence on the original terrain of an essential function in the world of economic production, creates together with itself, organically, one or more strata of intellectu-

als which give it homogeneity and an awareness of its own function not only in the economic but also in the social and political fields. (Gramsci 1971: 5; Q12§1)

Yesterday's organic intellectuals are today's *traditional* intellectuals in the sense that every new rising class 'has found (at least in all of history up to the present) categories of intellectuals already in existence and which seemed indeed to represent an historical continuity uninterrupted even by the most complicated and radical changes in political and social form' (Gramsci 1971: 6–7; Q12§1). Because they have survived the social formation from which they emerged, traditional intellectuals often see themselves as autonomous and independent from the current ruling classes. In other words, the terms 'organic' and 'traditional' are not absolute but relative categories, in accordance with the perspective of a specific class (see De Smet 2015: 99).

During the French Revolution the Jacobin society became the most important of the political clubs. Most members of the Jacobin club were from a bourgeois or petty-bourgeois background, although by 1791 most of the wealthy right-wing members had split from the group. Their leader was the lawyer Maximilien Robespierre (1758–94), who was strongly influenced by Rousseau's political thought, and who favoured a radical popular democracy as an alternative to absolutist rule. In contradistinction, the majoritarian 'right wing' (literally) of the National Assembly, which represented moderate aristocratic, bourgeois, and clerical forces, was in favour of the institution of a constitutional monarchy according to the English model. The Commons 'initially only posed those questions which interested the actual physical members of the social group, their immediate "corporate" interests' (Gramsci 1971: 77; Q19§24). However, the King's attempts at retaking his lost power, especially through diplomatic and military pressure by allied foreign monarchs and the failure of the new government to address the social and economic problems exacerbated the organic crisis instead of solving it. It also encouraged the formation of 'a new élite ... which did not concern itself solely with "corporate" reforms, but tended to conceive of the bourgeoisie as the hegemonic group of all the popular forces' (Gramsci 1971: 77; Q19§24). The crystallization of a radical opposition around the Jacobins, developing a hegemonic politics, and growing popular resentment towards the monarchy pushed the revolutionary process forward, '[preventing] it from stalling in its early stages' (Q3§103).

Leaning on the *sans-culottes*, the Jacobins became the directive force in the Paris Commune, which began to compete with the Assembly for power in the capital. The Assembly was superseded in 1792 when a National Convention was elected, which became France's unicameral, legislative, and executive body. The Convention merely recognized an existing reality when it proclaimed the nation a republic. The subsequent execution of King Louis XVII, voted for by the Convention, also dealt a mortal blow to absolutism as a *system* in the whole of the Continent, as it placed popular sovereignty above divine right.

In the Convention, the 'party' of the bourgeoisie split into two factions: the politically moderate Girondists,[13] who favoured a federal state, and the radical Montagnards,[14] who consisted mostly of Jacobins and who preferred a centralized and united France. As the revolution progressed, the Girondists looked to the right for class allies, which they found in the Church and the nobility, while the Montagnards sought the support of the *sans-culottes*. These two political factions represented diverging projects for a new historical bloc. Whereas the Girondists preferred a republican model that integrated the interests of the old ruling classes under the direction of the bourgeoisie, the Montagnards evolved towards a perspective of a radical popular democracy that was much closer to the hegemonic concept of an 'organic passage'.

By 1793 the factional fight between Girondists and Montagnards intensified as the economy was faltering and the French army was suffering defeat at the hands of a Coalition of Austria, the Dutch Republic, Great Britain, Portugal, and Spain. Gramsci observed that 'the Jacobins were able to utilize the external threat as a spur to greater energy internally: they well understood that in order to defeat the external foe they had to crush his [sic] allies internally' (Gramsci 1971: 81; Q19§24). From within their stronghold of the Paris Commune, the Jacobins organized an uprising of *sans-culottes* against the Girondists in the paralysed Convention, which catapulted the Montagnards to power. Counter-revolutionary and popular rebellions, war at the borders, rising prices, and incidents such as the murder of the popular politician Jean-Paul Marat increasingly pushed the Convention to the use of dictatorship and violence to protect revolutionary achievements. The Committee of Public Safety and, to a lesser degree, the Committee of General Security functioned for all purposes as the revolutionary government and concentrated executive power into their hands. Forced by circumstances of food shortages and war, the regime hesitantly took control over the economy, regulating production and allocating goods. State planning – 'economic Jacobinism' (see Gramsci 1971: 67; Q19§24) – was concentrated on the forging of a powerful, modern war machine able to defeat the Coalition forces. More importantly, the French armies would export the revolution far outside the borders of the nation.

Gramsci claimed that 'the Jacobins ... were certainly a "categorical embodiment" of Machiavelli's Prince ... an exemplification of the concrete formation and operation of a collective will which at least in some aspects was an original, *ex novo* creation' (Gramsci 1971: 130; Q13§1). The Jacobin leaders did not tail-end the twists and turns of the revolutionary process, nor did they represent 'the immediate needs and aspirations of the actual physical individuals who constituted the French bourgeoisie' (Gramsci 1971: 78; Q19§24). Instead they developed a concept of 'the revolutionary movement as a whole, as an integral historical development' (Gramsci 1971: 78; Q19§24), and of the necessity to subsume all classes under the bourgeois project. Moreover, they were able to connect this concept to a successful politics of persuasion by speaking the particular cultural–historical language of their epoch and nation. Finally, they understood that the success of the revolution consisted in defeating the counter-revolutionary forces and offering the allied classes solutions to their corporate problems (for example by building a coalition with the peasants around the agrarian question; see Gramsci 1971: 102; Q19§26). This required the construction of politico-military and hegemonic apparatuses that could subjugate internal enemies through revolutionary terror, defeat external foes through revolutionary wars, and forge new class alliances. Thus, according to Gramsci, the Jacobins went much further than securing bourgeois domination: 'They created the bourgeois State, made the bourgeois into the leading, hegemonic class of the nation, in other words gave the new State a permanent basis and created the compact modern French nation' (Gramsci 1971: 79; Q19§24; Gramsci 1971: 399; Q16§9).

However, by 1794 the hegemony of revolutionary government was shrinking. On the one hand, the bourgeoisie was intimidated and alienated by the terror and the radical economic policies, while, on the other, the spontaneous movement of the popular classes was contained, leaders of the *sans-culottes* were executed, and the powers of its chief organ, the Paris Commune were absorbed by the Committee of Public Safety. Not the use of terror in itself, but the loss of both its bourgeois and its popular-class base led to the demise of the Jacobin faction. Gramsci commented that

> the Jacobins ... 'imposed' themselves on the French bourgeoisie, leading it into a far more advanced position than the originally strongest bourgeois nuclei would have spontaneously wished to take up, and even far more advanced than that which the historical premises should have permitted – hence the various forms of backlash and the function of Napoleon I. (Gramsci 1971: 77; Q19§24)

With regard to the *sans-culottes*, the Jacobins remained within a strictly bourgeois framework, for they denied workers the right to organize and bargain collectively (see Gramsci 1971: 63, 79; Q19§24). As there was no organized force more progressive than the Jacobins, the revolution was no longer able to move forward – its movement was stalled and began to collapse (see Marx 1979a: 124).

Restoration

In the summer month 'Thermidor' of 1794 the Convention turned against the Committee of Public Safety, executed Robespierre and his companions, and abrogated the political and economic dictatorial powers of revolutionary government. The collapse of the centralized economy caused food shortages and inflation, which prompted a final popular uprising in May 1795. The new government succeeded in quelling the revolt and this signalled the end of the revolutionary process 'from below'. The executive powers of the Committees were transferred to the five members of the *Directoire* (Directory), the Convention was supplanted by a bicameral legislature, and political and social rights were reduced in the new, more conservative constitution. The rule of the *Directoire* represented, in a technocratic form, a return to the Girondist project of a bourgeois republic. In its attempts to suppress Jacobin opposition from the left and royalists from the right, the *Directoire* came to rely increasingly on the revolutionary army, led by Napoleon Bonaparte (1769–1821). On '18 Brumaire' (9 November 1799) Bonaparte overthrew the *Directoire* in a military coup, establishing the Consulate, before crowning himself Emperor in 1804.

Gramsci mused that the victory of Napoleon I 'represents in the last analysis the triumph of the organic bourgeois forces over the Jacobin petit-bourgeois forces' (Gramsci 1971: 112; Q15§15). Almost a century earlier, in 'The Holy Family' (1844) Marx had stressed that the Napoleonic appropriation of the French Revolution did not halt the bourgeois rev-olutionary process, but continued to modernize the economic structure and civil society in a top-down manner 'by substituting permanent war for permanent revolution' (Marx and Engels 1975a: 123). Furthermore, the Napoleonic wars persuaded other European nations 'under the whip of external necessity' (Trotsky 2001: 28) to start modernizing their own historical blocs: 'From then on, the processes of state-integration and economic – that is to say, capitalist – development went hand-in-hand' (Wood 2012: 134). Finally, under Napoleon's Empire, the revolutionary wars became imperialist wars, provoking wars of national liberation against the imperial aggressor, which became forces of modern state formation in their own right (Losurdo 2015: 110–1).

When Napoleon I was defeated by Coalition forces in 1814 (and again in 1815), France was returned to its pre-Napoleonic borders and Louis XVIII of the House of Bourbon was put on the throne. Although the state was purged from Napoleonic officials and sympathizers, the restoration did not signal a return to absolutism. Careful not to provoke the anti-royalist opposition, the new king favoured a relatively moderate and liberal politics, which angered the ultra-royalist faction. When Louis XVIII died in 1824, his brother Charles X, head of the ultra-royalist group, became the new king. Charles X imagined that the monarchy could simply return to the heydays of the Ancien Régime. His autocratic style, alliance with wealthy landowners, and inability to solve the enduring economic crisis between 1827 and 1830 alienated political actors ranging from radical republicans to constitutional monarchists, and social factions from the popular classes to the financial and industrial bourgeoisie. In July 1830 the king's decision to dissolve the liberal-dominated parliament, curb press freedom, and restrict the electoral body, were the signal for a new popular uprising in Paris, supported and encouraged by liberal newspapers. In three days the monarchy had fallen.

The July Revolution did not lead to a new republic: as a compromise the aristocratic businessman Louis Philippe of the House of Orléans, a distant cousin of Charles X, was crowned as King of *the French*: as the head of state within an explicitly liberal–constitutional framework that recognized the people's sovereignty. The Belgian Revolution, which followed the July Revolution, had a similar outcome. Marx contemplated that:

> in 1830 the bourgeoisie put into effect its wishes of the year 1789, with the only difference that its political enlightenment was now completed, that it no longer considered the constitutional representative state as a means for achieving the ideal of the state, the welfare of the world and universal human aims but, on the contrary, had acknowledged it as the official expression of its own exclusive power and the political recognition of its own special interests. (Marx and Engels 1975a: 124)

The bourgeoisie was revealed as 'an exclusive, limited mass, not an all-embracing one' (Marx and Engels 1975a: 82). The epochal distinctions between 'feudal aristocracy', 'absolutist monarchy', and 'capitalist bourgeoisie' had become nonsensical, as the nobility and the House of Orléans had become deeply embedded within the circulation process of capital. The differentiation *between* dominant classes had become *internal to* capital; that is, between different fractions of capital: commercial, landholding, industrial, and financial. The idea of bourgeois political emancipation through an organic passage of society was discredited, but there was as yet no new concept that could express the project of the subaltern classes.

Even though the social composition of France's state personnel – the bureaucracy – remained roughly the same, finance capital entered politics directly in the form of bourgeois bankers such as Jacques Laffitte and Casimir Perier, who headed governments.[15] According to Marx, Lafitte triumphantly declared: 'From now on the bankers will rule' (Marx 1978: 48). Even when it did not formally *govern* France, conservative finance capital certainly *ruled* the country, largely excluding the industrial capitalist and petty-bourgeois class from power, and using state expenditure and debt as lucrative sources of speculation and profit. Marx famously claimed: 'The July monarchy was nothing but a joint-stock company for the exploitation of France's national wealth, the dividends of which were divided among ministers' (Marx 1978: 50).

Strikes, demonstrations, insurrections, and cabinet shuffles continued to destabilize the regime and revealed its failure to forge a lasting historical bloc. Although industrialization did not reach the same levels as in England, France's industry became the most developed on the continent (Marx 1978: 56); this was reflected in the growing number of factories, which partly employed the increasing surplus rural population. The commodification and commercialization of landed property had led to rising debts among small plot holders, subjugating them to the interests of loan capital, and driving them from their lands (Marx 1978: 122). The first 'modern' industrial overproduction crisis, starting in 1846, coincided with a 'traditional' agricultural underproduction crisis, leading to unemployment and unrest among the popular classes and the petty bourgeoisie, which faced ruin.

After 1835 public meetings had been forbidden, stimulating the formation of conspiratorial secret societies and gatherings disguised as 'banquets'. When the King prohibited the last banquet in February 1848, this became the trigger for a new revolt. An uprising in Paris led to the abdication of Louis-Philippe, which, in turn, provoked a revolutionary wave in Europe and some of its (former) colonial territories. The revolutionary government that came to power in France reflected the broad opposition to the July Monarchy: the industrial bourgeoisie, the petty bourgeoisie, and the urban proletariat (Marx 1979a: 113). Although the working class had only two representatives in the new government, the relations of force in the capital were strongly in its favour, putting pressure on the bourgeoisie to proclaim the Second Republic on the basis of universal suffrage (Marx 1978: 54). Ironically proletarian mobilization completed bourgeois rule, in the sense that it politically emancipated *all* propertied classes and brought them into the political community: 'whereas a limited section of the bourgeoisie ruled in the name of the king, the whole of the bourgeoisie will now rule on behalf of the people' (Marx 1979a: 110). The provisional government dealt with unemployment by organizing national workshops for the urban proletariat. However, the *ateliers* could not keep up with the demand for work, nor did they offer interesting, well-paid work, which disappointed the working class (Marx 1978: 65). Moreover, as these state initiatives were financed by new land taxes that did not target the large landholders, but the small proprietors, the regime alienated the peasantry from its project. Therefore, it came as no surprise that elections for a new National Constituent Assembly granted the moderate and conservative political factions a large majority.

Permanent Revolution

In June the working class rose up in protest to the conservative turn of the revolution. The appearance of the proletariat as an autonomous political force, expressed in 'the bold slogan of revolutionary struggle: Overthrow of the bourgeoisie! Dictatorship of the working class!' (Marx 1978: 69) – signalled that a new epoch-making class was emerging at a time when the European bourgeoisie was fighting an increasingly unconvincing 'permanent revolution' against the forces of the Ancien Régime. While the bourgeoisie and the proletariat shared a democratic struggle against the waning feudal–absolutist order, bourgeois property rights were already becoming an immediate obstacle to the much more radical project of *communism*. Moreover, the absorption of the old aristocratic elites into the expanding capital relation rendered the opposition between feudal–absolutist and capitalist modes of production largely irrelevant: 'the landlord now is but the sleeping partner of the capitalist' (Marx 1986c: 335). The political front in February between workers and the industrial bourgeoisie against finance capital was short-lived: 'The reduction of [the industrial bourgeois's] profit by finance, what is that compared with the abolition of profit by the proletariat?' (Marx 1978: 117). The development of industrial capitalism and the process of primitive accumulation and proletarianization revealed the growing contradiction between the democratic project of the liberal bourgeoisie and the human misery in the new factories and working-class neighbourhoods. In this sense the June uprising represented 'the first great battle ... fought between the two classes that split modern society. It was a fight for the preservation or annihilation of the bourgeois order' (Marx

1978: 67). June 1848 hinted at the possibility of an alternative hegemony to that of the bourgeoisie: the leadership of the proletariat as a genuine 'universal class' – a class whose self-interested struggle for self-emancipation could liberate society in general.

The modern working class is the historical result of capital's creation of a wage labour population for the process of production. In order to defend their specific interests and rights workers organize themselves and struggle regardless of capitalist considerations. Draper underlined that '[a]s labor presses for more – including more social responsibility, more control over its conditions of existence – the class drives the logic of its own life situation outside the bounds of the capitalist framework and tends to create the conditions for exploding that framework' (Draper 2011b: 44). The proletariat's revolutionary and universalist potential is not an inherent quality but immanent to its position within the capitalist production process and the logic of its struggle (see De Smet 2015).

The reaction of the bourgeoisie and its frightened petty-bourgeois allies was violent. In France, the new government ordered General Louis Eugène Cavaignac to quench the uprising in blood. After the proletariat was defeated as a force in the streets, its attention turned to presidential elections as a means to defeat Cavaignac, who was the candidate of the bourgeoisie. However, the vote of the working class, along with the disillusioned petty bourgeoisie and the peasantry, catapulted Charles-Louis Napoleon-Bonaparte (1808–73), the nephew of Napoleon I, into power (Marx 1978: 79–81). Convinced of his destiny to lead France, Louis Napoleon had staged a coup in 1836 and again in 1840, but both attempts had failed quite embarrassingly. Now, thanks to his exile – and therefore his disconnection with the violent counter-revolution and political infighting in 1848 – and his mythical pedigree, Louis Napoleon became an empty signifier in which every disenchanted class could pour its desires and expectations: 'Just because he was nothing, he could signify everything save himself' (Marx 1978: 81).

Cunningly the new president maintained a balance between the left and the right wings of the political order in order to increase his own base of power. In 1849 he repressed a leftist uprising, pushing the radical democrats and the socialists out of the Assembly. Then he turned against the conservatives, dissolving the National Assembly with support of the army and the people. Through the means of a plebiscite, based on universal (male) suffrage, the Bonapartist coup was ratified and grounded 'from above' within a collective popular will. In December 1852 Louis Napoleon was crowned Napoleon III, Emperor of the French. Although it seemed 'that the state only returned to its oldest form, to the shamelessly simple domination of the sabre and the Cowl', under the

Emperor's centralist reign the country became thoroughly industrialized and modernized.[16] With Napoleon III the 'permanent revolution' of the French bourgeoisie against the Ancien Régime had come to an end: capital had absorbed and reconstituted the old precapitalist elites and, conversely, a reborn 'absolutism' had subsumed the bourgeois class under its imperial rule.[17]

In other European nations the revolutionary wave of 1848 had a similar outcome. On the one hand, the rise of the bourgeoisie as a political actor was curtailed by conservative monarchical and aristocratic forces. Proletarian and peasant uprisings were violently quelled. On the other hand, the bourgeois revolution 'from below' continued as a revolution 'from above' (see Engels 1990a: 431; 1990b: 513), in the sense that bourgeois property relations and rights were gradually introduced, serfdom was abolished, and capital slowly absorbed and transformed precapitalist relations and elites. Nations such as England or the Netherlands, which remained relatively stable in this period, had pre-empted the revolutionary wave by introducing constitutional reforms 'from above'.

Despite the workers' defeat, the year 1848 was a cathartic experience: 'It had revealed that here bourgeois republic signifies the unlimited despotism of one class over other classes' (Marx 1979a: 111). Although the bourgeoisie had been discredited as a revolutionary actor, the European 'revolution in permanence' continued – albeit with a different protagonist and a different script. The autonomous movement of the workers had clearly assembled and exposed the forces of the counterrevolution, illuminating possible class alliances and revolutionary tasks (Marx 1978: 69–70; see Thomas 2009: 145). In his March 1850 'Address of the Central Committee to the Communist League' Marx posited that although the German proletariat, organized as a separate political faction, should support the democratic petty bourgeoisie in its fight against Prussian absolutism:

> it is our interest and our task to make the revolution permanent, until all more or less possessing classes have been forced out of their position of dominance, the proletariat has conquered state power, and the association of proletarians, not only in one country but in all the dominant countries of the world, has advanced so far that competition among the proletarians in these countries has ceased and that at least the decisive productive forces are concentrated in the hands of the proletarians. (Marx 1978: 281)

Positioning himself on the standpoint of the proletariat, Marx stressed that the revolution had to be made permanent, in the sense that when the radical petty bourgeoisie had attained its democratic reforms the working class should continue *its own* struggle until it 'conquered state power'.[18] Hence the permanency of revolution consisted in the independent class action of the proletariat and the organic growth of communist revolution from the conditions of bourgeois revolution (Thomas 2015: 299). The concept of permanent revolution served as a means to frame and direct class politics at a time when the capacity of the bourgeois and petty-bourgeois classes to act as a revolutionizing actor was eclipsed by the emerging power of the proletariat and its promise of a communist society. Permanent revolution did not concede to any 'duration' of the capitalist mode of production: the epoch of the bourgeoisie had only just begun and the era of the proletariat seemed already on the horizon. Finally, permanent revolution also conceptualized the necessary dynamic of class struggle in the context of the uneven development of capitalism on a world scale.

3. A Criterion for Interpretation

Italian Unification

The process of Italian unification – the Risorgimento – presented a historical path towards a bourgeois-capitalist order that differed qualitatively from the English and French experiences. A profound study of this period led Gramsci to the development of the concept of 'revolution/restoration'[1] or 'passive revolution'. He borrowed the term 'passive revolution' from the conservative historian Vincenzo Cuoco (1770–1823), who described the absence of popular initiative 'from below' in the Neapolitan revolution of 1799, which was accomplished through an intervention 'from above' by the bourgeoisie and the French army. Whereas Cuoco used 'passive revolution' in the sense of a normative political strategy that avoided violent insurrections such as the French Revolution, Gramsci deployed the term 'not as a programme ... but as a criterion of interpretation' (Gramsci 1971: 114; Q15§62) for the peculiar trajectory of Italian history and for the *absence* of such a bourgeois revolution (Gramsci 1971: 108; Q15§11).

Gramsci's point of departure was that the medieval 'Italian bourgeoisie was incapable of uniting the people around itself, and this was the cause of its defeats and the interruptions in its development' (Gramsci 1971: 53; Q25§5; see Gramsci 1971: 98; Q19§26). Unlike the historical development in the Netherlands, where the merchant class was able to establish a unified republic, the Italian communal[2] bourgeoisie remained locked in a corporate, feudal position within the 'mechanical' state and was unable to constitute a modern, 'organic' state. The distinction between the estates – clergy, nobility, and the 'commons' – was complicated by a sharp division between city and countryside, ideologically and affectively articulated through a reciprocal aversion between rural and city folk. There was no organic bond between the city and the countryside; instead there emerged 'two vast territories of very different civil and cultural tradition' (Gramsci 1971: 92; Q19§26). The communal bourgeoisie did not succeed in developing organic intellectuals who could articulate the domination of their class as an encompassing, hegemonic project. Ironically the intellectual cosmopolitanism of the city-based Renaissance acted as a brake on the development of an Italian national–popular intelligentsia. The opposition between the urban and the rural life-world was represented geographically by the regional division between, respectively, the North and the Mezzogiorno – the South.[3] The historical legacy of a failed bourgeois hegemony would burden attempts during and after the Risorgimento to forge a unity between the peasants and the urban classes.

The rise of strong Italian city-states during the Renaissance and the growing social division between north and south Italy prevented a development towards a modern nation state along either the English 'agricultural capitalist' or the French 'absolutist' trajectory. From the sixteenth century onwards, foreign intervention and occupation by Austria, France, and Spain consolidated the territorial and political fragmentation of the cultural nation. Through the Napoleonic wars Italy was temporarily united and bourgeois property rights, ideas, and state structures were forcefully introduced in Italy, abolishing feudal relations, but strengthening autocratic rule. As the Congress of Vienna (1815) restored the rule of the European powers, especially Austria, over Italy, the struggle against autocracy became necessarily entwined with a fight against foreign domination.

Like France's Jacobins the Italian nationalist bourgeois vanguard, the *Carbonari*, was primarily composed of the petty bourgeoisie. The two most important leaders of the movement were Giuseppe Mazzini (1805–72) and Giuseppe Garibaldi (1807–82). Mazzini, a lawyer and journalist from Genoa, was directly influenced by Jacobin thought through his father, and became a passionate proponent of a popular uprising from below that would establish a united Italian republic. He established the Young Italy movement and led a number of armed insurrections, which, however, were all suppressed. Garibaldi was a merchant sea captain hailing from Nice. He joined Mazzini's Young Italy movement and participated in the 1834 uprising in Piedmont. The July Revolution of 1830 in France had encouraged the *Carbonari* to rise up in the Papal states, Modena, and Parma proclaiming a united Italy. Austria intervened to crush the rebellion. Garibaldi had to flee to South America, where he recruited an 'Italian Legion', which developed guerrilla tactics.

Insurrections in 1848 in Milan, Naples, the Papal States, Sicily, Tuscany, and Venice led to the first Italian war of independence against Austria. Garibaldi returned to his homeland, deploying his Italian Legion in the struggle. The revolutionary movement created alliances between new Italian republics, which expelled their autocrats and introduced democratic reforms, and conservative monarchies such as Piedmont, which merely desired independence from Austrian domination. By 1850, however, the Italian forces were defeated by Austria's military superiority. From that moment on, the initiative of Italian unification shifted to Victor

Emmanuel II (1820–78), king of Sardinia–Piedmont, and his liberal prime minister Count Camillo Benso di Cavour (1810–61). Despite its centralized character, this constitutional monarchy was one of the most economically liberal and industrially developed regions of Italy. Not the *Carbonari*, but Piedmont's powerful diplomatic and military state apparatus would become the main agent of Italian unification. Cavour became the main leader of the Moderate Party, the liberal–constitutionalist right wing of the nationalist movement. Not interested in the goal of Italian unification per se, Cavour hoped to acquire the wealthy northern provinces of Italy in a first wave of expansion. Mazzini opposed Piedmont because of its monarchist leadership over the nationalist movement and its pragmatic, top-down, and gradualist attitude towards the unification process. He founded the Action Party, which represented the popular and radical republican wing of the nationalist movement.

Whereas the Action Party tried to rally the masses for a process of unification 'from below', Cavour began to seek international allies to isolate Austria. The Kingdom struck a deal with Napoleon III and in 1859 Cavour was able to provoke Austria, creating a case for war in which France could join in the hostilities. During the second war for Italian independence Garibaldi was appointed as a military commander in the service of Piedmont – thus recognizing the leadership of the King over the nationalist movement, which caused a rupture with the republican Mazzini. Garibaldi revived Mazzini's slumbering Action Party in order to mobilize support for his campaign.

Although the Franco-Piedmont alliance won, Napoleon III negotiated a separate settlement with the Austrian Emperor Franz Joseph, which minimized the gains for Piedmont and the losses for Austria. However, Sardinian insurrectionary forces simply ignored the treaty and began to occupy and unite the central Italian states. Through skilful diplomacy, maintaining a balance between the European great powers, Cavour succeeded in annexing these territories. Despite the personal and political enmity between Cavour and Garibaldi, the statesman was also able to direct the revolutionary's efforts to Sicily, which he liberated, operating under the flag of King Emmanuel II. After Naples and the Papal States had been annexed, Garibaldi freely relinquished command to Emmanuel II, who was declared King of Italy in 1861 by the first Italian Parliament in Turin. To the frustration of Garibaldi, Nice, Rome, and Venice remained outside the new kingdom – as Emmanuel II was loath to provoke the European powers. Instead Emmanuel II patiently waited until the Austro-Prussian War of 1866. Garibaldi was mobilized again by the King and despite his misgivings he performed his military service dutifully. By supporting Bismarck's Prussia, Italy was able to wrest Venice from Austria. The next war, of Prussia against France in 1870, offered an opportunity to annex Rome. The defeat of Napoleon III, whose troops protected the Papal State, led the Italian army to a quick invasion and defeat of Rome. In 1871 Rome formally became Italy's capital.

Risorgimento as Passive Revolution

In order to understand the success of the Moderate Party in pursuing its elitist project of Italian unification compared to the failure of the popular–republican Action Party, Gramsci investigated their hegemonic politics. He concluded that:

> the Moderates represented a relatively homogeneous social group, and hence their leadership underwent relatively limited oscillations ... whereas the so-called Action Party did not base itself specifically on any historical class, and the oscillations which its leading organs underwent were resolved, in the last analysis, according to the interests of the Moderates. In other words, the Action Party was led historically by the Moderates. (Gramsci 1971: 57; Q19§24)

This compact observation stressed the crucial differences between the party of Cavour and Emmanuel II and that of Garibaldi and Mazzini. The Moderate Party did not become a genuine bourgeois–hegemonic force, but it was able to solve the problem of class leadership (hegemony) through *technical* instead of purely *political* means: 'It was precisely the brilliant solution of these problems which made the Risorgimento possible, in the form in which it was achieved (and with its limitations) – as "revolution" without a "revolution", or as "passive revolution"' (Gramsci 1971: 59; Q19§24).

Although France had faced foreign enemies throughout its revolutionary trajectory, the problem of external domination, especially by the Austrian Empire, was much more profound in Italy's case (see Gramsci 1971: 107; Q15§17). The hope for a revolutionary solution of simultaneously overthrowing the Ancien Régime in Austria and Italy was temporarily dashed in the botched revolts of 1848. Conversely, a purely military victory of Piedmont over the formidable Austrian armies was inconceivable (Gramsci 1971: 85–6; Q19§28; see Callinicos 2010: 494). Under the cautious leadership of the Moderates, the military strategy was therefore expanded diplomatically and politically. On the one hand, Piedmont allied itself first with France, then with Prussia, making use of the wars between these great powers to gradually absorb Italian territories. On the other hand, the military efforts of the Piedmont state were reinforced by 'the politico-insurrectional mobilisation of popular forces who would rise in revolt at the enemy's back ... and which would give the "technical" army an atmosphere of enthusiasm and ardour' (Gramsci 1971: 87; Q19§28). In other words, the subordination of the Action Party and chiefly of its popular and experienced guerrilla leader Garibaldi was also a crucial element for the military success of Piedmont (see Gramsci 1971: 112; Q15§15). Whereas in France military campaigns served to *strengthen* an already hegemonic regime, in Italy they actively *constructed* the leadership of Piedmont (Gramsci 1971: 81–2; Q19§24).

The party that acted as the main force for Italian modern state formation was, in fact, the Piedmont state, which the Moderates served as intellectual personnel. Gramsci claimed that the organic intellectuals of the Moderate Party 'were a real, organic vanguard of the upper classes, to which economically they belonged. They were intellectuals and political organisers, and at the same time company bosses, rich farmers or estate managers, commercial or industrial entrepreneurs, etc.' (Gramsci 1971: 60; Q19§24). However, because these fractions of capital and remnants of the Ancien Régime remained locked in their own corporate positions, unable to unite politically and constitute a national bourgeois party, the Piedmont state functioned as a directive class in their stead (Gramsci 1971: 104; Q15§59). Gramsci claimed that this historical function of Piedmont

> is of the greatest importance for the concept of 'passive revolution' – the fact, that is, that what was involved was not a social group which 'led' other groups, but a State which, even though it had limitations as a power, 'led' the group which should have been 'leading' and was able to put at the latter's disposal an army and a politico-diplomatic strength. (Gramsci 1971: 105; Q15§59)

Piedmont was not only an instrument for Italian state formation through military and diplomatic expansion, but it also 'provided a model of what a future unified State would do' (Gramsci 1971: 104; Q15§59). Its organizational cohesion and coherence of thought attracted other intellectuals who were not organically connected to either Piedmont or the bourgeois class. Leadership was not achieved by an 'organic passage' of society – the masses – to the ruling class, but by means of a restricted transition of its intellectuals to the Piedmont state apparatus – that is, by a politics of *trasformismo* or *transformism*: 'the gradual but continuous absorption ... of the active elements produced by allied groups – and even of those which came from antagonistic groups and seemed irreconcilably hostile' (Gramsci 1971: 58–9; Q19§24).[4] Furthermore, the incorporation of the Action Party 'in molecular fashion by the Moderates' led to the 'decapitation' of the popular masses and their exclusion from the new state (Gramsci 1971: 97–98; Q19§26; see Coutinho 2012: 161). The bourgeois politics of transformism that subordinated the Action Party was already taking shape from 1848 onwards, and after the Italian unification it continued in a parliamentary form (Gramsci 1971: 97; Q19§26). In a first phase, between 1860 and 1900, individual opposition leaders were integrated into the Moderate-dominated coalition; in a second period, whole groups were absorbed by the ruling bloc (Q8§36; see Q1§44).

In contradistinction, the Action Party was unable to articulate its popular republicanism as a class project. In order to counter the 'spontaneous' attraction of the Piedmont project, the republicans had to actively organize their own hegemony (Gramsci 1971: 61; Q19§24). Moreover, as Marx had observed, because of the radical–popular dimension of the 1848 revolutions, the bourgeoisie was no longer an objective ally in the struggle against autocracy. Instead the bourgeois class sought alliances with Ancien Régime forces, such as feudalist or commercial landowners, protecting its corporate interests *against* revolutions 'from below'. In order to accomplish their republican project, the petty-bourgeois *Carbonari* had to ally themselves with the popular classes, especially the peasantry, which were exploited by feudal landholding and capitalist classes (Gramsci 1971: 82; Q19§24).

However, the leaders of the Action Party did not succeed in forging a relation of leadership between their political faction and the popular masses. Here Gramsci allotted a great weight to the 'subjective factor': the agency of a social group. Internal strife and competition between leaders weakened and fragmented the organizational capacity of the Action Party (Gramsci 1971: 62; Q19§24). Whereas the Jacobins were able to impose their radical democratic project on the French bourgeoisie, the *Carbonari* struggled to organize *themselves*. This organ-izational weakness was reflected in their political perspectives; unlike the Moderates, the Action Party 'lacked even a concrete programme of government' (Gramsci 1971: 62; Q19§24).

Furthermore, the Action Party was not able to 'translate' its revolu-tionary ideas to the masses. The notion of 'translation' should be taken almost literally, as Gramsci stressed the incapacity of the intellectuals of the Action Party to speak the language of the popular classes:

[they] confused the cultural unity which existed in the peninsula – confined, however, to a very thin stratum of the population, and polluted by the Vatican's cosmopolitanism – with the political and territorial unity of the great popular masses, who were foreign to

that cultural tradition and who, even supposing that they knew of its existence, couldn't care less about it. (Gramsci 1971: 63; Q19§24; see Gramsci 1971: 117–8; Q10ii§61)

The Action Party leaders displayed a 'paternalistic' attitude towards the peasant masses. In other words, there was no organic bond between the republican, cosmopolitan intellectuals and the classes they wished to liberate. Furthermore, those intellectuals who did realize the necessity of a 'Jacobin' element, such as Giuseppe Ferrari (1811–76),

applied to Italy French schemas, which represented conditions considerably more advanced than those to be found in Italy.... Ferrari did not see that an intermediary link was missing between the Italian and French situations, and that it was precisely this link which had to be welded fast for it to be possible to pass on to the next. Ferrari was incapable of 'translating' what was French into something Italian. (Gramsci 1971: 65; Q19§24)

Here 'translation' means the adaptation and rearticulation of a universalist programme to particular circumstances. Although the Action Party *emulated* Jacobinism in the sense of its 'extreme energy, decisiveness and resolution' (Gramsci 1971: 66; Q19§24), it did not *translate* its universality to Italian conditions. It was Jacobin in *form*, but not in *content* (Gramsci 1971: 74, 117; Q19§24; Q10ii§61). In other words, Garibaldi and Mazzini did not offer the popular classes a political and civil 'organic passage' to their own narrow group. Although the radical republicans arguably captured the myth[5] of a united Italy and the Jacobin 'temperament' more successfully than the Piedmont faction, they could not translate this abstract idea in a concrete national–popular programme of transition.

The lack of an organic class programme was expressed most clearly in the incapability of the Action Party to rally the peasant masses behind its banner. The penetration of capital had dispossessed numerous farmers from their lands, but the class position of these agricultural labourers was still 'the same as that of the farmer and the small-holder' (Gramsci 1971: 75; Q19§24). There was no real subsumption of rural labour under capital, because there was no 'agricultural industry developed through concentration of capital and the division of labour' (Gramsci 1971: 75; Q19§24). Astutely, Gramsci remarked that the organization of rural relations of production, and especially the differentiation of the agricultural labour population into labourers and sharecroppers, was politically motivated by the large landowners, who could, consequently, divide the peasantry and ally themselves with the wealthier layers (Gramsci 1971: 76; Q19§24). In this manner the peasantry was integrated in a reactionary bloc dominated by Ancien Régime forces, such as, at the local level, large proprietors and the clergy and, at the (fragmented) national level, autocratic monarchies and the papacy. For Gramsci, this was probably one of the most important distinctions between the successful Jacobin project and the failure of the Action Party: 'The Jacobins strove with determination to ensure a bond between town and country, and they succeeded triumphantly' (Gramsci 1971: 63; Q19§24). This bond had been achieved in political and cultural–historical terms. Politically the French peasants had been mobilized through the implementation of land reforms. In Italy, such a programme for land reform never materialized (Gramsci 1971: 74; Q19§24). From a cultural–historical perspective, 'the necessity of binding the town (Paris) to the countryside had always been vividly felt and expressed' (Gramsci 1971: 63; Q19§24). Whereas the French Revolution was deeply embedded within a national cultural framework, the cosmopolitan outlook of most Italian intellectuals had prevented such an articulation. In France bourgeois culture was universalized as the ideological form of the popular 'organic passage' to the dominant class; in Italy elitist intellectualism remained an obstacle to such a hegemonic process. Moreover, the leaders of the Action Party 'considered as "national" the aristocracy and the landowners, and not the millions of peasants' (Gramsci 1971: 101; Q19§26). The Action Party could and would not rally 'the intellectuals of the middle and lower strata by concentrating them and stressing the themes most capable of interesting them' (Gramsci 1971: 74; Q19§24) to the cause of the peasantry. On the contrary, in 1860 Garibaldi's troops crushed the Sicilian independent peasant movements, and Mazzini's project of religious reform alienated the peasants (Gramsci 1971: 101–2; Q19§26).

Finally, apart from their failure to create an adequate leadership, a transitional programme, and an organic connection with the popular classes the Action Party did not develop a correct concept of the national particularities of the Italian historical context and of its own immediate and future position and tasks within these concrete circumstances. Gramsci claimed that 'whereas Cavour was aware of his role (at least up to a certain point) in as much as he understood the role of Mazzini, the latter does not seem to have been aware either of his own or of Cavour's' (Gramsci 1971: 108, Q15§11). Cavour and Emmanuel II gained the upper hand over Garibaldi and Mazzini not because they subjugated them directly, but because they had a better understanding of their own time and place, which empowered them to make better tactical and strategic decisions: 'thanks to this awareness, their "subjectivity" was of a superior and more decisive quality' (Gramsci 1971: 113; Q15§15). This insight was the result of the Moderates' analysis and self-criticism of the failed campaign for independence of 1848 (Gramsci 1971 110–1; Q15§11). Naturally, as Gramsci pointed out, this advantage of intellectual 'clairvoyance' over the Action Party would have been of little use without the will and the means of the Piedmont state (Gramsci 1971: 113; Q15§25).

In conclusion, Gramsci's comments on the Italian Risorgimento provide the raw materials for a concept of passive revolution. The historical trajectory of Italy's political economy, geopolitical relations, and geographical fragmentation had resulted in a weak and dependent bourgeoisie that had to ally itself with Ancien Régime groups in order to deflect popular initiative 'from below' by gradual transformations 'from above'. Within the complex of Italian states the Piedmont state emerged as the most powerful actor, assembling a coalition of the 'corporate' bourgeois and Ancien Régime forces under its political leadership, which was complemented by military and diplomatic agility in the international arena. Whereas the political weakness of the ruling classes was solved in this roundabout way, the subaltern groups remained locked in their corporate state. A lack of organization, vision, and a dialectical pedagogy[6] between leaders and masses blocked the formation of a successful popular counter-hegemony. This allowed the Piedmont state to substitute the organic passage of the population into the bourgeois project with a politics of transformism: the absorption of opposition leaders and groups through a limited and mostly technical extension of the state.

Europe's Passive Revolution

Gramsci stressed that the comparison between France's revolutionary trajectory and that of the other European nations was 'vitally important' (Gramsci 1971: 114; Q10ii§61). A classic case of modern capitalist state formation that did not take the French path was Germany, where 'Industrial development took place within a semi-feudal integument that persisted up to November 1918' (Gramsci 1971: 19; Q12§1). Gramsci compared the fusion between the old landowning classes and the bourgeoisie in Germany to the process in England, and concluded that bourgeois *rule* should not be confused with its capacity to *govern*. Although the commercial and industrial bourgeoisie was not able to dethrone the Ancien Régime forces by directly conquering state power, the gradual introduction of modern property rights, the development towards an integral state (for example the increasing role of constitutionalism, parliamentarianism, and the press), and the expansion of the capitalist mode of production signalled a process of economic transformation that favoured the owners of the means of production engaged in capital accumulation. Conversely, the *Junkers*, the German landed nobility, not only maintained in their hands political, economic, and military power, but they also developed their own intellectuals and an *esprit de corps*, which was vital to their survival, perhaps not as a proper ruling class, but certainly as a governing body (Gramsci 1971: 19, 83, 270; Q12§1; Q19§24; Q15§18).

A central figure in the unification of Germany was Otto von Bismarck (1815–98) a Prussian prince and statesman. Comparing German unification to the Risorgimento, Bismarck played the role of Cavour, and absolutist Prussia that of Piedmont. Like Napoleon III, who had introduced 'top-down' social reforms, the right to strike, and education for women without 'touching the essential' (see below), Bismarck carefully weighed the interests of the liberal factions of the bourgeoisie against those of the ultraconservative Prussian aristocracy. In an 1867 constitutional reform, the Bismarck government introduced the *Reichstag*, a parliament elected by (male) universal suffrage, and the federal council of the *Bundesrat*. Without freedom of speech and association, elections by universal suffrage[7] were deployed as a means of curtailing the power of the liberal bourgeoisie, petty bourgeoisie, and workers. The transformist policies of 'Royal Prussian government socialism' (Engels 1985: 225) brought even socialist movements such as the Lasalleans into the orbit of the Bismarck government.

Just as Napoleon I had continued the French Revolution of 1789 with military means, Bismarck promised to pursue German unification – one of the primary goals of the German revolutionary movement of 1848 – with 'iron and blood' (Draper 2011a: 327). The German 'revolution from below' was replaced by the initiative of the Prussian state, which still operated with a precapitalist, imperial logic (Wood 2012: 134). Through military campaigns against Denmark (1864), Austria (1866), and France (1870–71) Prussia united the German states from above. Although the popular element was even less present than in the case of the Risorgimento, Bismarck was able to play up nationalist sentiments and rally the German population against 'foreign' aggression. As with the process of Italian unification, war played a key role in Germany's passive revolution, displacing political revolt from below by military agency. After France's defeat in 1871, King Wilhelm I of Prussia was declared Emperor of the Germans in Versailles.

The Italian and German paths were not *exceptions* to the process of 'bourgeois revolution', they rather represented the *rule* of capitalist transformation (Cliff 1984: 65–6; see Davidson 2012: 443). The 'bourgeois revolutions' relied much more on top-down military interventions and cautious negotiations with Ancien Régime forces than on the revolutionary mobilization of popular classes. The dominant organic passage was that of landowning classes into the bourgeoisie, not of the subaltern groups into the integral state (see Draper 2011a: 328). The Glorious Revolution and the Continental passive revolutions in the nineteenth century are in this regard much more representative of the ideal typical 'bourgeois revolution' than the radical rupture of the French Revolution. In fact, one could argue that there is no such thing as a bourgeois *revolution*, only *transformation*. I return to this idea in the next chapter.

Nevertheless, in the nineteenth century the historical fact of France's 'radical and violent transformation of social and political relations' (Gramsci 1971: 115; Q10ii§61) became a political force in the whole of Europe, for it saliently projected a future of political emancipation, which served as a model to revolutionaries, and as a warning to the ruling classes. The myth of the French Revolution became a 'spectre' (Gramsci 1971: 82; Q19§24) that continued to haunt the Ancien Régime classes during the revolutions of 1830 and 1848. Callinicos rightly emphasized that '[o]ne of the most important general propositions about bourgeois revolutions is their cumulative impact. Each revolution alters the terms for its successors' (Callinicos 1989: 141). Different lines of capitalist development and class struggle became nationally and internationally intertwined, creating new conditions for subsequent transformations (see Engels 1975a: 473; Wood 2012: 33). The event of the French Revolution allowed conservative forces 'to prevent the formation of a collective will of this kind, and to maintain "economic-corporate" power in an international system of passive equilibrium' (Gramsci 1971: 132; Q13§1). The foreknowledge of an impending revolution following the French pattern permitted conservative elites to prepare for a similar uprising in their own countries, which directly influenced the outcomes of these struggles and rendered a simple repetition of the French experience historically impossible. The result was that the 'mode of formation of the modern States of continental Europe [developed] as "reaction – national transcendence" of the French revolution' (Gramsci 1971: 117; Q10ii§61). Returning to the exceptionalism of the French Revolution: it was precisely because the archetype of the French Revolution became the *political norm* of bourgeois revolution (see Wood 2012: 35) that it ended up as a *historical exception*.

The constitution of post-1789 European states was concretely achieved by

> successive small waves of reform rather than by revolutionary explosions like the original French one. The 'successive waves' were made up of a combination of social struggles, interventions from above of the enlightened monarchy type, and national wars – with the two latter phenomena predominating. (Gramsci 1971: 115; Q10ii§61)

The periods of restoration after 1815 and 1848 did not block but decelerated and diffused the process in which the bourgeoisie gained power and capitalist relations were constituted (see Gramsci 1971: 119; Q10i§9). The bourgeois class could mobilize the fear for popular revolt in order to transform the state into the guardian of capital accumulation (by the introduction of property rights, constitutionalism, etc.). Conversely, Ancien Régime forces could pre-empt their complete downfall by integrating the bourgeoisie in the historical bloc and/or by turning themselves into a fraction of capital (see Davidson 2010). It was simply a question of 'transform' or 'succumb' (Callinicos 2010: 495). Gramsci observed that in this process:

> The old feudal classes are demoted from their dominant position to a 'governing' one, but are not eliminated, nor is there any attempt to liquidate them as an organic whole; instead of a class they become a 'caste' with specific cultural and psychological characteristics, but no longer with predominant economic functions. (Gramsci 1971: 115; Q10ii§61)

The end result of this gradual process of transformation from above, as Engels observed, was 'that in Europe the independence and internal unity of the great nations, with the exception of Poland, had become a fact' (Engels 1990b: 513). One could say that in his discussion of the 1815–71 'revolutions from above', Gramsci expanded his 'Italian' concept of passive revolution, incorporating the trajectory of most European nations. However, the reverse holds true as well: the meaning of Italy's particular path to modernity was rendered comprehensible by its integration in a continental-wide historical process (see Bruff 2010: 411). From a criterion for the interpretation of Italian history, passive revolution evolved into an interpretative concept for the institution of capitalist modernity as a whole (see Thomas 2006). After 1815 and certainly after 1848, Jacobin politics and the popular–democratic project of the French Revolution had made way for the cynical, technocratic management of society by cautious elites. The essence of 'bourgeois permanent revolution' now appeared explicitly as a *passive* revolution.

The Stubborness of Capitalism

The abstract language of the 'Preface', repeated in *Capital*,[8] concealed the fact that, in opposition to the almost natural rise and fall of previous modes of production, the transition from bourgeois society to communism was anything but an automatic process. The constitution of a communist society required a conscious, mass intervention of human agency – that is, the development of a revolutionary subject – leaving the 'prehistory of human society' behind. The contradiction between the development of the productive forces and restrictive relations of production in capitalism had to be solved *politically* (see Q10ii§36). Communism was humanity's *project*, not its *destiny*.

This emphasis on the 'subjective factor' – the development of class organization – raised the question of what would happen when relations of production turned into fetters at a time when the revolutionary subject had not (sufficiently) developed itself, or when the emancipatory mass struggle was defeated. At this juncture, '[t]he crisis consists precisely in the fact that the old is dying and the new cannot be born: in this interregnum, morbid phenomena of the most varied kind come to pass' (Gramsci 1971: 276; Q3§34). The tendency of relations of production to constrict the development of productive forces appeared as an absolute and universal historical law, whereas the movement of the workers from a class 'in itself' towards a class 'for itself' – from a corporate to a political group – was articulated as a highly contingent, relative, and fragmented process, conditioned by particular political and economic 'situations of development' (see De Smet 2015).

The vision of a failure of the proletariat to develop and organize itself politically, lead an alliance of subaltern classes, and conquer state power had already brought Marx and Engels in the *Communist Manifesto* (1848) to conjecture about a catastrophic outcome of the class struggle as 'the common ruin of the contending classes' (Marx and Engels 1976: 482). In his 'Anti-Dühring' (1877) Engels reiterated that 'If the whole of modern society is not to perish, a revolution in the mode of production and distribution must take place' (Engels 1987: 146). In *The Erfurt Program: A Discussion of Fundamentals* (1892), Karl Kautsky (1854–1939) concluded: 'As things stand today capitalist civilization cannot continue; we must either move forward into socialism or fall back into barbarism' (Kautsky 1910, see Angus 2014; Hampton 2009). This general idea was picked up by Rosa Luxemburg (1871–1919) in her 'Junius Pamphlet'

(1916). Writing in 1915 and facing the unprecedented devastation wrought by the First World War Luxemburg perceived the systemic crisis of capitalism in the almost chiliastic terms of a 'dilemma of world history' between socialism and barbarism. The triumph of imperialism would lead to 'the collapse of all civilization as in ancient Rome, depopulation, desolation, degeneration – a great cemetery' (Luxemburg 1916). The great urgency that speaks to us from Luxemburg's writings betrays a profound sense for the epochal character of the world war, which the Russian Revolution of 1917 appeared to vindicate. Similarly, witnessing the triumph of Fascism and Nazism in the 1930s, Trotsky concluded that humanity stood before the epochal choice of a new global war, economic collapse, and barbarism, or world revolution and socialism (Davidson 2012: 429). Since the second half of the twentieth century the dystopian vision of extinction looms permanently over the class struggle. The risk of a nuclear holocaust after the Second World War and, since the 1970s, mounting ecological problems pose direct threats, not only to the existence of civilization, but to the very survival of humanity as a species.

Nevertheless, world capitalism has neither been overcome by a socialist revolution, nor has it led to 'the collapse of all civilization'. Although capitalist relations continue to fetter human development, time and time again the concrete forms of capitalism have been successfully reconstituted in the face of structural crisis and social revolution (see Achcar 2013: 21–2; Harvey 2004). Even the spectre of human extinction has been commodified and turned into a concept for mass consumption, leading to a situation in which 'it's possible to imagine the end of the world; it's not possible to imagine the end of capitalism' (Žižek 1999; see Jameson 2003). The punctuated drama of the capitalist epoch has made way for the protracted farce of its duration.

The empirical fact of the 'stubbornness' of capitalism invites us to investigate

> the persistent capacity of initiative of the bourgeoisie which succeeds, even in the historical phase in which it has ceased to be a properly revolutionary class, to produce socio-political transformations, sometimes of significance, conserving securely in its own hands power, initiative and hegemony, and leaving the working classes in their condition of subalternity. (Losurdo in Thomas 2009: 197)

Confronted by imperialism, the failure of European revolutionary movements in the wake of the First World War, the rise of Fascism and Fordism–Americanism (see below), Gramsci wondered to what extent passive revolution could function as a criterion of interpretation, not only for the period of the constitution of modern bourgeois societies, but also for their endless reconstitutions in order to solve ever returning organic crises (Gramsci 1971: 114–5, 118; Q15§62).

He speculated that:

> there is a passive revolution involved in the fact that – through the legislative intervention of the State, and by means of the corporative organisation [the trade union] – relatively far-reaching modifications are being introduced into the country's economic structure in order to accentuate the 'plan of production' element; in other words, that socialisation and co-operation in the sphere of production are being increased, without however touching (or at least not going beyond the regulation and control of) individual and group appropriation of profit. (Gramsci 1971: 119–120; Q10i§9)

In order for capitalism to survive organic crises as a *system*, concrete *historical blocs* have to be reconfigured by modifications to their economic structure and superstructures. Here passive revolution comes to signify a top-down, elite-driven, and state-led mode of transition, not only from the Ancien Régime to capitalism 'in general', but also from one particular form of capitalist society to another (see Buci-Glucks-mann 1979: 222). In the jargon of the 'Preface', the 'absolute' fettering of productive forces by capitalist relations of production can be stalled by the displacement of subaltern agency and their reconfiguration 'from above' (see Jessop 1990: 213; Morton 2007: 501). This creates 'a period of expectation and hope [and] reinforces the hegemonic system and the forces of military and civil coercion at the disposal of the traditional ruling classes' (Gramsci 1971: 120; Q10§I§9). Here Gramsci, together with Lenin, emerges as the philosopher *par excellence* of the *particularity* of capitalism. Whereas Marxism 'is usually very much better at distinguishing the large features of different epochs of society, as commonly between feudal and bourgeois' Lenin and Gramsci allow for historical materialism to distinguish more clearly 'between different phases of bourgeois society, and different moments within these phases: that true historical process which demands a much greater precision and delicacy of analysis than the always striking epochal analysis which is concerned with main lineaments and features' (Williams 1991: 413).

Imperialism and Fascism

In his seminal work 'Imperialism, the Highest Stage of Capitalism' (1916) Lenin offered a brief outline of the capitalist historical bloc that was emerging in the decades before the outbreak of the First World War.

At the level of the economic structure, the concentration of capital had gradually transformed free trade and competition into price fixing and monopolies, and stimulated the vertical integration of different phases of the production process by single companies.[9] The process of real subsumption of labour under capital, of which Marx only discussed the germ cells in his chapter on 'Machinery and Large-Scale Industry' in *Capital* (1990: 492–639), was expanded and deepened.

However, at the same time, monopolization began to fetter capital's expanded reproduction. Because of monopoly prices 'the motive cause of technical and, consequently, of all other progress disappears to a certain extent, and, further, the *economic* possibility arises of deliberately retarding technical progress' (Lenin 1964a: 276). Although monopolization never becomes absolute, monopoly capital displays a tendency to restrain the development of productive forces. This 'parasitic' aspect is worsened by the subordination of industrial capital to the interests of finance capital: 'although commodity production still "reigns" and continues to be regarded as the basis of economic life, it has in reality been undermined and the bulk of the profits go to the "geniuses" of financial manipulation' (Lenin 1964a: 206–7). The vast amounts of money capital required by the concentration of industrial capital called into being a powerful financial sector, in which the larger banks absorbed or subordinated the smaller ones. The traditional *technical* role of banking, facilitating the process of circulation and accumulation, became *political*:

> for they are enabled ... first, to *ascertain exactly* the financial position of the various capitalists, then to *control* them, to influence them by restricting or enlarging, facilitating or hindering credits, and finally to *entirely determine* their fate, determine their income, deprive them of capital, or permit them to increase their capital rapidly and to enormous dimensions, etc. (Lenin 1964a: 214–5)

The expansion of money capital bred a class of rentier capitalists, whose appropriation of surpluses was only indirectly based on the production process, but was firmly grounded in financial control. These rentier relations were internationalized as well. The concentration of capital within capitalist nations coalesced with the concentration of capital within the world economy at large, giving rise to 'the monopolist position of a few very rich countries' (Lenin 1964a: 241). As the appropriated surpluses were too large to be consumed in the form of commodities by the populations of the 'advanced' nations, capital could not find a profitable outlet in these home markets and had to be exported to more 'backward' countries. The competition between national capitalists for the home market was turned into a competition between international trusts and cartels for foreign markets. The process of monopolization was globalized, its economic division of the world leading to peaceful price fixing on the one hand, and increasing geopolitical and military conflict on the other. In less than four decades the six great powers – Great Britain, the United States, France, Germany, Japan, and Russia – carved up the world, increasing their total colonial possessions by half. Through the infamous 'scramble for Africa', the European powers, which in 1870 controlled merely ten per cent of the content, had by 1914 subjugated all African regions and nations, except for Abyssinia (Ethiopia) and Liberia.

Lenin contrasted 'imperialism in general', which could be found throughout the ages, or even colonialism during the previous form of capitalism, with imperialism as 'the latest stage in the development of capitalism' (Lenin 1964a: 254), which was 'the colonial policy of finance capital' (Lenin 1964a: 260). Whereas before the 1870s processes of empire-building and colonization were largely external to the process of capital accumulation, with the rise of monopoly capital they became an integral part of capitalist development. The control of the financial elites in the core capitalist countries divided the world 'into a handful of usurer states and a vast majority of debtor states' (Lenin 1964a: 277). Capitalist development directed by monopoly capital attributed to economic unevenness *between* and *within* nations (Lenin 1964a: 300).

A part of monopoly super-profits was not exported, but was used to support a politics of transformism of the working class in the heartland of capitalism: 'Imperialism ... makes it economically possible to bribe the upper strata of the proletariat' (Lenin 1964a: 281; see also 193, 301). In this regard imperialism was as much a *political* reaction to the development of strong workers' movements in Europe, as the *economic* consequence of the gradual concentration of capital. Imperialism favoured the creation of a dual labour market consisting of, on the one hand, privileged, high-earning, often white, male workers; and, on the other, low-waged, mostly immigrant[10] and/or female labourers (Lenin 1964a: 282–3). This tendency would be reinforced throughout capitalism's subsequent Fordist and neoliberal reconfigurations.

Lenin remarked that the economic structure of imperialism corresponded to new superstructures (Lenin 1964a: 262). The ideological forms of nationalism, patriotism, and jingoism not only expressed the geopolitical competition of nationally organized fractions of monopoly capital, but also penetrated the working class, rallying it behind the colonial and 'civilizational' successes of 'its' nation (Lenin 1964a: 285–6).

Gramsci recognized the parallels between imperialist powers and colonial countries and the geographical relations of domination within nations (Rosengarten 2009: 140). In the case of Italy he observed that the main obstacle for economic development was 'the semi-feudal and parasitic elements of society which appropriate an excessive tithe of surplus value and ... the so-called "producers of savings"' (Gramsci 1971: 291; Q22§6), rent-seeking fractions of capital that were not (sufficiently) integrated with the 'industrial–productive bloc'. A passive-revolutionary scenario 'could be the only solution whereby to develop the productive forces of industry under the direction of the traditional ruling classes, in competition with the more advanced industrial formations of countries which monopolise raw materials and have accumulated massive capital sums' (Gramsci 1971: 120; Q10i§9). Here the crisis of a particularly *Italian* capitalism vis-à-vis more powerful competitors had to be resolved by a dynamic of revolution/restoration of the existing historical bloc.

The First World War served as a catalyst for the formation of new historical blocs. The immense war effort led to the subordination of individual capitalists and companies to the state's planning, regulation, and control of the industries. Political society became a direct actor in the economic structure. The prestige of national bourgeois leaderships either leading the nation to a shared destiny of greatness or collabora-tively defending the homeland from foreign aggression offered a shortcut to hegemonic policies, which split the working class and its organ, the Second International. War presented the whole population with a violent organic passage to the nation, as political society, the state proper, appeared to subjugate civil society and the economic structure to the interests of the common good. In Italy, a group of 'nationalist' socialists under the leadership of Benito Mussolini (1883–1945) rejected the idea of the necessity of the international struggle of the proletariat, promoting the idea of a nationalist solution to the domination of finance capital.

In its mythical modernist and futurist form, Fascism represented the merging of workers and industrial capital (as the dominant force) into a national, productivist, 'urban' bloc (Gramsci 1971: 94; Q19§26). Workers would lose their independent collective class agency as their parties and trade unions were to be dismantled and their right to strike severely restricted, but their economic interests would be met by the state, which had to supervise corporatist structures and progressive labour legislation. Gramsci keenly observed that in Italy 'it was precisely the workers who brought into being newer and more modern industrial requirements and in their own way upheld these strenuously.... [S]ome industrialists understood this movement and tried to appropriate it to themselves' (Gramsci 1971: 292; Q22§6). However, in its practical form, Fascism was not able to solve the problem of unproductive money capital – that is, rentier capitalism – in a revolutionary way as it 'shore[s] up crumbling positions of the middle classes ... and is becoming, because of the vested interests that arise from the old foundations, more and more a machinery to preserve the existing order just as it is rather than a propulsive force' (Gramsci 1971: Q22§6). Ironically, these middle classes, squeezed by capitalist development, constituted the social base of Fascism. Moreover, Fascism's alliance with the Italian industrial bourgeoisie, rentier capitalists, the monarchy, and the Catholic Church against the vibrant socialist and communist movement undermined its imaginary of a revolutionary, modernist movement that was elevated above the classes.

Instead of the confrontational formation of a productivist bloc, which would subjugate commercial, landed, and finance capital to the interests of industrial capital, industrialize the Mezzogiorno, and commence a new wave of real subsumption of labour under capital, the Italian ruling classes chose to solve the problem of accumulation and development in an imperialist way. Internally, the Mezzogiorno functioned as 'a semi-colonial market, a source of savings and taxes' (Gramsci 1971: 94; Q19§26), subdued by police repression, institutionalized corruption, and the tranformism of the clergy – the intellectuals of the South. The nationalist bloc was externally oriented towards competition with foreign powers in order to get 'a piece of the cake' and not to 'fall behind'. This resulted in the relatively meagre bounty of Libya. After the Fascist takeover, Italy sought to increase its influence in the Mediterranean, intervening in Corfu and Albania, and to expand its colonial possessions by an invasion of Ethiopia.

Fascism can be understood as a reaction against the organic crisis of Italian capitalism and its ruling class – both active cause and passive consequence of a displacement of proletarian struggle in the wake of the 1917 Russian Revolution. Although the Fascist leadership objectively supported capitalist class power, its conquest of civil and political society, liquidating bourgeois state power, showed that in the 1920s 'no group, neither the conservatives nor the progressives, has the strength for victory, and that even the conservative group needs a master' (Gramsci 1971: 211; Q13§23). Through the mediation of Fascist dictatorship (see Gramsci 1971: 269–70; Q15§18), opposing fractions of capital were forcefully united in a more or less stable ensemble and social instability was pacified. Despite the bourgeoisie's inability to *govern*, its class *rule* continued. I return to this theme in the next chapter.

Fordism and Americanism

The trend towards greater state regulation of production after the First World War was not limited to Italy. Fascism was but a distorted form of a general process of capitalist development (see Buci-Glucksmann 1980: 310–4), propelled, on the one hand, by the wartime mobilization and central planning of resources and labour; and, on the other, by the political, economic, and cultural rise of the United States. The United States appeared as unburdened by a history of feudalism, able to develop a pure industrial society starting with a clean slate.[11] Gramsci remarked that Europe's rich civilizational heritage worked as a burden on its economic and social development: 'This past history has left behind a heap of passive sedimentations produced by the phenomenon of the saturation and fossilisation of civil-service personnel and intellectuals, of clergy and landowners, piratical commerce and the professional ... army' (Gramsci 1971: 281; Q22§2). In the European workplace, man-ufacturers still relied on a combination of premodern and capitalist disciplinary practices, such as the daily selection of unskilled workers at the factory gate, the contractual binding of expert craftsmen, and the direct subjugation of the labour force through a system of social rules, monetary penalties, overseers, and kinship bonds (Versieren and De Smet 2014: 201). In contradistinction, the management theories of the American engineer Frederick Winslow Taylor (1856–1915) injected the ongoing process of real subsumption of labour under capital with a scientific rationality, developing the technical division of labour in the workplace in order to increase labour productivity. The master-servant form of capitalist production relations, which still lingered in Europe, was gradually transformed into 'a layered system of molecular co-optation of workers into the daily management of the production process' (Versieren and De Smet 2014: 202). The increased technical division of labour was a mechanism of passive revolution at the level of the workplace, as it atomized the social body of workers, obstructing both precapitalist protests based on communal subjectivities and fully developed proletarian struggles. At the other end of the spectrum, the class power of the paternalist capitalist owner–manager became differ-entiated into ownership, managerial control, industrial expertise, etc.

At the factory floor, scientific organization of the labour process was complemented by an increasing mechanization and automation of manufacturing. The old craft-based system was slowly (and unevenly) replaced by capital-intensive, large-scale production of standardized commodities for a mass market (Kiely 2005: 52). The Taylorist frag-mentation of the production process in its component parts allowed for a deskilling of labour, while at the same time it required new forms of specialized – and therefore privileged – labour. The expansion of what was essentially the modern factory system established the economic base of a new accumulation strategy: *Fordism*, named after Ford Motor Company owner Henry Ford (1863–1947).[12] At the core of Fordism was a focus on the production of *relative* surplus value (by reducing necessary labour time) instead of the production of *absolute* surplus value (by lengthening the working day). Whereas the latter form of exploitation still represented the moment of formal subsumption of labour under capital, Fordist accumulation based on relative surplus extraction or 'the production of surplus value based upon the increase and development of the productive forces' (Marx 1986a: 335) represented the moment of real subsumption – of the direct integration of the processes of labour and production. In this regard, Fordism was 'simply the most recent phase of a long process which began with industrialism itself' (Gramsci 1971: 302; Q22§11).[13]

Ford reintegrated the Taylorist fragmented worker back into the mechanical unity of the company (Smith 2000: 4), realizing that '[i]t would be uneconomic to allow the elements of an organic whole so laboriously built up to be dispersed, because it would be almost impossible to bring them together again, while on the other hand reconstructing it with new elements, chosen haphazardly, would involve not inconsiderable effort and expense' (Gramsci 1971: 312; Q22§13). Mass manufacturing of the standardized 'Model T' Ford automobile lowered its production costs. Ford used this productive edge to lower the price of the car, turning it into a product for mass consumption. In addition, Ford combined modern methods of coercion and discipline with the payment of higher wages, social benefits, and 'subtle ideological and political propaganda', to secure workers' loyalty, moral behaviour, and productivity at the 'point of production': 'hegemony here is born in the factory' (Gramsci 1971: 285; Q22§2; see Gramsci 1971: 312; Q22§13). Moreover, the 'rational' spending of high wages directly created a consumer base for the company (Gramsci 1971: 303; Q22§11). In turn, private car ownership would establish the base for a transport revolution, which changed the dynamics of capitalist redistribution, as well as urban–rural social relations (Clarke 1990: 14).

Fordist transformism in the economic sphere was complemented by corporatist modifications to the integral state, often involving the organization of mass education, the recognition of trade unions and the right to strike, and state supervision of negotiations between workers and capitalists at the enterprise, sectorial, and/or national level. Instead of attempting simply to destroy the powerful trade unions, as Fascism had done in Italy and Germany during the interwar years, the Fordist state incorporated trade union leaders and sometimes even absorbed entire syndicalist structures into a subordinated position within the domain of the state. Syndicalist transformism was not only introduced to increase labour productivity, but also to deflect the more radical demands of the workers' movement, especially after the Second World War (Kiely 2005: 52). Various forms of workers' co-management locked the class in a corporate state and prevented workers' control and self-management (Barfuss 2008: 845). High wages for a section of the predominantly white and male labour population went hand in hand with low wages for unskilled women and migrant workers, who were increasingly drawn into the labour market, reinforcing the dual labour market (Clarke 1990: 38).

Following the logic of industrial monopolization, the ideal typical Fordist company was a large-scale company, which vertically integrated as many components of the production process as possible. Short- and long-term decision making with regard to the production process was top-down and bureaucratically organized. The workforce was divided along 'mental' and 'manual' labour lines and further fragmented in hierarchical positions with different wage scales and bonuses (Smith 2000: 4–5). Fordist companies operated with large stocks of raw materials, parts, and finished products, which guaranteed the continuity of the production and valorization processes. As capital-intensive production required large sums of money the interventionist role of the state as creditor, investor, and salvager of losses increased in the private sector (Gramsci 1971: 314–5; Q22§14). This might give the impression of a state elevated 'above' the economic structure, disciplining non-industrial forms of capital. Nevertheless, 'its structure remains plutocratic and it is impossible for it to break its links with big finance capital' (Gramsci 1971: 315; Q22§14).

Culturally, Fordism was accompanied by 'Americanism', consisting, firstly, of the top-down idea of 'a new type of man suited to the new type of work and productive process' (Gramsci 1971: 286; Q22§2), which was actively supported by the state; for example through prohibition, which channelled high wages into 'rational' consumption (Gramsci 1971: 302–4; Q22§11); and through new forms of sexual regulation (Gramsci 1971: 294–301, 304–5; Q22§3,9–11). The rigid organization of the Fordist factory was extended to society at large. Secondly, everyday life in the United States also projected new ways of living 'from below'. However, Gramsci claimed that these cultural forms did not represent a new global civilization, but merely a critique of the old European order in a predominantly material form. Put simply, the import of Americanism would not give birth to an American civilization in Europe, but to a variety of European Americanisms. In Americanism Europe recognized its own stasis (Gramsci 1971: 317–8; Q22§15). The rationale of the Fordist historical bloc was theoretically articulated in (neo-)Keynesian theories, which stressed the importance of market demand, a balance between wages and profits achieved by collective bargaining, (nearly) full employment for economic growth, and the establishment of a welfare state.[14]

Franklin Delano Roosevelt's (1882–1945) 'New Deal' policies constituted a first attempt at assembling the different technical, social, political, and ideological elements of a Fordist accumulation strategy into a new historical bloc (Barfuss 2008: 845).[15] The New Deal offered the population a new myth, which strengthened the collapsing bourgeois hegemony in the wake of the 1929 crisis. Moreover, by recognizing trade unions as an integral part of a properly functioning bourgeois democracy the New Deal blocked their political development (Clarke 1990: 29). However, it was the Second World War and its aftermath that served as a catalyst for a rapid, global reconstitution of capitalism. The 1944 system of Bretton Woods reorganized world-market relations. Whereas international free trade was encouraged, monetary policies and global capital flows were strongly regulated. New international institutions such as the IMF, the World Bank, and GATT were established. The implementation of the dollar as the international means of payment reflected the growing economic, cultural, political, and military hegemony of the United States in the wake of the devastation wrought by the Second World War and the perceived threat of the Soviet Union (Harvey 2004: 76; Kiely 2005: 49–51). The combination of a post-war economic boom structured around trade liberalization and the regulated internationalization of capital on the one hand, and the threat of a communist politicization of trade unionism on the other, stimulated the global diffusion of Fordism.

The post-war creation of Fordist historical blocs *emulated* the organic passage of the American and European industrial working class to bourgeois society. The 'bribing' of the upper layers of the proletariat, already discussed by Lenin in 'Imperialism', became the material pillar of a much more profound and stable class alliance. Whereas high wages and mass consumption provided the material base for hegemonic consent, universal suffrage and a further democratization of parliamentary bourgeois regimes opened up the political community to the proletariat. However, the passive-revolutionary mechanisms of consumerism and indirect representation through reformist political parties and labour bureaucracies would become sources of discontent in the following decades.

Neoliberalism

In the second half of the 1960s, the Fordist historical bloc entered an organic crisis, which was revealed in a series of conjunctural crises, ranging from the so-called oil crisis of 1973–74, through riots in black American communities, to the US war in Vietnam (1955–75). In the sphere of the economic structure, Fordist accumulation hit its limits.[16] Gramsci had claimed that Fordist high wages would be a transitory phenomenon, as they resulted from the monopoly position of companies deploying new production methods. When the global diffusion of these methods put an end to monopoly advantages, profits diminished, and wages came under pressure (Gramsci 1971: 310–1; Q22§13). Fordist capitalism suffered a crisis of *over-accumulation*: a surplus of labour, expressed by rising unemployment; and a surplus of capital, reflected by stocks of commodities that could not be valorized on the market (overproduction), machines that were running below their capacity, and money capital that could not be channelled into profitable investments (Harvey 2004: 64; see Kiely 2005: 34–5). As mass consumption markets became saturated with standardized products, capitalists began to differentiate commodities, which required more flexible and 'lean' production units. Japanese firms pioneered such lean production systems replacing the serial automation of the assembly line 'by programmable multifunctional machines, capable of switching from one production application to another at low cost' (Smith 2000: 13). In the case of information technology, the Fordist centralized mainframe was swapped for decentralized networks of personal computers. Traditional bureaucratic boundaries between R&D, production, marketing, and administration become much more fuzzy and osmotic. Better estimation of market demand and more efficient communication with suppliers and subcontractors permitted companies to replace Fordist stockpiling of finished goods, parts, and resources with 'just-in-time' production and distribution (Smith 2000: 14–5).[17]

Such a production process necessitated a new wave of real subsumption of labour under capital – that is, a modification of the content of the labour process – by developing a privileged layer of flexible, agile, innovative, and multi-skilled workers, able to solve problems creatively and collaborate as a team (Barfuss 2008: 840; Smith 2000: 13). On the other hand, 'lean' production also meant trimming the fat of the cost of variable capital (wages) by combining a high profile workforce with a low-waged, deskilled labour population. For the capitalist class the traditional, bureaucratic Fordist corporatist structures became an obstacle to maintaining, let alone increasing, the rate of accumulation and profit.

However, industrial workers as well began to reject the Fordist system, which, despite providing high wages and job security, was based on the dull, repetitive work of the assembly line and a rigid, hierarchical division of labour. Astutely, Gramsci commented that 'the fact that [the worker] gets no immediate satisfaction from his work and realises that [his employers] are trying to reduce him to a trained gorilla, can lead him to a train of thought that is far from conformist' (Gramsci 1971: 310; Q22§12). Workers' alienation at the 'point of production' coincided with their estrangement from their social bodies – the trade unions and social democratic parties – which were becoming appendages of the integral state and immediate barriers to proletarian self-emancipation. The transition of the working class to bourgeois society through the route of direct consumerism and indirect social democratic representation now appeared as a dead end, an empty 'anti-myth' that could no longer sustain popular enthusiasm. The workers' rejection of alienating systems of mass production and inadequate forms of class representation went hand in hand with a broad popular refusal of mass consumption and traditional authoritarian and patriarchal relations that were still predominant in the spheres of the family, the workplace, and civil and political society. Along with workers' protests new civil and social movements emerged, addressing issues of equal citizenship, women and LGBT rights, and ecology. Internationally, US hegemony was weakened by its involvement in the Vietnam war, which led to a powerful peace movement. Similarly, the military interventions of the Soviet Union in Hungary (1956), Czechoslovakia (1968), and Afghanistan (1979–89) increasingly diminished its prestige as a global counter-hegemon.

In the intellectual domain, these social movements concurred with the rise of (post)structuralist critiques of modernist subjectivities, which underlined the heterogeneous, multi-vocalist, non-linear, and anti-essentialist character of identities. As power was revealed as a decentralized force that (also) operated at the 'microscopic' level (see Foucault 1980: 73–4), research into contestation and struggle was diverted from traditional institutions (for example the trade unions) and spaces (for example the workplace) to everyday social and cultural forms. In Marxist Autonomism the centrality of the Fordist 'mass worker' as a revolutionary subject was replaced by the 'social worker' – that is, the whole population involved in the social reproduction of capital (Negri 1982). The emphasis on class struggle beyond the workplace reflected both the fragmentation of capital in global commodity chains and production networks and the integration of production, distribution, and consumption.

The Fordist organic crisis could not be solved 'by a frontal assault, which would only serve to polarize the class struggle even more, but only by a more selective offensive which would secure the decomposition of the working class by opening new sectional divisions' (Clarke 1990: 39). The conjunctural crises of 1974–76 and 1979–81 became catalysts of the process, forcing the workers' movement on the defensive and the capitalist class on the offensive. Although the restructuring of the Fordist historical bloc had already begun in the economic structure, where systems of flexible accumulation and lean production had begun to seep in, the superstructural forms that once stimulated capital accumulation now inhibited it. State regulation of capitalist production had turned bourgeois political society into a site of the economic struggle, subjecting spheres of the economic structure to democratic debate, if not control. Instruments for capital accumulation had been partially appropriated by the workers' movement to improve its own living conditions. In order to increase or at least maintain the rate of profit, the capitalist class had to reassert its class power by recapturing its full state power.

The apparent withdrawal of the state from its Fordist function of economic regulation concealed its real removal from the control of national parliaments.[18] The dictatorship of capital was reaffirmed in 'independent' supranational institutions such as the IMF and the World Bank, banks, and financial markets, which escaped democratic control. The role of the state was not diminished, but 'rescaled' and differentiated within national, regional, and global spheres. Moreover, the United States was able to maintain its supremacy within the global economy by evolving from the world's biggest creditor and exporter of capital to the number one debtor and importer of capital (Kiely 2005: 65) and by establishing a financial regime backed up by Wall Street and the Treasury, which directed the policies of institutions such as the IMF and supervised credit flows to national economies. The declining competitiveness and productivity of the United States had eroded the dollar as an international currency, which led to the collapse of the Bretton Woods agreement between 1971 and 1973 and of fixed exchange rates (Kiely 2005: 56–7). Through compensating for its diminishing advantage in the realm of production by establishing control over finance, the US state became the main actor in the restructuring of the Fordist bloc, integrating its geopolitical agenda with the economic interests of (especially financial) capital (Harvey 2004: 70, 77–8; Kiely 2005: 66).

The deregulation of global capital flows from the 1970s onwards served the intertwined purposes of restructuring state power and restoring the rate of accumulation. Lean production, which could be regarded as a real development and transformation of productive forces to overcome Fordist barriers, was complemented by an increasing financialization of the economy. Over-accumulation was partly displaced by a 'temporal fix' (Harvey 2004). Marx already observed that in the development of capitalism the flow of money capital is increasingly diverted to investments in claims to *future* income, which, in turn, become part of the circulation process (market) as *fictitious* capital in the form of traded bonds, credit, debt, shares, speculation, etc. This dynamic multiplies the value of the original investment of money capital, expanding credit and therefore demand, but it also multiplies the claims to the same income, creating a financial crisis when claimants desire to convert their fictitious capital *en masse* into real or money capital (see Marx 1991: 525–42). The expansion of fictitious capital from the 1980s onwards strengthened the position of finance capital in relation to other capital fractions, and, vice versa, the central role of finance stimulated the circulation of fictitious capital.

The temporal fix is combined with a geographical fix (Harvey 2004). Capital becomes fixed into social space in the form of factories, infrastructure, roads, schools, power plants, etc. The appropriation and transformation of new spaces by capital consumes surplus labour and capital, functioning as a geographical fix for over-accumulation. Lenin had discussed the necessity for capital to be exported in 'Imperialism'. The growth of transnational corporations (TNCs) after the world war allowed capital to transcend, momentarily and partly, the limits of the nation state. The production process of a single commodity became increasingly geographically fragmented. In order to articulate a commodity chain as a global process, its pre-existing elements had to be disjoined and reassembled into a new transnational ensemble. The constitution of global commodity chains represented a process not only of connection and inclusion, but also of 'disarticulation': disconnection and exclusion (see Bair and Werner 2011). Furthermore, as Lenin had already pointed out, the geographical fix displaced a class confrontation 'at home' due to increased exploitation by accumulation 'abroad' (Harvey 2004: 69). Similarly, in the form of credit, the temporal fix may cause a brief consumer-led boom, momentarily compensating for a drop in real wages, as happened during the Thatcher and Reagan years in the second half of the 1980s (Kiely 2005: 66).

Other possible 'fixes' are military state expenditure[19] and 'accumulation by dispossession': the fraudulent, predatory, and violent appropriation of values and their injection into the already ongoing process of capital accumulation and circulation (see Harvey 2004: 76). Apart from a reconfiguration of the economic structure and the capitalist state apparatus, the transformation of the Fordist bloc also entailed a reformulation of the dominant ideological forms. The failure of neo-Keynesian policies to overcome the accumulation crisis attracted the intellectuals of capital towards monetarist, neoconservative, and neoliberal theories, which were, to a degree, explicitly adopted in the second half of the 1970s by the United States and Britain.[20] Although the concrete economic practices of the new historical bloc did not reflect the purity of neoliberal doctrine, the term 'neoliberal bloc' is relevant and adequate because it expresses the myth of 'freedom through the market' that underlies the whole project. Neoliberal theories established a conceptual base for a coherent accumulation strategy, which, by the end of the 1980s, was expressed at the level of international policy through the so-called Washington Consensus: the liberalization and deregulation of trade and markets, the privatization of public enterprises, fiscal discipline, and the strengthening of private property rights. At the deeper ideological level, a new common sense, based on 'clever, agile and ironic individualism' (Barfuss 2008: 838) corresponded to the neoliberal accumulation strategy.

Despite – or rather because of – vocal subaltern movements, the global crisis of Fordist accumulation and US supremacy was gradually solved in a 'passive-revolutionary' way, by reconstituting the historical bloc along neoliberal lines.[21] Neoliberal restructuring cannot be understood as a blatant counter-revolution against a more 'progressive' Fordist bloc. Its practical and ideological success can only be comprehended as an appropriation and reactionary reorientation of genuine subaltern concerns regarding capitalist state power and alienation.[22] The desire for autonomy, freedom, and creativity often expressed by the working class and the so-called new social movements in the wake of the late 1960s was channelled into the new flexible production process. This development underlined Gramsci's concern that '[s]ubaltern groups are always subject to the initiative of the dominant groups, even when they rise up and rebel' (Gramsci 1971: 55; Q25§2). Those privileged layers of the labour population that could transform themselves into flexible and highly skilled workers became the new subordinate allies of the capitalist class, for they benefited materially from the dismantlement of trade unions and systems of collective bargaining, as their own agility and success was rewarded by individualized systems of payment, bonuses, and prestige. For the wider population, freedom, individuality, and creativity were realized virtually through a differentiation of products, which allowed for the self-creation of identities for which product consumption was but the material mediation.

Permanent Passive Revolution?

Throughout the *Prison Notebooks* the meaning of passive revolution is expanding from a criterion of interpretation for the individual process of Italian state formation, through a particular mode of constitution of capitalist states in Europe in the nineteenth century, to the universal 'stubbornness' of capitalist modernity. Moreover, the concept sheds light on these historical processes in many hues: top-down transformation or 'revolution from above', gradual modifications to the existing historical bloc, the extension of the state, a technical solution to hegemony, displacement of subaltern agency, the duration of capitalism, uneven and combined development (see above), reformism, etc. There is no clear 'definition' of passive revolution to be found in Gramsci as he deploys the term with different and even contradictory nuances, which leads, according to Callinicos (2010: 492), to an over-extension of the concept.

Callinicos recognizes the usefulness of passive revolution as a type of bourgeois revolution, a theoretically enriched version of the concept of 'revolution from above', applicable to the era of the constitution of capitalism, both in nineteenth-century Europe and in modernizing countries in the Global South (for example Turkey) in the twentieth century (2010: 495). He concedes that later developments within capitalism such as Fascism and Fordism could be interpreted within a broader conceptual framework of passive revolution as 'socio-political processes in which revolution-inducing strains are at once displaced and at least partially fulfilled' (Callinicos 2010: 498). However, Callinicos underlines that, whereas the transition from precapitalist states to bourgeois societies in the nineteenth century implied a qualitative, systemic *transformation*, Fascism, Fordism, and neoliberalism merely *reconfigured* existing capitalist relations.

Although the opposition between the process of constitution and reconstitution of capitalist relations is analytically correct, it is misleading simply to equate the 'external' transition between pre-capitalist formations and capitalism with a 'qualitative' transformation, and 'internal' transitions within capitalism with 'quantitative' modifications. Instead of examining the character of capitalist development on the basis of a general concept of 'transformation', the social and technical acceleration unleashed by the capitalist mode of production forces us to rethink the very character of transformation in this epoch. Transformation has become 'integral' to the capitalist mode of production. No longer does 'transition' represent a bridge between external, separate societies, but it has become an internal function of capitalism itself. As I discussed earlier, the constitution of capitalism as a proper mode of production requires a process of both formal and real subsumption of labour under capital. In this sense, the internal transitions to Fordism and neoliberalism should not only be understood as alternations of 'finished' forms of capitalism on a 'flat' temporal axis, but as new waves of real subsumption embedded within the ongoing historical development of capitalism.

This perspective appears to undermine Marx's view in the 'Preface' that, at a certain point, capitalist relations of production come into conflict with the productive forces unleashed by them, creating the conditions for a social revolution that destroys bourgeois society. However, as Gramsci commented, this merely offers a 'necessary corollary' to the argument (Gramsci 1971: 114; Q15§62; see Gramsci 1971: 106–7; Q15§17), showing how the essence of a systemic crisis of the capitalist mode of production (for example induced by the tendency of the rate of profit to fall; see Gramsci 1971: 280; Q22§1) always appears as the organic crisis of a particular historical bloc (see Thomas 2009: 156).[23] Marxists have often been seduced, for example for strategic reasons, to represent a specific organic crisis of capitalism as the final crisis of the system. However, when such an explosive moment is displaced, capitalism catches it breath and continues its development through the elements of a newly constituted historical bloc – until systemic contradictions force new moments of crisis. The function of passive revolution as a concept is to probe into the dynamic of this revolutionary displacement.

The claim that Gramsci began to 'stretch' his concept of passive revolution from the original case of the Risorgimento – the historical constitution of capitalism – to the reconfiguration of capitalism is misleading. Callinicos recognizes that passive revolution already existed in Gramsci's thought in a 'practical state' before its first explicit appearance in his fourth prison notebook (Q4§57). He confines the concept to Gramsci's early comments on the Risorgimento (Callinicos 2010: 492). Nevertheless it was already present as an implicit problematic in Gramsci's writings on the 'Southern question' (Morton 2010: 326), and in his study of Fascism (Hoare and Nowell-Smith in Gramsci 1971: 45). The failure of the *biennio rosso* – the two years of intense class struggle in Italy between 1919 and 1920 – and the subsequent reconfiguration of capitalism led Gramsci to 'the search for an adequate theory of proletarian hegemony' (Thomas 2009: 136) that could explain the 'stubbornness' of capitalism as well as offer a normative–strategic framework for the creation of a powerful and authentic proletarian subject. Arguably, Gramsci's historical investigation of the Risorgimento functioned as a conceptual mediation in comprehending the contemporary phenomenon of Fascism and the political need of formulating an adequate communist policy (see Fontana 2004: 176–7; Thomas 2009: 145). The study of the more primitive historical form of passive revolution during the Risorgimento allowed Gramsci to develop a *concept* of passive revolution, which then served as a criterion of interpretation for the historically more advanced phenomenon in his own time.

As a second critique, Callinicos distinguishes between passive revolution as a type of *bourgeois revolution* that institutes capitalism, and essentially *counter-revolutionary projects* such as Fascism and neoliberalism, which do not move capitalism forward – let alone the position of the working class (Callinicos 2010: 503). Similarly, Countinho (2012: 156–61) makes a distinction between passive revolution and *counter-reformation* and claims that in the neoliberal age the restoration/ revolution dialectic is absent, because the suppression of the welfare state and workers' rights represent a historical step backward. The problem with such an evaluation is that it underestimates the neoliberal accumulation strategy as a *revolutionary* restoration. We have to take seriously Gramsci's remark that 'it is certain that in the movement of history there is never any turning back, and that restorations *in toto* do not exist' (Gramsci 1971: 219; Q13§27). Neoliberalism represents a clear restoration of capitalist class power in the face of Fordism's organic crisis. However, it would be erroneous to conceive of the neoliberal era in terms of a 'turning back' in the movement of history. Neoliberal accumulation overcame the limits to capital drawn up by the Fordist bloc, not only through financialization and the repression of organized labour, but also by breaking open rigid units of production and universalizing production by global commodity chains. Modern ICT, social media, and P2P, for example, are productive forces that were much more easily developed within the economic structure of the neoliberal era than they would have been in the context of Fordism. For all imperialism's sins, Lenin was able to recognize its 'progressive' aspect: the increased socialization of human production (Lenin 1964a: 205). Gramsci, likewise, recognized the 'progressive' character of Fascism and Fordism in their promotion of 'planned' society. Similarly, neoliberal accumulation stimulated new forms of collaborative production and the global integration of human production, distribution, and consumption. The reactionary character of imperialism and neoliberalism is not their absolute incapacity to develop the productive forces in new ways, but their chaining of the real potential of socialized production by capitalist relations and private property rights. From the standpoint of capital, the passive-revolutionary aspect of neoliberalism was its agency to transform an organic crisis into an opportunity.

Furthermore, the success of the neoliberal project can only be comprehended by taking its ideological claims seriously – obviously this does not mean that we should *accept* them – in the sense that it offered, on the one hand, a critique of the Fordist bloc that was (only superficially and not organically) connected to the demands of subaltern movements, and, on the other, the myth of the market as a source of freedom, autonomy, creativity, and prosperity. By considering neo-liberalism merely as a counter-revolution or counter-reformation, as an opposed movement, one cannot account for its capacity to function as a substitute for anti-Fordist resistance. Its brutal role in destroying trade unions, uprooting economies, and curtailing welfare states should not blind us to the fact that it 'displaced' 'revolution-inducing strains' by 'at least partially' fulfilling them.

Nevertheless, Callinicos and Coutinho have a point when they underline important differences between Fordism and neoliberalism as 'cases' of passive revolution. These differences centre on the position of the working class vis-à-vis capital, with the labour movement obviously being much weaker in the era of neoliberalism than it had been in the Fordist period. As Thomas highlights, a process of revolution/restoration could entail 'a cautious, defensive measure' as well as 'a form of cautious attack' (Thomas 2009: 151). If passive revolution encompasses both 'defensive' and 'offensive' movements of capital,[24] the concept appears to be 'stretched' once more. When used as a concept to discern a clearly delineated *type* of process, passive revolution tends to become an empty signifier, applicable to all cases of transition, elite-driven transformation, or reformism. If everything since the French Revolution can be categorized as a passive revolution, nothing is a passive revolution.

However, I would like to stress that there is no such *thing* as passive revolution. To paraphrase Marx, passive revolution 'does nothing' and 'wages no battles'. Explaining specific forms of capitalist development and state formation through the 'model' of passive revolution runs the risk of 'making what is a principle of research and interpretation into a "historical cause"' (Morton 2007: 67). Instead of trying to pinpoint a clear and exact definition of passive revolution, Morton encourages us to embrace the 'continuum of passive revolution' (2010). He argues that passive revolution is a 'portmanteau concept that reveals continuities and changes within the order of capital' (2007: 41; 2010: 322). Passive revolution is not a concept that can be simply 'applied' to particular cases (Morton 2010: 331). Instead of a mirrored ideal type of the 'classical' (French) form of capitalist state formation or a model for alternative modernization, passive revolution functions as a research *theme*, a 'criterion of interpretation' (Gramsci 1971: 114; Q15§62), which allows for a comparative study of transformations *within* a nation's modern trajectory (see Hesketh 2010: 384; Morton 2007: 70–1). Thus Gramsci mused: 'is it not precisely the fascist movement which in fact corresponds to the movement of moderate and conservative liberalism in the last century?' (Gramsci 1971: 119; Q10i§9).

Like hegemony, passive revolution is neither an analytical concept that is the outcome of critical thinking that abstracts from reality 'until one arrived at the simplest determinations' (Marx 1986a: 37), nor is it a synthetic concept that is the result of a conceptual movement that 'leads from abstract determinations by way of thinking to the reproduction of the concrete' (Marx 1986a: 38). Instead it is a 'practico-indicative' concept (see Thomas 2009: 134) that is deployed to orient the whole thought process, in the sense that it functions as a methodological searchlight, illuminating phenomena that should be investigated in their concreteness (De Smet 2014c).

Furthermore, I would suggest that passive revolution should not only function as a historicist *theme* but also as a politicized *programme* for critical research. The continuum of passive revolution – the 'various concrete historical instances in which aspects of the social relations of capitalist development are either instituted and/or expanded' (Morton 2010: 316) – is the heterogeneous outcome of the actual deployment of the concept, of which the essence remains, in my view, quite straightforward, namely: *the problematic of the continuous absence of permanent revolution or proletarian hegemony.*

The failed European revolutions of 1848 underlined the hard limits of the bourgeois project and the struggle for political emancipation. Marx remained optimistic, however, as the experience had differentiated the proletariat as a political subject from the petty bourgeoisie. The democratic struggle, which would be waged in alliance with the petty bourgeoisie against both the lingering Ancien Régime and the frightened bourgeois classes, constituted the first step for the working class to wage its own fight, conquer state power, and pursue its project of human or social emancipation. The notion of permanent revolution expresses the *universal strategic possibility and expectation of human emancipation in capitalism*, developing from the conditions of a struggle for political emancipation 'from below', when the proletariat becomes a leading class and organizes a real organic passage of society into itself, thereby abolishing class society. For Gramsci, the notion of hegemony was simply 'the present form of the Forty-Eightist doctrine of permanent revolution' (Gramsci 1971: 56n5; see Gramsci 1971: 242; Q13§7; see Thomas 2015: 297). Unlike permanent revolution, which was an abstract and generalizing concept, a mobilizing battle cry born from the fluid character of society before 1870 (see Gramsci 1971: 243; Q13§7), the notion of hegemony inquired into those concrete relations and forms of class leadership that were adequate and necessary with regard to specific historical and national contexts.

However, the strategic possibility of human emancipation did not materialize on a world scale. For Gramsci the stubborn survival of capitalism – especially in its grotesque Fascist form – testified, on the one hand, to the inability of the working class to fulfil its historical expectations, and, on the other, to the capacity of the ruling groups to maintain class power and deflect revolutionary transformations 'from below' (see Löwy 1981). In the first instance,

> the working classes – for different reasons in different countries, but with the same result – had not yet been able to socialise the ideological forms that corresponded to their own experiences of the conflicts within the economic structure of bourgeois society and thus lay the foundations for transforming it. (Thomas 2009: 156–7)

In other words, the proletariat was not able to constitute itself successfully and sufficiently as a 'class for itself', as a collective political subject, as a 'Modern Prince'. This political pathology was not only the result of an incomplete or distorted internal development, but it was also the outcome of the agency of the dominant classes: 'the choice of the ruling classes to develop strategies to disaggregate those working classes and confine them to an economic–corporative level within the existing society' (Thomas 2009: 156). As a methodological searchlight, passive revolution highlights the agency and agility of the dominant groups in the process of the class struggle, which are all but automatically replaced by the sweep of history, but fight to reproduce the conditions of their social existence.

Permanent and passive revolution emerge as twin concepts that struggle for predominance at the juncture of an organic crisis. Just as passive revolution 'presupposes, indeed postulates as necessary, a vigorous antithesis' (Gramsci 1971: 114; Q15§62) – permanent revolution assumes its antithesis in the form of passive revolution: the partial fulfilment and displacement of subaltern needs, demands, and expectations 'from above' (Callinicos 2010: 505). If permanent revolution holds the promise of subaltern self-emancipation through proletarian hegemony, passive revolution functions as its negative concept, exploring the driving forces behind the continuous absence of permanent revolution. In this sense passive revolution is the 'blocked dialectic' (Buci-Glucksmann 1980: 315) of permanent revolution, as it displaces and stalls the moment of revolutionary negation. The possibility of permanent revolution, saliently displayed in the 1848 revolutions, the uprising of the Paris Commune in 1871, and the Russian Revolution of 1917, prompted the dominant classes to consider

> the necessity for the 'thesis' to achieve its full development, up to the point where it would even succeed in incorporating a part of the antithesis itself – in order, that is, not to allow itself to be 'transcended' in the dialectical opposition. The thesis alone in fact develops to the full its potential for struggle, up to the point where it absorbs even the so-called representatives of the antithesis; it is precisely in this that the passive revolution or revolution/restoration consists. (Gramsci 1971: 110; Q15§11).

If permanent revolution imagines a revolution that develops beyond its initial modest, democratic project towards the epoch-constituting 'social revolution' Marx is speaking of in the 'Preface', passive revolution envisions a counter-revolution that is forced to go beyond simple restoration in order to block this subaltern dynamic (see Q8§25; Sassoon 1987: 210).

Considering permanent and passive revolution from this perspective also means that the constitution and reconstitution of historical blocs is tightly connected to class formation, both at the 'top' and at the 'bottom'. In the Marxist tradition this has created confusion about defining revolution in terms of its actual consequences – that is, political and/or social transformation – or in terms of its 'substance' – that is, as a process of self-emancipation from 'below' and a prefiguration of an alternative society. The next chapter engages with the difference between a 'political' and a 'social' revolution, between an objectivist and a subjectivist approach, between 'war of movement' and 'war of manoeuvre', and with the concept of *Caesarism*.

4. Caesarism

Revolution: Process or Outcome

Two years after the 2011 uprisings in the Middle East, the initial enthusiasm of many scholars and commentators was turning into cynicism and pessimism. Facing the rise of Islamism in Tunisia and Egypt, enduring civil war in Libya and Syria, an aborted insurrection in Bahrain, etc., they voiced concerns that the region's 'spring' was degenerating into an authoritarian 'winter'. Revolutions remained unfinished, or were smothered in the violence of counter-revolution. As the Egyptian political and economic system had not been transformed in any substantial way since the fall of Mubarak, labour historian Joel Beinin provocatively stated: 'The January 25 Revolution is not over. Rather, it has not yet occurred' (Beinin 2013b). Beinin rightly criticized those analysts who identified the *event* of the 25 January uprising with a process of *revolution*, which he defined as

> social, political, and economic transformations involving social movements and political mobilizations, one or more moments of popular uprising, and a longer-term process of reconstructing a new socio-political order involving the replacement of the former ruling coalition with new forces of a substantially different social character and interests. (Beinin 2013b)

Indeed, the mass uprising of 25 January was the high point of a gradual accumulation of political and social protests that had been building up since the early 2000s, which, in turn, were propelled by the emergence of a new generation of activists and novel political, labour, and human rights organizations in the 1990s. Street politics returned to Egypt with mass demonstrations in solidarity with the Second Palestinian Intifada in 2000, protests against the wars in Afghanistan, Iraq, and Lebanon, and the civil-democratic movement of Kefaya (literally, 'Enough'). Political discontent was fertilized by the development of 'virtual' activism by bloggers, Facebook users, and tweeters, who were able to escape state censorship. Separately from these democratic, explicitly political protests, workers went on strike and protested against the threat of privatization, the rise of unemployment, and deteriorating working conditions.

Slowly they started to throw off the weight of the state-controlled trade unions, trying to organizing their own independent and democratic representative bodies. In the countryside, small farmers struggled against increasing land rents and the dispossession of their lands by landed capital in league with the Mubarak state. They occupied their plots and organized production cooperatives. Protesting against cuts in the water or electricity supply, villagers blocked roads, railways, and canals.

I have argued that the 25 January insurrection was not the beginning of a revolutionary process, but the moment when the slow 'original accumulation' of organized discontent came to recognize itself as a revolution (De Smet 2015: 124–6; see also Chapter 7). The uprising concentrated and massified the previous political and social protests, elevating them to a new level, rendering explicit and salient what had already been present in an undeveloped, implicit, hidden, and fragmentary form. Consequently, the 25 January Revolution was an unfinished revolutionary process that was already building up in the decade before 2011.

In contradistinction, Beinin's assertion that the revolution *has not yet occurred* (see Achcar 2013: 15) strongly echoed Theda Skocpol's classic definition of revolution in her seminal work 'States and Social Revolutions' (1979). Skocpol differentiated between political and social revolutions. Whereas social revolutions were characterized by 'rapid, basic transformations of a society's state and class structures ... accompanied and in part carried through by class-based revolts from below', political revolutions 'transform state structures but not social structures, and they are not necessarily accomplished through class conflict' (Skocpol 1979: 4). Distinguishing her method from earlier approaches, Skocpol stressed that 'this definition makes successful socio-political transformation – actual change of state and class structures – part of the specification of what is to be called a social revolution, rather than leaving change contingent in the definition of "revolution" as many other scholars do' (Skocpol 1979: 4). Her emphasis on the societal *outcomes* or *consequences* of a revolutionary process was shared by other authors, such as Huntington (2006). The essence of revolution is *change* and the main difference between a political and social revolution is the *extent* to which society is transformed.

For Skocpol the focus on change was primarily a methodological decision: 'Because I intend to focus exactly on this question in my comparative historical analysis – in which actual social revolutions will be compared to unsuccessful cases and to non-social-revolutionary transformations – my concept of social revolution necessarily highlights successful change as a basic defining feature' (Skocpol 1979: 4). However,

there is a fundamental contradiction in this outcome-centred or consequentialist approach. If 'successful change' is a 'basic defining feature'
of social revolutions, how can 'unsuccessful cases' be treated as failed
revolutions? If the success of a revolutionary process – i.e, societal transformations – becomes the primary determinant for its definition, the
very notion of a failed revolution – an *unsuccessful* successful transformation – becomes nonsensical. The idea of a failed, blocked, or unfinished
revolution requires a concept of the process that happens *before* the
victorious conquest of power and the 'rapid, basic transformations of a
society's state and class structures' – a process that encapsulates the *effort*
(Goldstone 2001: 142), *intention* (Achcar 2013: 16), *expectation*, and
prefiguration towards a revolutionary outcome. Hence the explicit claim
of protesters during the 18 Days that they were making a revolution.
Ironically, investigating the conceptual negative of a successful transformation discloses the real substance of revolution: a developmental
process of 'class-based revolts from below' that may or may not lead to
the conquest of state power and the transformation of society.[1]

The Consequences of Revolution

I refer to the standpoint that conceives of revolution as essentially a
developmental process of collective political actors and their prefigurative activity of a new society – i.e. subject formation – as the *subjectivist*
approach. Conversely, I deem the Skocpolian view an *objectivist*
approach, in the sense that it focuses on the consolidated externaliza-
tions – societal transformations – of the revolutionary subjects. The first
approach is necessarily the constructivist perspective of the immediately
involved political activist, who needs a concept of his ongoing activity
in order to actively determine its outcome; whereas the second one is
the critique of the distant historian, who has the luxury to 'wait out' the
process before evaluating it with the advantage of hindsight (see Marx
1986b: 57).

The two approaches presuppose each other logically and function
as moments in the internal interpretation of the revolutionary process
by the actors involved. Revolutionary subjects are as much constituted
by the objective possibility of societal change as they are the agents of
such transformations. A political activist needs to put herself in the
position of a future historian, with the aim of unravelling potential lines
of development towards her goal; just as a historian has to understand
the dynamic of subject formation with the purpose of understanding
the victory or failure of the revolutionary process. The Marxist tradition
offers examples of both subjectivist and objectivist approaches, but their

analytical difference is often not rigorously distinguished. Retracing the lineages of these approaches throughout the literature requires an investigation in its own right. For the discussion at hand a few examples will have to suffice.

When in 1848 Marx discussed the English and French Revolutions, he claimed that

> [t]hey did not represent the victory of a particular class of society over the old political order; they proclaimed the political order of the new European society. The bourgeoisie was victorious in these revolutions, but the victory of the bourgeoisie was at that time the victory of a new social order, the victory of bourgeois ownership over feudal ownership, of nationality over provincialism, of competition over the guild, of the division of land over primogeniture, of the rule of the landowner over the domination of the owner by the land, of enlightenment over superstition, of the family over the family name, of industry over heroic idleness, of bourgeois law over medieval privileges. (Marx 1977: 161)

The historical meaning of 1688 and 1789 as bourgeois *revolutions* is clearly the transformation of society, not by a mere change of rule, but by 'the victory of a new social order'. Even if the bourgeoisie as a class did not formally conquer state power and was excluded from governing, it still 'won': 'That interest was so powerful that it was victorious over the pen of Marat, the guillotine of the Terror and the sword of Napoleon as well as the crucifix and the blue blood of the Bourbons' (Marx and Engels 1975a: 81). What matters here is not the protagonists, but the outcome of the revolutionary process: bourgeois society.

More recently,[2] Callinicos (1982, 1989, 2013) and Davidson (2005, 2010, 2012) have offered a similar 'consequentialist' interpretation of bourgeois revolutions: 'The emphasis must shift from the class which makes a bourgeois revolution to the effects of such a revolution – to the class which benefits from it' (Callinicos 1989: 124; see Morton 2010: 318). The success of a bourgeois revolution should be judged 'by the degree to which it succeeds in establishing an autonomous centre of capital accumulation' (Callinicos 1982: 110). The consequentialist approach emerged as a critique of the archetype of the bourgeoisie as an insurrectionary class and the concept of the tasks of the bourgeois revolution.[3] Marx and Gramsci had already underlined that the bourgeoisie never stood at the helm of its own 'class-based revolts'. During the French Revolution, it was actually the petty-bourgeois Jacobins who drove 'the bourgeois forward with kicks in the backside' (Gramsci 1971: 77;

Q19§24). With regard to the July Revolution of 1830 and the February Revolution of 1848, Marx writes: 'Just as the workers in the July days had fought for and won the bourgeois monarchy, so in the February days they fought for and won the bourgeois republic' (Marx 1978: 55).

Nevertheless, even in the clear absence of a leading bourgeois class, revolutions were often still categorized as bourgeois because of the 'historical tasks' they fulfilled: political emancipation in the sense of establishing a democratic republic', elimination of (rural) precapitalist modes of surplus extraction, and national liberation (Löwy 1981: 161). Callinicos (1982) questions the universality of these tasks, as they were derived from the archetype of the French Revolution, which appeared rather as the historical exception to the general process of bourgeois transformation than as its model (see Chapter 3). The concrete outcomes of the French Revolution presented a normative ideal type of the 'pure' bourgeois revolution, which subsequently no country could ever fully attain.

Here Davidson's problematic of 'how revolutionary were the bourgeois revolutions?' (Davidson 2012) becomes pertinent. In general, bourgeois transition was not 'revolutionary' in the sense of the imaginary of a popular insurrection led by the bourgeoisie (see also Ginsborg 2014). It was revolutionary in the narrow, technical sense of 'basic transformations of a society's state and class structures', which were not necessarily 'rapid' or 'accompanied and in part carried through by class-based revolts from below'. The institution of 'an autonomous centre of capital accumulation' appears as the objective consequence of qualitatively different processes, ranging from subaltern mass mobilizations 'from below', through civil and imperialist wars, to state-led, gradual transformations 'from above'. These processes could result in the total eradication of precapitalist relations or their incorporation into a capital-dominated circulation process; to democratic republics, constitutional monarchies, or military dictatorships; and to nation states or multi-ethnic empires. Consequentialism groups these distinct outcomes, which nevertheless share the formation of an 'autonomous centre of capital accumulation', under the common denominator of the 'bourgeois revolution'.

It is evident that the formation of an 'autonomous centre of capital accumulation' is not a short-term and linear historical process. As demonstrated in the case of France (see Chapter 2), the road to bourgeois society was paved with republican uprisings, Bonapartist coups, and royalist restorations. Skocpol claimed that there are, in fact, two *types* of revolution: political and social ones (see above). In *The Revolution Betrayed* (1936), Trotsky remarked that: 'History has known elsewhere not only social revolutions which substituted the bourgeois for the feudal regime, but also political revolutions which, without destroying the economic foundations of society, swept out an old ruling upper crust (1830 and 1848 in France, February 1917 in Russia, etc.)' (Trotsky 1972: 287–8).

Similarly, Draper compared a political revolution – 'changes in governmental leadership and forms, transformations in the superstructure' – to a social revolution – 'involving the transference of political power to a new class; and this change in ruling class tends to entail a basic change in the social system (mode of production)' (Draper 2011b: 18–9; see Davidson 2010). A bourgeois revolution, for example, represents a *political* change in state power that brings about a *social* transformation (Callinicos 1989: 124). Finally, Marx's claim in the 'Preface' that 'changes in the economic foundation lead sooner or later to the transformation of the whole immense superstructure' (Marx 1987: 263) underlines the reverse process, in which a transformation of productive forces and relations pushes forward a change of the entire society. Draper called this long-term, molecular process of transformation which lacked any central agent a *societal* revolution (Draper 2011b: 19). Likewise, Engels observed that England's political revolution was long since eclipsed by its soci(et)al revolution, in the sense of 'comprehensive and far-reaching' societal transformations of the 'conditions of life' (Engels 1975a: 469).

The 'bourgeois revolution' appears as a broad category of historical interpretation, encompassing societal revolutions such as the centuries-long and decentred process of transformation in England towards commercial and industrial society, social revolutions such as the French Revolution and its Bonapartist offspring, which lasted a few decades and reorganized class power, and political revolutions, such as February 1848, which merely reconfigured state power over the span of a few years (Davidson 2010). Following such a typology, the 'passive-revolutionary process' in Italy and Germany could, perhaps, be interpreted as the drawing together of the societal, social, and political revolutions in a decades-long process of transformation 'from above'.

However, as Marx observed in 1844, real revolutions defy the simple methodological binary between 'political' and 'social': 'Every revolution dissolves the old order of society; to that extent it is social. Every revolution brings down the old ruling power; to that extent it is political' (Marx 1975a: 205). Draper recognized that '[o]ur aim is not to make a hard and fast distinction between political revolutions and social revolutions but, if anything, the reverse: to recognise how often they are mingled in given revolutionary situations, so that the two elements must be distinguished by analysis' (Draper 2011b: 20). The goal is not to create a neat typology of political and social revolutions, but to understand why some revolutions entail the change of only state forms, and others the transformation of whole societies.

In order to understand the causality of effects, we have to look at the processes that produce specific outcomes. This question reorients the investigation from the 'basic transformations of a society's state and class structures' towards the dynamic of 'class-based revolts from below'. Such a subjectivist approach to revolution can be summed up by Trotsky's reflection in his 'History of the Russian Revolution' (1930):

> The most indubitable feature of a revolution is the direct interference of the masses in historic events ... [The masses] break over the barriers excluding them from the political arena, sweep aside their traditional representatives, and create by their own interference the initial groundwork for a new régime. The history of a revolution is for us first of all a history of the forcible entrance of the masses into the realm of rulership over their own destiny. (Trotsky 2001: 17–8)

Here revolution is understood not in its technical sense of political or social change, but as a collective emancipatory process that develops a new society from its own self-directing activity. Revolution is, firstly, 'the direct interference of the masses in historic events'. Similarly, Gramsci emphasized 'popular initiative' as the key element that distinguished genuine revolutions from revolutions from above (see Gramsci 1971: 108; Q15§11). Secondly, revolution is not the mobilization of a mindless mob, directed by external agitators, but the politicization – a 'living political school' (Luxemburg 1970: 172) – of subaltern actors who are normally legally or practically excluded from political society. Revolution is a political learning process 'because the class overthrowing [the ruling class] can only in a revolution succeed in ridding itself of all the muck of ages and become fitted to found society anew' (Marx and Engels 1975b: 53). Moreover, the masses 'sweep aside their traditional representatives' and establish means to govern themselves. Revolution represents the organic passage of the popular masses to a state of their own. Thirdly, by their collective, self-directed activity they construct 'the initial groundwork for a new regime'. Likewise, Lenin commented that the Paris Commune and the Russian Revolution of 1905 were popular revolutions,

> since the mass of the people, their majority, the very lowest social groups, crushed by oppression and exploitation, rose independently and stamped on the entire course of the revolution the imprint of their

own demands, their attempt to build in their own way a new society in place of the old society that was being destroyed. (Lenin 1964c: 421)

Hence revolution appears not only as a means to an end, for the goal is already materially prefigured in the movement of the masses, which creates the embryo of a new society.

The Soul of Revolution

The subjectivist approach draws our attention to the substance of revolution as a process of emancipation; as class struggle rather than the agentless progression of productive forces. Furthermore, it denotes that true emancipation is always self-emancipation, a crucial idea that goes back to the 'battle cry' that 'the emancipation of the working classes must be conquered by the working classes themselves' (Marx 1985a: 441; see Marx and Engels 1989: 269; Engels 1989a: 215). At the time of the First International, this slogan constituted a revolutionary principle that rejected previous paternalist traditions whereby an enlightened elite, Blanquist[4] vanguard, or benevolent 'Saviour–Ruler' (see Draper 1971) acted as the emancipator of a subaltern group, substituting their own power for the agency of those who desired liberation (see Levant 2012). Real emancipation, however, entails the development of the capacity of a group to emancipate itself.

From a subjectivist perspective the distinction between political and social revolution is directly connected to the difference between political and social (or human) emancipation in the modern era. Instead of talking about two different *types* of revolution, in his early writings Marx differentiated between two *souls* of the revolutionary process. Marx mused about political emancipation as the 'political soul' of revolution, which 'consists in the tendency of classes having no political influence to abolish their isolation from statehood and rule' (Marx 1975a: 205). Historically, the political emancipation of the bourgeoisie consisted of its inclusion in the state by transforming the very nature of feudal state power. The particular emancipation of the bourgeoisie as a class from feudalism was achieved by the universal emancipation of the whole society from the inequality of the Ancien Régime order. By offering the other classes an 'organic passage' to its own 'democratic' project, the bourgeoisie established its class power as state power. However, this universal emancipation did not eliminate the social basis of inequality, but abstracted the political community from real society as a separate sphere in which citizens enjoyed equal rights. This sphere, which represented the universal idea of humanity, stood in opposition to the real, individual existence of bourgeois society's members. The bourgeois state can only function as long as it remains abstracted from the inequalities of real life, offering a space in which real class differences are sublated in a roundabout, legal way. Marx concluded that the political soul of revolution was limited and only replaced one ruling stratum with another: 'however universal a political uprising may be, it conceals even in its most grandiose form a narrow-minded spirit' (Marx 1975a: 205).

Conversely, the social soul of revolution 'represents man's [sic] protest against a dehumanised life' (Marx 1975a: 205) as it springs not from political exclusion, but from real conditions of exploitation and alienation. A social revolt may appear as a partial, limited conflict over living conditions, but this everyday concreteness 'contains within itself a universal soul' (Marx 1975a: 205). For Marx, the collective body to which this social soul belongs, is the proletariat. By freeing itself from the exploitative wage–labour relation, the working class emancipates other social groups from capitalism.[5] Social emancipation substitutes 'for the old civil society an association which will exclude classes and their antagonism, and there will be no more political power properly so-called, since political power is precisely the official expression of antagonism in civil society' (Marx 1976: 212). In other words, the administration of people – governance – returns to the administration of things when society as an organic whole regains control over the production, appropriation, and distribution of economic surpluses.

The character of a revolution is determined by the class that achieves hegemony in the course of its development. The historical form of the political revolution is the bourgeois revolution, which *cannot* go beyond political emancipation without losing its bourgeois character. The character of the bourgeois revolution is necessarily short-lived; 'soon they have attained their zenith, and a long crapulent depression seizes society before it learns soberly to assimilate the results of its storm-and-stress period' (Marx 1979a: 106).

Conversely, the historical form of the social revolution is the proletarian revolution, which *has* to go beyond political emancipation in order to liberate the working class from its social conditions. This creates a *permanent* dynamic. Firstly, proletarian revolutions are permanent in the sense that they

> criticise themselves constantly, interrupt themselves continually in their own course, come back to the apparently accomplished in order to begin it afresh, deride with unmerciful thoroughness the inadequacies, weaknesses and paltrinesses of their first attempts, seem to throw down their adversary only in order that he may draw new

strength from the earth and rise again, more gigantic, before them, and recoil again and again from the indefinite prodigiousness of their own aims, until a situation has been created which makes all turning back impossible. (Marx 1979a: 106–7)

Here 'permanency' refers to the non-linear course of the revolutionary process, which consists as much of defeats and temporary setbacks as of victories and progress. Marx turned Hegel's philosophical comment that '[n]ecessity is blind only so long as it is not understood' (Hegel 1975: 209) into a practical, political problem: a social revolution is a long-term learning process driven by the contradiction between the unwillingness of subaltern actors to confront their social predicament in a revolutionary, society-shattering way, and the material necessity to do so.

Secondly, proletarian revolutions are permanent because, in the fluidity of historical process, the activity of the proletariat pushes for the social soul of a political revolution to appear. Draper remarked that '[t]he modern tendency is for political revolution, however narrowly initiated, to waken the elements of social revolution from dormancy or to raise them to new levels' (Draper 2011b: 20). Even in his early writings, Marx had already developed an implicit concept of the 'revolution in permanence', in the sense that a revolution that begins as a political revolt may morph into a social revolution:

Revolution in general – the overthrow of the existing power and dissolution of the old relationships – is a political act. But socialism cannot be realised without revolution. It needs this political act insofar as it needs destruction and dissolution. But where its organising activity begins, where its proper object, its soul, comes to the fore – there socialism throws off the political cloak. (Marx 1975a: 206)

This paragraph does not merely advocate 'a telescoping of bourgeois-democratic and proletarian-socialist/communist revolutions into a unitary, short-term process' (Thomas 2015: 289); it transmits a crucial idea, namely that a revolution which is political in form reveals its social soul at the point 'where its organising activity begins'. The potential outcome of the revolutionary process is materially prefigured in the development of the activity of the masses. Whereas in political revolutions 'the words went beyond the content', in a social revolution 'the content goes beyond the words' (Marx 1979a: 106). The revolutionary movement is not defined by its goal, but the goal becomes defined by the movement (see Draper 2011b: 27). Here the fundamental meaning of permanent revolution resurfaces as the transition of emancipatory struggle from its political form to its social essence – a potentiality that becomes universal with the institution of modern capitalist society. Instead of distinct, clearly delineated outcomes or phases, political/bourgeois and social/ proletarian revolution become moments of one and the same process of subaltern emancipation.[6]

From this point of view every modern political revolution that is the outcome of popular initiative is essentially an *incomplete* revolution of which the social soul remains undeveloped. Moreover, it invites us to reverse Davidson's (2012) problematic: instead of asking ourselves 'how *revolutionary* were the *bourgeois* revolutions?' – we should ask ourselves: 'how *bourgeois* were the bourgeois *revolutions*?' If we take the idea seriously that the French Revolution was not the model of bourgeois transformation and that the bourgeois class has never offered leadership to mass movements (*pace* Davidson 2012: 479), then the 'class-based revolts from below'-type of bourgeois revolution is a *fata morgana*. Genuine revolutions have always been subaltern movements with a prefigurative logic of their own. In the French case, it had been the radicalization of a faction of the bourgeoisie's political personnel, the Jacobins, that created the illusion of a bourgeois-led mass movement. Gramsci's concept of passive revolution, which related to the earlier notion of 'revolution from above', revealed the essence of bourgeois hegemony as the gradual, negotiated, and coercive acquisition of state power through a displacement and substitution of popular initiative. In other words, popular revolution is simply neither the historical nor the logical mode of struggle through which the capitalist class conquers state power (see Poulantzas 1973: 183). In reality, the only groups to which the bourgeoisie offered a material 'organic passage' were the Ancien Régime elites, by turning them into fractions of capital.[7] In 1789 the Jacobins not only functioned as the organic intellectuals of the bourgeoisie, but also as placeholder intellectuals for the *sans-culottes*, moving the revolutionary struggle far ahead of the bourgeoisie's own aims. Apart from its far-reaching and all-encompassing project of political emancipation, the French Revolution already displayed a strong social soul, going beyond the 'struggle for this or that form of State': 'The French Revolution was a social movement from beginning to end, and after it a purely political democracy became a complete absurdity' (Engels 1976: 5).

In principle, the germ of a certain type of socialism was already present in the development of the French Revolution, flowing from the self-organizing activity of the masses. Marx claimed that the French Revolution was a failure for the popular masses because they could not develop their own revolutionary principle but were subjugated to the idea of the bourgeoisie (Marx and Engels 1975a: 82; see Marx 1975a:

204). After 1848 the kernel of bourgeois hegemony, which was originally articulated as a progressive project of political emancipation, revealed itself as the active displacement of the immanent social soul of revolution – that is, as passive revolution.

Movement and Position

The Paris Commune of 1871 represented both the high point and the final phase of the classical era of permanent revolution: 'an historical period in which the great mass political parties and the great economic trade unions did not yet exist, and society was still, so to speak, in a state of fluidity from many points of view' (Gramsci 1971: 243; Q13§7). In the nineteenth century the bourgeois integral state was still in development. Society was characterized by 'a greater backwardness of the countryside', 'almost complete monopoly of political and State power by a few cities or even by a single one', 'a relatively rudimentary State apparatus', 'greater autonomy of civil society from State activity', 'a specific system of military forces and of national armed services', and 'greater autonomy of the national economies from the economic relations of the world market' (Gramsci 1971: 243; Q13§7). In the core or 'advanced' capitalist countries the economic transition to imperialism and the rise of strong trade unions and workers' parties developed the bourgeois integral state into a complex ensemble of civil and political organs. This transformation required a development of proletarian strategy. Gramsci famously claimed that

> the Forty-Eightist formula of the 'Permanent Revolution' is expanded and transcended in political science by the formula of 'civil hegemony'. The same thing happens in the art of politics as happens in military art: war of movement increasingly becomes war of position, and it can be said that a State will win a war in so far as it prepares for it minutely and technically in peacetime. (Gramsci 1971: 243; Q13§7)

Continuing his deployment of the military metaphor of 'war of movement' (or manoeuvre) and 'war of position', Gramsci observed that

> [t]he massive structures of the modern democracies, both as State organisations, and as complexes of associations in civil society, constitute for the art of politics as it were 'trenches' and the permanent fortifications of the front in the war of position: they render merely 'partial' the element of movement which before used to be 'the whole' of war, etc. (Gramsci 1971: 243; Q13§7)

Similarly, the Italian Marxist argued that Lenin understood that 'change was necessary from the war of manoeuvre, applied victoriously in the East in 1917, to a war of position which was the only form possible in the West' (Gramsci 1971: 237; Q7§16). This was because '[i]n Russia the State was everything, civil society was primordial and gelatinous; in the West, there was a proper relation between State and civil society, and when the State trembled a sturdy structure of civil society was at once revealed' (Gramsci 1971: 238; Q7§16).

A superficial reading of these passages might lead to the conclusion that Gramsci advocated reformism for the West and revolution for the East. However, Thomas (2009) has convincingly refuted the idea that the concept of 'war of movement' is identical to that of 'revolution' and that this strategy is only appropriate for the Western epoch of capitalist institution or for contemporary nations without a developed integral state, such as Russia and the colonial countries. Arguably, the distinction between 'movement' and 'position' is based neither on absolute historical nor on geographical differences, as they constitute discrete moments *within* the development of bourgeois society and of its proletarian antithesis. Gramsci distinguished between three broad modes of class struggle: war of movement, war of position, and 'underground' warfare: 'Boycotts are a form of war of position, strikes of war of movement, the secret preparation of weapons and combat troops belong to underground warfare' (Gramsci 1971: 229–30; Q1§134). Whereas the war of movement represents a frontal attack on state power, a 'concentrated and instantaneous form of insurrection', the war of position is a more '"diffused" and capillary form of indirect pressure' (Gramsci 1971: 110; Q15§11), a deliberate and steadfast siege of the state. The development of capitalism and the integral state did not *replace* the war of movement with the war of position, but it led to the *incorporation* of the war of movement as an element within the war of position. Gramsci stressed that 'the concentrated and instantaneous form of an insurrection' became impossible, but only 'in so far as that concentrated and instantaneous form was not preceded by long ideological and political preparation organically devised in advance to reawaken popular passions and enable them to be concentrated and brought simultaneously to detonation point' (Gramsci 1971: 110; Q15§11). If at any one moment one mode of struggle functions as an overall strategy, it subsumes the other mode as a tactic (see Gramsci 1971: 235; Q13§25). If the war of position is leading the development of proletarian hegemony, this mode does not rule out sudden and sharp 'attacks' – assertive strikes, demonstrations, and even uprisings – that reinforce the position of the class vis-à-vis the bourgeois state. Therefore Thomas asserts that a war of position can be both 'permanent' and 'offensive' (Thomas 2009: 79, 150). Conversely, when the war of movement is the dominant strategy, this does not absolve the working class from gradually developing its organizational and ideological forms (Gramsci 1971: 110; Q15§11).[8]

As it takes two to tango, neither the bourgeoisie nor the proletariat freely picks its mode of class struggle in isolation from the other 'unless from the start one has a crushing superiority over the enemy' (Gramsci 1971: 234; Q13§24). Here things become complicated because war of movement and position appear not only as carefully chosen strategies, but also as a 'territory' that is shared by antagonistic forces. In a war of movement the moments of revolution and counter-revolution are much more explicit because of the saliency and centrality of the popular insurrection and its often violent repression. On the other hand, in a war of position, popular initiative is much more diffused and indirect – and the reaction of the ruling class is equally deliberated and restrained. This made Gramsci wonder:

> Can the concept of 'passive revolution' ... be related to the concept of 'war of position' in contrast to war of manoeuvre? ... In other words, does there exist an absolute identity between war of position and passive revolution? Or at least does there exist, or can there be conceived, an entire historical period in which the two concepts must be considered identical – until the point at which the war of position once again becomes a war of manoeuvre? (Gramsci 1971: 108; Q15§11)

This might be interpreted in a reformist way: that a proletarian war of position is, in fact, a process of passive revolution. However, as I have outlined in the previous chapter, passive revolution is not a political programme or strategy but 'a criterion of interpretation, in the absence of other active elements in a dominant way' (Gramsci 1971: 114; Q15§62). The fact that the proletariat and the bourgeoisie became locked in a war of position can be interpreted by a deployment of the concept of passive revolution: an investigation into the capacity of the ruling classes to displace popular initiative and survive organic crises by reconfiguring the historical bloc. The concepts of war of position and of passive revolution become identical only when the 'territory' of struggle is completely dominated by the capitalist class. From the perspective of the proletariat, the war of position becomes a defensive one. However, the identity between war of position and passive revolution is not a necessary relation: the territory of struggle can be appropriated by the working class for its own project through the development of hegemonic politics. Thus proletarian hegemony appears as the form of permanent revolution that is necessary for waging a successful offensive war of position (see Gramsci 1971: 243; Q8§52; Thomas 2009: 149).

Class and State

In Chapter 2 I defined 'the state' loosely as the objectification of a ruling class, which mediates relations between that class and subaltern groups. Gramsci remarked that the relation between state and class is at the same time one of identity, representation, and autonomy (Gramsci 1971: 269; Q15§3,§18). For a class, the act of establishing its hegemony is nothing else than the act of 'founding' or 'becoming' a state (Gramsci 1971: 52, 269; Q25§5; Q15§3,§18). A party, in its specific sense of a hegemonic apparatus, represents 'an embryonic State structure' (Gramsci 1971: 226; Q3§42). With regard to the French Revolution, Marx had already observed that the political clubs were 'a coalition of the whole working class against the whole bourgeois class, the formation of a workers' state against the bourgeois state' (Marx 1978: 91). After Thermidor the apparatus of the clubs morphed into secret societies, which, in turn, became proper political parties in the late nineteenth century (see Gramsci 1971: 259–60; Q1§47).

As a concept, hegemony stresses the identity of class and state formation. Bourgeois hegemony superseded the *mechanical* ensemble of feudal corporate bodies, which existed in political and social separation from each other, with one universal political state (see Gramsci 1971: 54n4; Q25§2). However, bourgeois society did not present a real *organic* solution. At this point it becomes necessary to develop Gramsci's dichotomy between 'mechanical' and 'organic' state relations by turning to Hegel's distinction between mechanical, chemical, and teleological (organic) as three moments of the subject–object relation. The character of mechanism is 'that whatever the connection that obtains between the things combined, the connection remains one that is *alien* to them, that does not affect their nature, and even when a reflective semblance of unity is associated with it, the connection remains nothing more than *composition, mixture, aggregate,* etc.' (Hegel 2010: 631). The relations between Ancien Régime estates were mechanical because these bodies constituted 'complete and self-subsistent objects that, consequently, even in connection relate to one another as each standing on its own, each maintaining itself in every combination as external' (Hegel 2010: 631). Here class power always presumes a direct relation of subordination between subject and object through means of state power, as they are purely external and alien to each other. There is no assimilation, no 'organic passage' between classes, only subjugation and incorporation: 'The weaker can be seized and invaded by the stronger only in so far as it accepts the stronger and constitutes one sphere with it' (Hegel 2010: 638).

The second moment is that of *Chemism* whereby subject and object 'in a state of reciprocal tension seek one another and then combine in a neutral product by means of a formal and external middle term' (Hegel 2010: 649). Subject and object have an *affinity*: their separate natures share a property, which becomes a means to mediate their relation. The bourgeois state is a chemical agent in the sense that it creates an apparently 'neutral' relation between the bourgeois class and other social groups on the basis of their shared property as citizens or belonging to 'the people' – that is, as equal members of political society, which functions as the 'middle term' that mediates class relations (see Marx 1979a: 165). Yet its representative function is merely a means to the end of achieving bourgeois class power – an end that is not shared by the subaltern groups. Moreover, as a 'universal capitalist', the bourgeois state effectively mediates the hierarchical relations between different fractions of capital. Even as a 'middle term' the state remains a coercive force: 'That the purpose immediately refers to an object and makes it into a means, as also that through this means it determines another object, may be regarded as violence inasmuch as purpose appears of an entirely different nature than the object, and the two objects are in like matter mutually independent totalities' (Hegel 2010: 663). Thus the Marxian conception that the bourgeois state is purely a class weapon does not preclude a more sophisticated understanding of its 'independence' from society and even from the capitalist class: 'it is a distinct advantage to the bourgeoisie if its own state – the state which assures its interests – is not simply its tool, if indeed this state enjoys sufficient autonomy from the ruling class so that, if need be, the former can even exert coercion on the latter' (Draper 2011a: 334).

Finally, *Teleology* or organicism describes a relation where subject and object recognize their own purpose in each other. The subject and object come together in a real, organic unity, in which both function as means to each other's ends. Identity of interests precludes the necessity for coercion either through direct subjugation or state mediation: 'There is no need, therefore, for the subjective purpose to exercise any violence to make the object into a means' (Hegel 2010: 667).

This conceptual detour illuminates that for Gramsci hegemony is not a *neutral* conception of class leadership in modern times, for the character of bourgeois hegemony differs fundamentally from that of proletarian hegemony (see Thomas 2009: 222).[9] With regard to bourgeois class power, which subordinates a social majority to the interests of a minority through the universalist mediation of the state, hegemony is the form of which domination is the inner content (see Gramsci 1971: 59; Q19§24). Consent is achieved by top-down reforms, paternalist concessions, and transformist policies – remaining essentially coercive. The formally organic passage of the subaltern classes into political society hides the essentially 'chemical' nature of bourgeois class rule and its 'neutral' state. If the political state wants to be the mirror in which the whole of society can recognize itself as bourgeois, it has to acquire an existence outside the bourgeois class. At the core of bourgeois hegemony is the logic of representation. The ideological and institutional forms of the state are objectifications, externalized expressions of the bourgeois class, which mediate between the ruling and subaltern groups (see Gramsci 1971: 269; Q15§3,§18). Because these state forms are external to the bourgeois class, they attain a semblance of class neutrality, which reinforces their hold over society as a whole.

Ironically, the completion of bourgeois hegemony and the perfection of the state as arbiter of the class struggle cause a breakdown of the chemical formula: 'The parliamentary regime leaves everything to the decision of majorities; how shall the great majorities outside parliament not want to decide?' (Marx 1979a: 142). Pure bourgeois hegemony expressed in the form of the democratic republic 'is also the type of state that frees the class struggle from its last fetters and prepares the battleground for it' (Engels 1988: 419). The abolishment of feudal and absolutist monarchical remnants not only completes the bourgeoisie's political rule, but it also 'undermines its social foundation, since they must now confront the subjugated classes and contend against them without mediation, without the concealment afforded by the crown, without being able to divert the national interest by their subordinate struggles among themselves and with the monarchy' (Marx 1979a: 129).

Because state power is differentiated from bourgeois class power, it can, for a period, obtain real independence, or it can be appropriated by other class forces. In this simple, abstract formula lies the key to understanding the complex 'nature' of the state, which, as the externalization of the bourgeois class, is both an instrument of class power and an independent subject in its own right. Paraphrasing Gramsci, we could conclude that if it is true that states are only the nomenclature for classes, it is also true that states are not simply a mechanical and passive expression of those classes, but react energetically upon them in order to develop, solidify, and universalize them (see Gramsci 1971: 227; Q3§119). The Jacobin moment of the French Revolution already began to transgress the merely chemical essence of bourgeois hegemony, only to find itself isolated on the island of the political state, squeezed between the *sans-culottes* who desired social emancipation and new and old elites vying for domination. Here, again, the French 'model' of popular bourgeois revolution appears rather as a transgression – a political enlightenment 'overreaching itself' (Marx and Engels 1975a: 122) – than as its pure expression. Conversely, the 'dictatorship of the proletariat' – class rule of the majority – represents hegemony as a content of which domination is the outward form. Inner consent is realized by a dialectical pedagogy: a continuous reciprocal exchange between 'leaders' and 'led' (see De Smet 2015; Thomas 2009: 437–8). For Gramsci this dialectical pedagogy was exemplified in the struggle of the factory councils during the *Biennio Rosso*, where intellectuals and workers came together in an organic unity. However, this movement fell short of developing a Modern Prince, a hegemonic apparatus that could organize this organic passage at the level of society as a whole. Other subaltern groups, such as the Southern peasants in Gramsci's Italy, have to find the conditions for their own social emancipation in the self-emancipatory struggle of the working class. Equally the proletariat needs to approach the emancipation of these groups as an end-in-itself, for it can 'build socialism only if it is helped and followed by the large majority of these social strata' (Gramsci 2005: 41). In this regard the working class has the potential to become a true 'universal class':

> A class claiming to be capable of assimilating the whole of society, and which was at the same time really able to express such a process, would perfect this conception of the State and of law, so as to conceive the end of the State and of law – rendered useless since they will have exhausted their function and will have been absorbed by civil society. (Gramsci 1971: 260; Q8§2; see Marx 1975b: 280; 1976: 212)

The first moment of concrete proletarian hegemony was the Paris Commune of 1871: 'the first revolution in which the working class was openly acknowledged as the only class capable of social initiative, even by the great bulk of the Paris middle class – shopkeepers, tradesmen, merchants – the wealthy capitalists alone excepted' (Marx 1986c: 336). When Prussia–Germany defeated the French Empire of Napoleon III in the battle of Sedan in the fall of 1870, representatives of the National Assembly in Paris proclaimed a new republic. As the German armies marched on Paris, the bourgeoisie and the affluent layers of the petty bourgeoisie fled the capital, leaving the working classes to face the siege. When it became clear that the provisional republican government, now operating from Bordeaux, wanted to surrender to Prussia–Germany, the proletarian and impoverished petty-bourgeois masses, joined by National

Guard soldiers, occupied the Parisian city council on 22 January. The capital was declared a self-governing Commune. After the Communal elections of March, which brought workers to power, Marx enthusiastically claimed that the Commune 'was essentially a working-class government, the produce of the struggle of the producing against the appropriating class, the political form at last discovered under which to work out the economical emancipation of Labour' (Marx 1986c: 334).

The historical experience of the Commune showed, for the first time, how a new state was prefigured in the struggle of the popular masses, led by the proletariat. This embryonic state represented both the completion of political emancipation and the beginning of a process of social emancipation. The insurrection entailed not simply the entry of proletarian representatives into bourgeois parliament, but the revolutionizing of democratic representation itself, for 'the working class cannot simply lay hold of the ready-made State machinery, and wield it for its own purposes' (Marx 1986c: 328; see Lenin 1964c: 393). The chemical bourgeois state had to become an organic popular one: 'While the merely repressive organs of the old governmental power were to be amputated, its legitimate functions were to be wrested from an authority usurping pre-eminence over society itself, and restored to the responsible agents of society' (Marx 1986c: 332–3). The Commune decided to abolish the standing army and supplant it with a popular militia; subjugate the police and state bureaucracy to direct Communal control; grant the population to elect and revoke municipal councillors, bureaucrats, and magistrates, hold them accountable, and pay them a worker's wage; combine executive and legislative functions in the 'working body' of the Commune; turn religion into a private affair; democratize education and free it from state and religious interference; etc. (Marx 1986c: 331–2). The model of the Commune was to be exported to other cities, provincial towns, and rural thorps. The self-governance of these local Communes would be complemented by a National Delegation in Paris, elected by them. Marx underlined that this would not mean the end of central government, but its reconstitution on a popular base (Marx 1986c: 334).

These political forms set in motion the process for social emancipation, for '[t]he political rule of the producer cannot coexist with the perpetuation of his social slavery' (Marx 1986c: 335). Marx conceived of social emancipation not as an intentional process, in the sense of a predetermined development towards an ideal, but as a learning process that *emerges* from the struggle, that had to be 'worked out' 'through long struggles, through a series of historic processes, transforming circumstances and men' (Marx 1986c: 335). The Commune only stood at the beginning of this 'immanent' process of social emancipation, implementing a few basic reforms such as the abolition of night work for bakers, the elimination of surplus extraction by employers through fines, the collectivization (with compensation) of closed workshops and factories, etc. Nevertheless the spirit of a new society waiting to be born was already gripping the masses, creating a festive atmosphere and the feeling that 'for the first time since the days of February, 1848, the streets of Paris were safe, and that without any police of any kind' (Marx 1986c: 341).

The uprising in Paris created a situation of 'dual power' between popular and bourgeois government, which, however, was primarily articulated along socio-geographical lines: national parliamentary elections, held in February, showed the great differentiation between the capital, where radical democratic and socialist candidates won an absolute majority, and the French hinterland, which was represented by conservative monarchist and bourgeois delegates. Proletarian hegemonic unity between the city, the provincial towns, and the countryside was not achieved, as Paris moved far beyond the rest of the nation and was not able to draw the whole population into its radical project. With the support of Bismarck, the French national government sent the army to Paris to pacify the rebels. Other Communes in regional cities were quickly and violently dismantled. By the end of May the Paris uprising was suppressed in a counter-revolutionary bloodbath that claimed thousands of civilian lives.

Marx on Bonapartism

What happens when the 'chemical' nature of bourgeois hegemony reveals itself, but the new, competing universal class is unable to offer the subaltern groups an organic passage of its own? What happens when the bourgeoisie retreats from pursuing its class project to its own logical conclusion of political emancipation, frightened by the prospect of social revolution? The historical experience of modern imperial rule by Napoleon I, Napoleon III, Bismarck, etc., demonstrated that the democratic republic was not the necessary end point of bourgeois rule. Moreover, it showed that the successful displacement of permanent revolution in 1789 and 1848 was not always the product of a crafty and agile bourgeoisie standing at the helm of the state apparatus. On the contrary, it was the *active dispossession* of the bourgeoisie of its *state power* that guaranteed its continued *class power*. By losing its power to govern, it succeeded in consolidating its rule.

With regard to the French Revolution we have concluded that the struggle for political emancipation was turning the revolution against the bourgeoisie itself. By taking its own organic claims of universal suffrage, human rights, and so on, seriously, the pure bourgeois political society was threatening the structure of its constituent civil society. The political state and its Jacobin petty-bourgeois personnel disconnected themselves from their class, but, by rebuffing the particular class demands of the *sans-culottes*, they found themselves isolated from society in general. Subsequently, the *Directoire* and the Orléanist constitutional monarchy of 1830 represented the rule of a bourgeois class that 'no longer considered the constitutional representative state as a means for achieving the ideal of the state, the welfare of the world and universal human aims but, on the contrary, had acknowledged it as the official expression of its own exclusive power and the political recognition of its own special interests' (Marx and Engels 1975a: 124).

By cynically recognizing the particularist base of its universalist state, bourgeois hegemony lost much of its Jacobin prestige. By replacing bourgeois leadership by the agency of the political state, Napoleon reasserted the bourgeois ideal of a political state elevated above the classes, but in an explicitly illiberal form. Bonaparte 'regarded the state as an end in itself and civil life only as a treasurer and his subordinate which must have no will of its own' (Marx and Engels 1975a: 123). Napoleon appeared as the stern guardian of bourgeois society, substituting the faltering leadership of the ruling classes with his own 'charismatic' direction (see Gramsci 1971: 210; Q13§23), which was primarily rooted in his capacity as a military leader. Not only was the state 'in the last analysis' conceptually reducible to 'bodies of armed men' (Lenin 1964c: 393–6), but national armies had become a material apparatus for the *constitution* of modern bourgeois states during and after the French Revolution. Marx mused: 'were not barrack and bivouac, sabre and musket, moustache and uniform finally bound to hit upon the idea of ... saving society once and for all by proclaiming their own regime as the highest and freeing civil society completely from the trouble of governing itself?' (Marx 1979a: 118). Becoming conscious of its power to constitute political society, the military could substitute its own 'praetorian'[10] agency as a national apparatus for that of civil politicians who appeared unable to govern. Bonaparte became the herald of modern military coups and regimes.

The rule of Bonaparte's nephew Napoleon III, famously discussed by Marx in 'The Eighteenth Brumaire of Louis Bonaparte' (1852) and in 'The Civil War in France' (1871), was of a different calibre. The rise to power of the uncharismatic Napoleon III illustrated the fact that the dynamic of Bonapartism could not be reduced to the agency of an individual; instead 'the class struggle in France created circumstances and relations that made it possible for a grotesque mediocrity to play a hero's part' (Marx 1985b: 57). The repression of the proletarian uprising of June 1848 caused a chain reaction of disintegrating class alliances: between the working class and the petty bourgeoisie, between the petty bourgeoisie and capital, and ultimately between different fractions of capital. Whereas the squabbling bourgeois factions in the National Assembly reflected the fragmentation of the nation, Louis Bonaparte, elected as president by universal (male) suffrage, appeared to express the popular will directly and in a concentrated form. With the claim that parliament represented the universal good discredited, the semblance of the state as a neutral 'middle term' was increasingly concentrated in the individual figure of the president. The fact that Napoleon III was a parvenu, a foreigner, and not in any way organically connected to a class in French society, allowed him to play a 'chemical' role. However, it also meant that he was but an individual, without a party or a state-in-forma-tion. A 'princely lumpenproletarian' himself, he bought elements of the lumpenproletariat, organizing them into a party apparatus of his own – the December 10 Society (Marx 1979a: 150–1; 157). This 'lumpenparty' was deployed to gain hegemony in civil society, rooting Louis Napoleon's imperial ambitions in the semblance of a popular will.

Bereft of their own hegemonic apparatuses, the popular masses called upon the president to defend their interests against the National Assembly. The conservative smallholding peasantry in particular, still the majority of the French population, which could not produce a political representation of its own, accepted Louis Napoleon as its benevolent caretaker, who would protect its property against the socialism of the working class and the liberalism of the bourgeoisie.[11] Conversely, Louis Bonaparte learned the value of mobilizing the unorganized popular masses against parts of the political state apparatus. By reintroducing universal (male) suffrage for presidential elections he appeared more democratic than the bourgeoisie, which had virtually restricted the electorate to its own ranks. The president could reach out directly to the whole of the French masses, outbidding parliament's democratic legitimacy. Top-down social reforms, employment by public work programmes, and financial measures such as state donations, lotteries, and easy loans relieved the direct predicament of the popular classes, but at the same time bound them as clients to the paternalist state.

The president's gradual usurpation of power, culminating in crowning himself Emperor Napoleon III in 1852, met with little resistance from the bourgeois politicians: 'the parliamentary party was paralysed by a double fear, by the fear of again evoking revolutionary unrest and by the fear of itself appearing as the instigator of unrest in the eyes of its own class, in the eyes of the bourgeoisie' (Marx 1979a: 153). Each victory of Louis Napoleon was greeted by the financial, industrial, and commercial bourgeoisie as a victory of order and stability over the chaos of parliamentarianism. The bourgeoisie muzzled its own organic intellectuals – especially liberal politicians and journalists who were defending the political rights of their class. The leadership of Napoleon III was primarily rooted in his negative ability to continuously break the independent political power of both the ruling and the subaltern classes.

While the modern structures of French executive, legislative, and judicial power were changed drastically over the decades after 1789, reverting from different forms of democratic republicanism to constitutional monarchy and vice versa, the bureaucratic and military state apparatus had gradually accumulated members, functions, and influence, representing a beacon of stability in the revolutionary storms. Unlike the proletarian revolutionaries of the Commune, the bourgeoisie had appropriated the Ancien Régime absolutist state apparatus, transforming, developing, and perfecting it as a modern instrument of centralized class domination. The bureaucracy became the instrument through which political society 'enmeshes, controls, regulates, superintends and tutors civil society' (Marx 1979a: 139). The growth of the bureaucracy went hand in hand with the dominance of the executive power over the legislative (Draper 2011a: 314). Every activity of civil society became the object of governmental control and supervision.

The dispossession of the bourgeoisie of its direct political power may give the impression that the political state became independent from its constituent class. As Marx stressed, however, 'the state power is not suspended in mid air' (Marx 1979a: 186; see Gramsci 1971: 211; Q13§23).[12] Although the state represented the peasantry, which constituted its *social* base for electoral mobilization, this representation was layered on top of the state's continued support for the accumulation of capital and its civil protagonists – its real *class* base (see Draper 2011a: 401–2). Even if the bourgeoisie lost political power, it still produced personnel for the state bureaucracy from its ranks. Moreover, the lingering form of the absolutist tax-office state gained a new capitalist content as the bourgeois class 'makes up in the form of state salaries for what it cannot pocket in the form of profit, interest, rents and honorariums' (Marx 1979a: 139). In this regard the state apparatus of the Second Empire remained a body controlled by the bourgeois class. The relation between class and state remained essentially chemical; the state functioned as a mediating 'middle-term' between bourgeois class interests and society as a whole. For the bourgeoisie it was much easier to be a ruling class that appeared to suffer the shared fate of all classes in society – to be subjugated in equal measure by imperial power – then to face the reality of being a class that cowardly refrained from completing its own emancipatory project.

Marx and Engels understood the emergence of Bonapartism and imperial absolutism in general in world-historical terms as 'the only form of government possible at a time when the bourgeoisie had already lost, and the working class had not yet acquired, the faculty of ruling the nation' (Marx 1986c: 330). The independent insurrection of the proletariat in 1848 had not only revealed 'the general content of the modern revolution', but also that this content 'was in most singular contradiction to everything that, with the material available, with the degree of education attained by the masses, under the given circumstances and relations, could be immediately realised in practice' (Marx 1979a: 109). At this point, the failure of permanent revolution in the face of the organic crises of bourgeois society was comprehended as a historical interlude between bourgeois and proletarian hegemony. Here Marx's *post factum* materialist interpretation becomes tragic: the self-determining movement of the proletariat in 1848 was doomed to defeat, as it went beyond 'the situation, the relations, the conditions under which alone modern revolution becomes serious' (Marx 1979a: 106).

The return of Ancien Régime forms such as monarchy and empire in the nineteenth century could be understood either as a *transitional* political form towards the democratic republic, or as the *end point* of bourgeois domination, which retreated before the radical consequences of its own political emancipation. Engels commented that Bonapartism or 'Caesarism' was the final form of the monarchy and that '[a]fter it, the only possible type of state left is the republic' (Engels 1988: 417). In Spain, for example, the constitutional monarchy was the result of a lack of capitalist development and unripe class. The democratic struggle for the bourgeois republic would create a political stage for a more open class struggle between the bourgeoisie and the working class (Engels 1988: 419). Similarly, with regard to the post-1905 concessions of czarism, Lenin remarked that:

Bonapartism is the manoeuvring on the part of a monarchy which has lost its old patriarchal or feudal, simple and solid, foundation – a monarchy which is obliged to walk the tightrope in order not to fall, make advances in order to govern, bribe in order to gain affections, fraternise with the dregs of society, with plain thieves and swindlers, in order not to rely only on bayonets. (Lenin 1963a: 269)

Here Bonapartism is the desperate gamble of a monarchy that 'cannot rely for support upon any one class of the population. It cannot even maintain its alliance with the landlords and the big bourgeoisie' (Lenin 1963c: 421).

In contradistinction, Marx's concept of 'the Caesarism of Paris' (Marx 1981: 385) flowed from his analysis that the French historical bloc was *overripe* after 1848; that the class struggle had already moved *beyond* the democratic republic; and that Empire was the final bourgeois stage before proletarian revolution. Here we can discern an anticipation of Lenin's argument in 'Imperialism'.[13]

Gramsci on Caesarism

The stubbornness of capitalism after the Paris Commune and the First World War and its rejuvenation not only in Fordism, but also in the clearly Bonapartist form of Fascism, brought Gramsci to contemplate 'Caesarism' as a concept that stood in a close family relation with the dynamic of permanent/passive revolution (Fontana 2004). In order to understand the role of Caesarism in the development of capitalism, Gramsci began with the simplest abstract determination of the concept: 'Caesarism can be said to express a situation in which the forces in conflict balance each other in such a way that a continuation of the conflict can only terminate in their reciprocal destruction' (Gramsci 1971: 219; Q13§27). When a subaltern class (A) struggles with a dominant class (B) for power, this can lead to the victory of one of the two parties, but 'it may happen that neither A nor B defeats the other – that they bleed each other mutually and then a third force C intervenes from outside, subjugating what is left of both A and B' (Gramsci 1971: 219; Q13§27). In other words, Caesarism describes a crisis that cannot be overcome by either the subaltern or the dominant class force, which leads to the mediation of a third party (see Gramsci 1971: 211; Q13§27). This crisis can be conjunctural or organic: the result of a 'momentary political deficiency of the traditional dominant force' or of an 'insuperable organic deficiency' (Gramsci 1971: 211; Q13§27).

However, as Marx underlined with regard to the state under Napoleon III, Caesarism only *feigns* neutrality. Its character depends on the side it supports in the class struggle: 'Caesarism is progressive when its intervention helps the progressive force to triumph, albeit with its victory tempered by certain compromises and limitations' (Gramsci 1971: 219; Q13§27). Gramsci considered Caesar and Napoleon I as examples of progressive Caesarism as they advanced the class interests of, respectively, the Roman *populares* and the French bourgeoisie against the patricians and the aristocracy.[14] Conversely, Caesarism 'is reactionary when its intervention helps the reactionary force to triumph

– in this case too with certain compromises and limitations, which have, however, a different value, extent, and significance than in the former [case]' (Gramsci 1971: 219; Q13§27). Napoleon III and Bismark were ideal types of this reactionary intervention.

In addition to the distinction between progressive and reactionary Caesarism, Gramsci distinguished between qualitative and quantitative variants. Qualitative Caesarism represented 'the historical passage from one type of State to another type – passage in which the innovations were so numerous, and of such a nature, that they represented a complete revolution' (Gramsci 1971: 222; Q13§27). Here 'revolution' is deployed in its objectivist sense. More specifically, it refers to 'bourgeois revolutions' or rather, from a passive-revolutionary criterion, the bourgeois transformations from above that took place in the absence of a strong, hegemonic bourgeois class. Napoleon III represented a merely quantitative type of Caesarism: 'there was no passage from one type of State to another, but only "evolution" of the same type along unbroken lines' (Gramsci 1971: 222; Q13§27). Under Napoleon III the opposition between capital and the popular classes became total. Imperial state power could not organically fuse and unite bourgeois and popular class interests, but it could present itself openly as a chemical solution that brought balance in society. In this case, the historical bloc was not fundamentally reconfigured.

Up until Napoleon III the general historical form of Caesarism was the 'praetorian' military coup. Gramsci highlighted the fact that not every military dictatorship has a Bonapartist character, but that military interventions become Caesarist when the army expresses the interests of a specific social stratum (see Marx 1986b: 465), such as the peasantry or the petty bourgeoisie, which are often mediated by the junior officers (see Gramsci 1971: 212; Q13§23). In situations when this class fraction is actively struggling, the military cannot simply crush the opposing force: 'the army has to remain neutral (up to a certain point, of course), since otherwise it might split horizontally' (Gramsci 1971: 216; Q13§23). In these circumstances the military leadership has to forge alliances in order to restore the equilibrium and ensure the survival of its own apparatus, by forcing political and social concessions from the dominant classes. Thus the military leadership 'succeeds in permeating the State with its interests, up to a certain point, and in replacing a part of the leading personnel' (Gramsci 1971: 217; Q13§23).[15] This idea will prove important for our analysis of Egyptian Caesarism in the second part of the book.

Gramsci was careful to emphasize that this abstract concept of Caesarism was 'a generic hypothesis, a sociological schema (convenient for the art of politics)' (Gramsci 1971: 221; Q13§27) that had to be oriented towards concrete historical cases in order to become useful. The Italian Marxist probably had in mind Marx's denunciation of the concept of 'so-called Caesarism' among his contemporaries:

> In this superficial historical analogy the main point is forgotten, namely, that in ancient Rome the class struggle took place only within a privileged minority, between the free rich and the free poor, while the great productive mass of the population, the slaves, formed the purely passive pedestal for these combatants…. With so complete a difference between the material, economic conditions of the ancient and the modern class struggles, the political figures produced by them can likewise have no more in common with one another than the Archbishop of Canterbury has with the High Priest Samuel. (Marx 1985b: 57–8)[16]

Gramsci's use of the term 'Caesarism' was an ironic appropriation of the comparison made by Fascists between Mussolini and Julius Caesar (see Hoare and Nowell-Smith in Gramsci 1971: 219n9): 'Caesarism is a polemical–ideological formula, and not a canon of historical interpretation' (Gramsci 1971: 220; Q13§27). He agreed with Marx that '[i]n concrete analyses of real events, the historical forms are individualised and can almost be called "unique". Caesar represents a very different combination of real circumstances from that represented by Napoleon I, as does Primo de Rivera from that of Živković, etc.' (Gramsci 1971: 217; Q13§23). The generic label of 'Caesarism' should not replace an analysis of the actual 'interplay of relations' (Gramsci 1971: 222; Q13§27). Gramsci did not conceive of Caesarism as a binary concept, but considered that there could be various gradations, intermediate forms, episodes, and successive waves of Caesarism, for example in Italy in the years between the March on Rome in 1922 and the end of parliamentary democracy in 1926 (Gramsci 1971: 220, 222; Q13§27). In fact, Gramsci's attention shifted to the qualitative differences in content between historical forms of Caesarism.

Although classical Caesarism reflects 'the particular situation in which *a great personality* is entrusted with the task of "arbitration" over a historico-political situation characterised by an equilibrium of forces heading towards catastrophe' (Gramsci 1971: 219; Q13§27; my emphasis), Gramsci stressed that '[a] Caesarist solution can exist even without a Caesar, without any great, "heroic" and representative personality' (Gramsci 1971: 220; Q13§27). Here the concept of Caesarism moves beyond the epoch of the institution of capitalism and migrates into the age of capitalist reconfigurations: 'In the modern world, with its great economic-trade-union and party-political coalitions, the mechanism of the Caesarist phenomenon is very different from what it was up to the time of Napoleon III' (Gramsci 1971: 220; Q13§27). Modern Caesarism emerged from the developed class conflict between the proletariat and the bourgeoisie, which, unlike the previous epochal struggle between the aristocracy and the bourgeoisie, could not end in a simple fusion of class interests (Gramsci 1971: 222; Q13§27; see Carver 2004: 124). The only organic passage that was achieved was that between the feudal aristocracy and the bourgeois class; even in cases such as Germany when the bourgeoisie did not succeed in formally governing, the gradual transformation of the mode of production had turned Ancien Régime elites into fractions of landed or financial capital. The constitutional monarchy, in both its early commercial and its late imperial forms, expressed the fundamentally *passive* condition of the bourgeoisie, which longed for a Cromwell or a Napoleon to safeguard its class interests in a roundabout way. The hegemonic moment of 1789, when the bourgeoisie seemed to express itself most clearly as a revolutionary class, elevating itself from a corporate to a political body, was only achieved by the liberal transgression of its Jacobin vanguard, mobilizing the popular classes. Although this transgression, the fight for a genuinely democratic republic, opened the Pandora's box of social emancipation, undermining the bourgeoisie's class interests, it also became its epochal myth and the ideological base of its pseudo-organic rule. The chemical formula of the democratic republic, the accomplished state form of political emancipation, was equally the most powerful means for generating consent among the subaltern groups and the gravest threat to bourgeois rule.

The development of the integral state after 1848 and 1871 turned Caesarism into a permanent *civil* characteristic of bourgeois hegemony, as state bureaucracies and even democratic coalition governments could be understood as a 'first stage of Caesarism' (Gramsci 1971: 212, 220, 228; Q3§119; Q13§23,§27; see Fontana 2004: 189). Instead of an authoritarian aberration, Caesarism appears as the naked chemical relation between the bourgeois class and the capitalist state – as the essence of bourgeois hegemony (see Carver 2004: 113–4). This could be interpreted simplistically: all bourgeois governments are Caesarist dictatorships (see Fontana 2004: 181n21). However, this abstract analysis cannot explain the concrete hegemonic form of the dictatorial content. Bourgeois Caesarism remains hidden, wrapped in the apparatus of the political state and its promise of an organic passage into bourgeois society – until the political parties, associations, and personnel of the bourgeoisie are no longer recognized as hegemonic, as able to lead society, by either the subaltern groups or the (allies of the) bourgeoisie itself, or both. This creates a situation of hegemonic crisis, which, if unresolved, may lead to the intervention of a third party, as I discussed earlier.

In its moderate form, the Caesarist actor *substitutes* its own agency for the weak, corporate, and fragmented ruling and subaltern political bodies, as was the case with the Piedmont state in Italy, or in a later stage, with 'those capitalist governments that, by exploiting the antagonisms between the proletarian and fascist camps and by leaning directly upon the military–police apparatus, raise themselves above parliament and democracy, as the saviours of "national unity"' (Trotsky 1956). In its strongest, most explicit form the military or civil third party 'set itself over and above the parties, not so as to harmonise their interests and activities within the permanent framework of the life and interests of the nation and State, but so as to disintegrate them, to detach them from the broad masses' (Gramsci 1971: 227; Q3§119). This is the radical form of Fascism, which creates an equilibrium between the classes by completely obliterating their political apparatuses, replacing them entirely with its own personnel, ideology, and practices.

Reflections on 'Progressive' Caesarism

Gramsci struggled with the intellectual legacy of Marx's 'Preface' in the face of the stubbornness of capitalism. A tragic understanding of the revolutions of 1848 implied that they came too soon, in the sense that the productive forces and society in general could still be developed under capitalist relations. Although the proletariat, swept forward by the war of movement, showed itself capable of leading society, it bumped into the backward conditions of France, unable to rally the peasant and petty-bourgeois masses of that era: 'The policy of alliances and of permanent revolution had finished by posing new questions which at that time could not be resolved; it had unleashed elemental forces which only a military dictatorship was to succeed in containing' (Gramsci 1971: 80; Q19§24). At this juncture the proletariat could merely reveal the inadequacy of the bourgeois democratic republic, but it was incapable of formulating a political project of its own (see Chapter 2). Moreover, Gramsci concluded that the success of Napoleon III illustrated that 'the existing social form had not yet exhausted its possibilities for development' (Gramsci 1971: 221–2; Q13§27).

However, he immediately added that 'a social form "always" has marginal possibilities for further development and organisational improvement, and in particular can count on the relative weakness of the rival progressive force as a result of its specific character and way of life' (Gramsci 1971: 222; Q13§27). Although the capitalist mode of production had become a fetter upon material development and human emancipation in an absolute and world-historical sense, there was not to be a 'final' crisis of capitalism followed by a universal social revolution. The transition to a new mode of production did not flow directly from the socialization of production under capitalism, but also needed an active, human agent – the proletariat as a universal class, whose political and social struggle prefigured the new communist society. The historical failure of this permanent-revolutionary dynamic, especially after the Russian Revolution of 1917, invited Gramsci to develop the interpretative criterion of passive revolution. From the perspective of passive revolution, Caesarism is the methodology to consolidate (quantitative) or reconstitute (qualitative) historical blocs in specific situations of conjunctural or organic crisis where neither dominant nor subaltern classes are able to assert their hegemony. Fascism, for example, emulated American Fordism in a Caesarist form (Buci-Glucksmann 1980: 310–4). Here the criterion of passive revolution does not illuminate the craftiness and agility of a dominant class that is able to continue its rule past its expiry date, but it highlights *the autonomous agency of their instruments of class rule*, which display a political initiative and will of their own to fill the political vacuum.

Still, in contrast to the qualitative forms of Caesarism in the nineteenth century, the transformative potential of modern Caesarism was limited. Such movements derived strength from 'their adversary's inability to construct, not by an inherent force of their own' (Gramsci 1971: 223; Q14§23). However, if the 'progressive' outcome is understood in a purely objectivist sense (see Fontana 2004: 179–80; 192) – that is, if a revolution from above can be altogether progressive, as Gramsci implied with regard to the rule of Napoleon I – can we conceive of a modern Caesarism that stands in a chemical relation, not with the bourgeoisie, but with a subaltern group and, in particular, the proletariat? Can we conceive of a Caesarism from the perspective of permanent revolution? Gramsci himself warned against 'an anachronistic and anti-natural form of "Napoleonism"' (Gramsci 1971: 241; Q14§68). He had in mind the dissemination of a permanent revolution 'from above' by the Red Army, as a parallel to Napoleon's military campaigns that spread the French Revolution throughout Europe (Hoare and Nowell-Smith in Gramsci 1971: 241n41). His rejection of such a strategy was probably born from Engels' and Lenin's assertion that the proletariat could not force its national achievements upon another country (see Losurdo 2015: 112).

From a subjectivist perspective, it is clear that 'subaltern Caesarism' cannot function as an adequate programme for proletarian action, as political substitutionism is the antithesis of self-emancipation. If communist society is prefigured by the hegemonic class activity of the proletariat, this development is essentially obstructed by the independent initiative of a third party. Nevertheless, the Russian Revolution and the decolonization movements seem to indicate that modern military and bureaucratic Caesarism does not have to represent the class interests of the bourgeoisie, but may be chemically connected to a popular base. This was, in fact, Trotsky's critique in 'The Soviet Union Today' (1935) of Stalinist substitutionism as a form of *proletarian Bonapartism*. Despite the proletarian seizure of power in 1917, the Soviet state bureaucracy emerged as a third party to resolve the contradictions between the minority working class and the peasant majority, between city and countryside, amongst different national groups, and so on. Implicitly deploying a chemical concept of hegemony, Trotsky claimed that '[t]he *social* domination of a class (its dictatorship) may find extremely diverse *political* forms. This is attested by the entire history of the bourgeoisie, from the Middle Ages to the present day' (Trotsky 1956). The class nature of the Soviet bureaucracy was not bourgeois, but proletarian, in the sense that *'the social content of the dictatorship of the bureaucracy is determined by those productive relations that were created by the proletarian revolution'* (Trotsky 1956; emphasis in original). Trotsky drew an analogy between the progressive Caesarism of Napoleon I, who continued to spread the political emancipation of the French Revolution through Empire and sword, and Stalin's top-down and coercive trans-formation of the mode of production. From such a 'neutral' objectivist perspective, the Soviet Union remained a workers' state, albeit deformed, because the outcomes constituted a social revolution to the benefit of the working class. However, after 1924, the initiative shifted to the state bureaucracy as the working class was too small and too weak to exert hegemony *after* the takeover of power, and the other classes had been politically, if not socially, eradicated.[17]

Trotsky correctly understood the chemical relation between the Bonapartist Soviet state and the working class, but despite his emphasis that 'in contradistinction to capitalism, socialism is built not automat-ically but consciously' (Trotsky 1956), he downplayed the essence of proletarian hegemony as self-emancipation and self-governance. The separation between 'political' and 'social' domination is highly artificial. The real content of a workers' state is not a nationalized and planned economy, but the organic connection between proletarian state and class power – the 'dictatorship of the proletariat'. This is the crucial difference with bourgeois hegemony, which is *essentially* Caesarist. Although the notion of 'modern progressive Caesarism' is useful as an analytical, objectivist criterion to interpret the relation between state and class power, it does not reflect a normative step forward in world history from the perspective of political and social emancipation.

Yet, there is a complementary approach to the question of contemporary progressive Caesarism; the position that outside the core capitalist countries *modern* Caesarism was in fact a bastard form of *classical* Caesarism, which was still fighting an epochal struggle against feudalism. A more sophisticated version of this argument is posited by the theory of deflected permanent revolution, which requires us first to investigate Trotsky's development of the theory of permanent revolution and his concept of uneven and combined development in relation to Gramsci's notion of passive revolution.

Part II
Gramsci in Egypt

5. Passive Revolution and Imperialism

From Absolutism to Colonialism

On 1 July 1798 Napoleon Bonaparte, at the time a general under the *Directoire*, landed in Alexandria, Egypt. Europe's revolutionary wars had left Britain as France's main antagonist. As Egypt connected the important Mediterranean and Red Sea commercial routes, Napoleon's army invaded the country probably with the intention of disturbing British trade with India. By the end of the eighteenth century, Mamluk[1] military and bureaucratic leaders had gradually wrested the Ottoman province from under the direct control of the Sultanate. The concentration of landed property, low agricultural prices, and the expansion of European markets between the 1740s and 1815 intensified trade relations between the Ottoman Empire and the West, incorporating Egypt into the developing world market. At the moment of the French invasion, Egypt was governed with an iron fist by the duumvirate of Murad Bey (1750–1801) and Ibrahim Bey (1735–1817). Thus, when Bonaparte came to Egypt, he presented himself not as a foreign conqueror, but as a progressive Caesar spreading the universalist ideas of the French Revolution – a liberator of the Egyptian people from the yoke of both Ottoman despotism and Mamluk domination. Like those parts of Europe that were invaded by the Napoleonic armies, Egypt was introduced to the fruits of modernity, both material (for example the printing press and military organization) and ideal (for example liberalism and nationalism), by 'iron and blood'. Murad and Ibrahim resisted the French, supported by local imams and *shuyukh* (sing. *shaykh*) who called upon the Arab population to rise up against foreign occupation, for example in the Cairo revolt of 22 October 1798.

One year later Bonaparte returned to France. His retreat was prompted by personal ambitions at home, as the power of the *Directoire* was waning, and by his realization that he could not hold Egypt against the combined force of the British and Ottoman Empires and a revolting populace. Notwithstanding its brevity, this episode had a lasting impact on Egyptian history. For Europe it marked Egypt's entry into the modern era, which was understood as drawing the country into the orbit of Western civilization. Yet modernity – the myth of bourgeois society – was not just imported into Egypt, but it was actively translated by the military and bureaucratic needs of the Mamluk rulers – just as the contemporary Western view of Egyptian civilization was the construction of an orientalist myth mediated by Europe's own interests and prejudices. The real importance of the French invasion lay in its abrupt disclosure of Egypt's growing connection to the geopolitics of the epoch. Ottoman weakness cleared the way for the rise of the country as a regional heavyweight in the 1830s, only to have its imperial ambitions crushed by the British Empire by the middle of the nineteenth century. British colonialism constituted a displacement of an 'indigenous' development – real or imagined – towards capitalism in Egypt. Thus lingering feudal relations and underdevelopment flowed from 'too little' capitalism. On the other hand, the introduction of colonialism was an active force that fettered the development of the productive forces at the national level. Hence Egypt's 'backwardness' was also the result of 'too much' capitalism.

Throughout the eighteenth century military confrontations with emerging European powers forced the Ottoman Empire and its provincial rulers to raise their income in order to modernize and expand their armies. Murad Bey imposed a state monopoly on customs collection and the government purchased and resold a large part of the wheat crop to pay for its military expenditures. This move anticipated the policies of Muhammad Ali (1769–1849), an ambitious commander of the Ottoman Albanian regiment, who was able to seize power after the French left Egypt, defeating both the Ottoman governor and Mamluk competitors between 1801 and 1805. Ali was able to forge a coalition with local Arab leaders, who secured his standing with the population.

Once in power, Muhammad Ali was granted the honorary title Pasha and Wali (governor) by the Sublime Porte.[2] The new Pasha continued Murad Bey's policy of building a modern army, while pursuing a more radical mercantilist policy. In order to gain fiscal autonomy from the landed elite, he adopted the reform programme of the French, who had seized tax farms, nationalized agricultural lands, and brought the urban guilds[3] under state supervision. In 1814 tax farming was abolished. Peasants kept the usufruct of their lands, but were obliged to sell their crops directly to the state at low set prices. This monopsony allowed the government to trade agricultural produce with a large profit margin on both local and international markets. Protectionist measures safeguarded the weak Egyptian industries – primarily textile and weapon manufacturing – against competition with Western capitalist countries. Through forced conscription wage labourers were recruited among the peasants and guild artisans (Owen 2005: 114–5; Tucker 2005: 234–5).

Muhammad Ali's centralized policies were primarily oriented towards the needs of the military and the bureaucracy, curtailing the power of urban guilds, landed elites, and merchant capital. His political economy closely resembled that of European absolutism (al-Khafaji 2004: 43). Although there was an undeniable development of state-led commercialization and manufacturing, there was *no evolution towards a capitalist mode of production*. Both the labour and production processes remained firmly precapitalist. Firstly, the command economy did not initiate a process of primitive accumulation as labourers were not wage workers, but peasants who were temporarily drawn into the production process by means of extra-economic coercion (*corvée*). In other words, there was no process of proletarianization, no creation of a permanent waged labour force that could be subsumed under capital (Beinin 1981: 14). The temporary workforce of the manufactories moved effortlessly back to its original occupations. The labour force involved in the public works during the reign of the Pashas in the second half of the nineteenth century was also based on *corvée* and did not represent a modern working class (Lockman 1994: 80). Secondly, the new state manufactories did not develop the technical production process, as they lacked mechanization, division of labour, and new energy sources (Beinin 2001: 42–3). Manufactured goods only entered the capitalist circulation process properly when they had crossed the Egyptian borders.[4]

Muhammad Ali's military expansionism in Africa, Syria, Turkey, and Europe and his protectionist policies led to increasing tensions with the European powers – especially Great Britain – which sought to stabilize the Ottoman Empire to preserve the balance of power in the region. Through the Anglo-Ottoman Commercial Convention (1838) and the Treaties of London (1840, 1841) the military power and economic sovereignty of Ali's Egypt were curtailed. The imposition of a free-trade regime reduced Egypt's markets and commercial income, undermining central state power. From 'below', the state was weakened by peasant struggles against conscription and heavy taxation, which led to a shortage of labour and a further decline of state revenues. In order to pay for its expenditures, the state began to redistribute the nationalized lands among loyal sections of the military and bureaucratic caste. By the mid-1840s, 53 per cent of lands were in private hands (Beinin 2001: 52). The reinstatement of tax farming, the delegation of state power to local landlords, and the introduction of the debt bondage system led to a 'refeudalization' of the countryside (al-Khafaji 2004: 19–20).

During the reign of Muhammad Ali's successors Ibrahim (1789–1848), Abbas (1812–54), Said (1822–63), Ismail (1830–95), and Tawfiq (1852–92), Egypt's 'feudal turn' was reinforced. Between 1850 and 1880 Egypt became fully integrated into the capitalist world market on the basis of raw cotton production (Chaichian 1988: 28). Although agricultural products, especially cotton, were sold as commodities to the world market, and despite the presence of cash-crop farming and money capital, there was still no process of capitalist accumulation in the Egyptian countryside: 'there was little investment, even by wealthy landowners, in either mechanization or in other means of raising productivity' (Beinin and Lockman 1987: 9).

The building of the Suez Canal (1854–63) generated more debts than revenues for the Egyptian state. This was compensated, at first, by the increased demand for Egyptian cotton during the American Civil War (1861–65). New revenues were primarily used for the modernization of the military, a costly war with Ethiopia, urban prestige projects, and as a guarantee for further loans with Europe's finance capital. When the Civil War ended, American cotton flowed back into the world market and global cotton prices plummeted, causing a fiscal crisis in Egypt. Between 1865 and 1868 taxes were increased by 70 per cent, which threw many peasants into debt and led to a further concentration of agricultural lands (Beinin 2001: 52). In 1871 new tax reforms made small landholders lose their lands and become an 'unpaid, bonded workforce' (Mitchell 2002: 73). Peasants were converted into labourers who received a small plot of land for themselves or who were paid in kind (Owen 2005: 119). Unable to repay his international loans, Ismail Pasha had to sell Egyptian shares in the Suez Canal Company to the British state.

The economic depression of 1873–96 led to a global decline of prices for agricultural produce, which caused the bankruptcy of several Ottoman provinces. Their inability to repay their loans instigated European intervention in their internal financial affairs. In 1876 the *Caisse de la Dette Publique* was established to oversee Egypt's treasury. In order to secure the interests of finance capital, Britain and France intervened in the Egyptian state by reducing the political and economic power of Ismail Pasha and by installing British and French ministers, imposing direct foreign control over government.

Growing dissatisfaction among the population, but especially in the ranks of the army, led to a revolt in 1879, led by Colonel Urabi. Junior officers were discontented not only with British and French intervention, but also with the monarchy, which had led the nation into a disastrous war against Ethiopia and international debt bondage. Fiscal austerity resulted in a drastic reduction of the Egyptian military. Urabi demanded that Ismail Pasha dissolve the foreign controlled government, which he did, having little choice in the matter. In retaliation, Britain and France pressured the Sublime Porte to depose Ismail, replacing him with his son

Tawfiq Pasha. The revolt continued, however, until in 1882 British troops invaded and occupied Egypt. This intervention concluded the period of Egypt's increasing subjugation to British and French imperialism and marked the beginning of the explicitly colonial era.

Too Much or Too Little Capitalism?

Marx's writings about colonialism in the early 1850s analysed the British occupation of India in terms of its world-historical role: 'England has to fulfil a double mission in India: one destructive, the other regenerating – the annihilation of old Asiatic society, and the laying of the material foundations of Western society in Asia' (Marx 1979b: 217–18). Although Marx recognized the debased motives of colonial capital, bent on violently plundering India's resources, he posited that the British Empire had introduced modern communication and transport into the subcontinent in order to plunder more efficiently, and that this in turn would have a snowballing effect on industrialization.[5] Marx emphasized that colonialism's violent institution of capitalism – like the process of primitive accumulation in Europe – was not an emancipatory force in itself, quite the contrary, but that its development of the productive forces was a necessary but insufficient condition for political and social emancipation. The real moment of emancipation would consist in the overthrow of the British bourgeoisie by British workers, or in the self-liberation of the Indian people. Colonialism was materially progressive in so far as it developed and socialized the productive forces; it was politically regressive in so far as it created new forms of exploitation and oppression, such as institutionalized torture to extract taxes from the peasant population.

The idea that communism needs a solid material base that overcomes the social problems and oppressive state forms resulting from systemic want, underproduction, and scarcity, was one of the main improvements of 'Marxism' over its 'utopian socialist' competitors. Capitalism not only changed the production process: its revolutionary transformation redefined the very nature of economic and social change. Discrete histories became world history. From this perspective, Marx appropriated capitalist development for the project of communism as it created an absolute material base for a new society. The problem with this view was, firstly, that it cast the subaltern struggles of bygone ages into a tragically determinist light, as they were doomed to fail due to the absolute deficiency of their material base – which was only discovered in the age of capitalism. Moreover, the history of the workers' movement from 1848 becomes equally tragic, as it failed to establish a communist society despite the presence, finally, of an adequate material base. Secondly, it raised the question of whether Marx himself wasn't too optimistic with regard to the material base achieved by capitalism in the nineteenth century. From the viewpoint of subsequent generations, Fordist automation and scientific management and neoliberal information technology might seem indispensable to a planned, democratically controlled economy and the removal of want. In other words, is the 'material base' an *absolute* achievement of gradually progressing world history, or a requirement of which the modalities are *relative* to each epoch? Here it suffices to say that Marx and Engels stressed the necessity of a capitalist and bourgeois 'stage' in the world-historical transition towards communism (see Engels 1989c: 39–40).

In the Preface to the first edition of *Capital*, Marx claimed that '[t]he country that is more developed industrially only shows, to the less developed, the image of its own future' (Marx 1990: 91). Marx compared the gradual transformation of the economic base to *natural* history (Marx 1990: 92), implying that, in contrast to communism, the expansion and development of capitalism was an automatic and agentless process. Lenin concluded in 'Imperialism' that the world market and modern means of transport and communication rendered the export of capital to 'backward countries' *possible* and that the creation of surplus capital in 'advanced' countries made it *necessary*. At the end of the nineteenth century, colonialism became capitalism's 'spatial fix' (see Chapter 3), profiting from the absence of competition and low costs of land, labour, and raw materials in the colonial countries (Lenin 1964a: 241–2). While paying attention to the monopoly position and rentier rationale of colonial capital, Lenin still posited that the export of capital 'influences and greatly accelerates the development of capitalism in those countries to which it is exported ... expanding and deepening the further development of capitalism throughout the world' (Lenin 1964a: 243).

If colonialism played the role of the 'bourgeois revolution', pushing forward the development of the productive forces and destroying precapitalist forms, the subaltern masses had merely to liberate the developing nation from foreign occupation and the colonial state apparatus. Yet, this perspective did not take into account the unevenness and contradictions of the geographical expansion of the capitalist mode of production. Colonialism in Egypt illustrated this ambiguity. Indeed, through the instrument of the colonial state, new capitalist relations and production methods were forcefully introduced at the end of the nineteenth century (Clawson 1978). *Corvée* labour was abolished and landed private property was officially recognized. Advanced irrigation techniques removed the dead season, which prompted landlords to exert full control over the labour of their farmers. The privatization and concentration of landed property drove peasants from their land and to Egypt's first industries: 'they could now be recruited not by physical coercion through the bureaucratic and repressive mechanisms of the state ... but rather through the less obviously coercive mechanism of the market, which just as effectively kept wages low and working conditions inhuman' (Lockman 1994: 83). A real process of primitive accumulation had begun, which gave rise to new forms of labour struggle (De Smet 2015: 140–1). Apart from a proletariat, colonialism also produced its own layer of organic intellectuals: the *effendiyya*, a group of modern middle-class professionals, engineers, journalists, lawyers, teachers, and bureaucrats with often a nationalist and Western cultural outlook.

In contrast, with regard to Italian uneven development, Gramsci observed that: 'the North concretely was an "octopus" which enriched itself at the expense of the South, and that its economic–industrial increment was in direct proportion to the impoverishment of the economy and the agriculture of the South' (Gramsci 1971: 71; Q19§24). The development of capitalism in one location was achieved by the underdevelopment of another space that existed in unity with the first one – an insight that gained prominence with the emergence of dependency theory and world-system analysis in the second half of the twentieth century. In Egypt, foreign capital de-industrialized most of the indigenous manufactories, preparing the home market for an influx of European commodities (al-Khafaji 2004: 41). In the early 1870s Ismail had implemented a modest industrialization programme, establishing some 40 state-owned enterprises. The state bankruptcy of 1876 led to either their destruction or their sale to foreign firms. From then onwards the initiative of industrialization shifted to foreign corporations and the *mutamassirun*: foreign capitalists living in Egypt (Beinin 2001: 68). The industrializing role of the colonial state was in fact restricted to the creation of large-scale transport, communication, service and (some) modern manufacturing enterprises.

In the countryside, the colonial state did not abolish feudal relations, because farming out the production of cotton to existing domestic landlords was more profitable for foreign capital. At the local level, agriculture remained controlled by large landholders with connections to urban centres of trade and petty commodity production (Bush 2007: 1601). Instead of organizing the distribution of lands among smallholding peasants, colonial capitalism reinforced bimodalism[6] in the countryside. The absolutist state of Muhammad Ali was replaced by a new historical bloc, composed of the colonial state and finance capital, and domestic landlords and urban money capital (Chaichian

1988: 30). The primary rationale of this class coalition was the provision of agricultural goods (primarily cotton) to international markets (primarily the British textile industry).

With regard to Germany, Marx had considered that

> we suffer not only from the development of capitalist production, but also from the incompleteness of that development. Alongside the modern evils, we are oppressed by a whole series of inherited evils, arising from the passive survival of archaic and outmoded modes of production, with their accompanying train of anachronistic social and political relations. (Marx 1990: 91)

Marx's use of the adjective 'passive' and 'anachronistic' presents these forces as but temporary bumps on the road to 'total' capitalism. As we have seen in Chapter 3, however, Gramsci posited that the precapitalist *Junker* elite survived as the political personnel of the new historical bloc. In the end, the *Junkers* were turned into a fraction of national capital. However, in the case of the colonial countries the alliance between foreign capital and domestic precapitalist elites *actively resisted* the emergence of a national bourgeoisie and therefore capitalist development. There 'forms which elsewhere have been superseded and have become anachronistic are still in vigour' (Gramsci 1971: 243; Q13§7). Underdevelopment, compared to the advanced nations, became the result of both 'too much' and 'too little' capitalism. As capital profited from this arrangement, questions should be raised about the geographical dynamics of capitalist development, which cannot be conceived of as a simple homogeneous expansion of identical labour relations and production forms.

Uneven and Combined Development

Even in the early notes that comprised 'The German Ideology' (1845–46) Marx and Engels mused about the unity of capitalism as a global system. The constitution of the capitalist mode of production in England, France, Italy, and Germany had followed distinct pathways, originating from different precapitalist social formations, until their historical trajectories – along with those of other European nations, the United States, and the colonial world, drawn into the global circulation of capital – became entwined in the nineteenth century. At this point the fragmented history of the world, which previously had been rendered coherent merely in thought, became, materially, world history: 'Thus, for instance, if in England a machine is invented which deprives countless workers of bread in India and China, and overturns the whole form of existence of these empires, this invention becomes a world-historical fact' (Marx and Engels 1975b: 51).

Previously, war and commerce had connected societies that existed in isolation from one another, constituting a 'mechanical' unity (see Chapter 4). The world market transformed these *external* relations between countries, regions, and empires into *internal* relations of a global system. The development of individual social formations became mediated by their relation to the world economy. A concept of capitalism was needed that embraced its essence as both a historical process that originated at a certain time and place and spread itself around the globe, and as a system with specific relations between the whole and its parts. In order to comprehend this diachronic and synchronic character, Trotsky introduced the notion of the uneven and combined development of capitalism, which he elaborated in the introductory chapter of his 'History of the Russian Revolution' (1930).

As discussed in Chapter 2, although embedded within a broader regional and global commercial and geopolitical context, capitalism – defined not merely as money capital, but as a mode of production that had originated in England – quickly spread itself to Western European nations and the United States. The qualitative difference between the productive forces that capitalism unleashed and precapitalist production processes created a deep dichotomy – 'unevenness' – between 'advanced' and 'backward' forms. Firstly, it created a differentiation between social forms *within* one and the same society. In nineteenth-century Europe this created a 'combination' of capitalist relations with an 'accompanying train of anachronistic social and political relations' (see Gramsci 1971: 90–1; Q19§26). Under the aegis of bourgeois state power, 'national' capital was able to subjugate and transform these relations.

Secondly, it created qualitative differences *between* advanced and backward states.[7] In the foreword to *Capital* Marx had postulated that '[o]ne nation can and should learn from others.... [S]ociety ... can neither leap over the natural phases of its development nor remove them by decree. But it can shorten and lessen the birth-pangs' (Marx 1990: 92). Trotsky recognized that, in principle, because of global trade, backward social formations could directly appropriate advanced forces of production without going through all the historical steps that the advanced nation had taken to develop these forces. Prussia–Germany and Japan stood out as historical examples of this 'privilege of backwardness'. Gramsci agreed that

the impetus of progress is not linked to a vast local economic development which is artificially limited and repressed, but is instead the reflection of international developments which transmit their currents to the periphery – currents born on the basis of the productive development of the more advanced countries. (Gramsci 1971: 116–17; Q10ii§61)

However, the privilege of backwardness was only an abstract possibility. The export of capital to less developed regions led to combinations that did not necessarily develop the whole social formation. The combined character of capitalist development meant that nations could not simply repeat the ideal typical trajectory of the first industrial countries, especially that of England. Moreover, most non-industrialized societies 'missed' the historical advent of the capitalist mode of production in the first half of the nineteenth century and were confronted with capitalism in its developed *imperialist* form (see Chapter 3). Uniting Trotsky's and Lenin's perspectives, Ernest Mandel (1923–95) argued that imperialism blocked the possibility for non-industrialized countries to develop along the same lines and at the same tempo as the first industrial nations (Mandel 1976). In other words, the often forceful introduction of capitalist relations immediately fettered or at least deformed the development of the productive forces in most precapitalist societies. In the imperialist stage of capitalism, these local deformations did not retard but enhanced capital accumulation at the global scale (see Hesketh 2010: 387).

In order to render the concept of combination more concrete, Davidson (2010) distinguishes between three broad groups of countries, each of which expresses a particular variant of combination. The first group is composed of the core, advanced capitalist states, containing both early starters such as England and latecomers such as Prussia–Germany, which made use of their privilege of backwardness, successfully turning precapitalist forms into fractions of wage labour and capital. However, even in the core countries a hierarchy between European nations developed, with some nations more strongly industrialized and powerful than others, often due to unresolved internal struggles. In Italy, for example, geographically uneven capitalist development and passive-revolutionary state formation produced 'a bastard' (Gramsci 1971: 90; Q19§28): a combination of a dominant industrial north and an economically backward Mezzogiorno. Yet in the imperialist era, the Italian historical bloc no longer represented a combination of capitalist and precapitalist forms, but of fractions of industrial, commercial, and landholding capital under the direction of finance capital.

A second group of countries comprises those nations who embodied a 'proper' combination between capitalist and precapitalist forms. Davidson differentiates between strong absolutist states such as Russia and the

Ottoman Empire, which, threatened by Western military successes, engaged in a limited industrialization from above. However, as Trotsky observed (Trotsky 2001: 25–37), sometimes more advanced forms were debased when they were embedded in a backward context, which paradoxically led to a strengthening of these backwards conditions instead of revolutionizing them. In czarist Russia urban pockets of industry, generalized commodity production, and capitalist accumulation existed within the larger, still dominant framework of an agrarian absolutist state. Other states such as China were not strong enough to repulse imperialist powers, but were not fully subjugated either. Here combination was much more mechanical, in the sense that imperialist powers established industrial centres that were not connected to the Chinese state. Finally there were states such as India, Algeria, and Egypt that were both industrialized and de-industrialized by their colonial masters, tailoring production to the needs of the colonizing heartland.

The third group consists of peripheral, colonial countries that were not at all developed or modernized by imperialist capital. Sometimes imperialism even supported or actively introduced a feudalistic elite that was dependent on the imperial centre. Here the development of capitalism in the core countries directly impeded the development of the periphery.

The above categorization is primarily descriptive and does not allow for a detailed and dynamic overview of a country's historical trajectory (Davidson 2010). Still, it highlights, firstly, that combination in general is an intrinsic aspect of capitalist development as it represents the interiorization of global processes into an individual social formation. Secondly, it shows that not all combinations are equal; that the specific character of combination is not an empty formula, but an object of investigation, taking into account the position of the country in the international state system, the internal relations between the classes, and the economic base and superstructures – in short, what Gramsci called the historical bloc.

The concept of historical bloc renders the abstract notion of 'combination' operational with regard to a specific social formation. While Trotsky emphasized the world economy as the starting point of analysis (Trotsky 2005), Gramsci suggested that 'the line of development is towards internationalism, but the point of departure is "national" – and it is from this point of departure that one must begin' (Gramsci 1971: 240; Q14§68). These two approaches are not mutually exclusive. Even though the general *framework* of analysis consists of capitalist world history, the world market, and the international state system, its concrete *unit* is the sphere of the national state, where unique combinations materialize (see Davidson 2010; Roccu 2012). For Gramsci, the scientific choice for a 'national' unit of analysis was also a *political* necessity: 'In reality, the international relations of any nation are the result of a combination which is "original" and (in a certain sense) unique: these relations must be understood and conceived in their originality and uniqueness if one wishes to dominate them and direct them' (Gramsci 1971: 240; Q14§68). Although essentially an internationalist class, the proletariat had to solve the riddle of hegemony by developing and leading a 'combination of national forces' (Gramsci 1971: 240; Q14§68).

The Uninterrupted Revolution

The combined character of Russia's social formation around the turn of the twentieth century meant that the young proletariat faced the dual predicament of feudal–absolutist and capitalist exploitation and oppression. With regard to the revolutionary 'tasks' of the proletariat, Georgi Plekhanov (1856–1918), the 'founder' of Russian Marxism, followed the 'orthodox' line of Marx's writings about permanent revolution. In the absence of a strong and independent bourgeoisie (as in Germany in 1848) the proletariat should take on a leading role in an alliance against czarist absolutism, constituting a democratic republic and abolishing feudalism in the countryside. Under the democratic leadership of the proletariat the economic base for socialism would be established, which would open up the possibility for social emancipation. In Plekhanov's two-stage approach, the proletariat would wage the bourgeois revolution, accomplishing political emancipation for all classes, but it could not initiate its own proletarian revolution until Russia had been sufficiently developed (Townshend 1996: 61).

After the experience of the 1905 Revolution, Russian Marxists became divided into broadly three groups with regard to the question of revolutionary strategy: Mensheviks, Bolsheviks, and Trotsky and his followers. The Mensheviks (and Plekhanov himself) abandoned the idea of proletarian hegemony, arguing that the Russian working class should support the liberal factions of the national bourgeoisie, which would, in a Jacobin fashion, lead a purely bourgeois revolution.[8] Workers should not act too militantly or too independently, as their agency could scare the progressive bourgeoisie back into the arms of absolutism (Townshend 1996: 62). In contradistinction, the Bolsheviks compared the Russian bourgeoisie rather to the reactionary liberals of 1848 than to the revolutionary class of 1789. Although the bourgeoisie desired political emancipation, its fear of the rising working class outweighed its antipathy towards absolutism. Moreover, ownership of large landholdings would prevent the bourgeoisie from initiating land reforms, pushing the smallholding peasantry to the cause of the proletariat. Whereas the Mensheviks saw the peasantry as the class base of czarist despotism, the Bolsheviks argued that exploited peasants were the natural allies of the urban workers in their struggle for emancipation. If the feeble and cowardly bourgeoisie led the class struggle, the result would be, at best, a constitutional monarchy, dominated by conservative landed property. This outcome would restrict the capacity of the proletariat to develop itself politically, and limit the development of the economic base of society. Conversely, an alliance between workers and peasants would establish a Jacobin democratic republic, a 'revolutionary democratic dictatorship of the proletariat and the peasantry', granting extensive political and social rights and implementing a programme of land nationalization that would free surpluses for the development of industry, which, in turn, would expand the proletariat. Importantly, a salient victory for the Russian proletariat would inspire other working classes in Europe to rise up and start a revolution of their own, which would push the democratic revolution in Russia into a socialist direction (Townshend 1996: 63–4).

After the 1905 Russian Revolution, Trotsky, in 'Results and Prospects' (1906), criticized the views of both the Mensheviks and the Bolsheviks, who relied too strongly on historical analogies with either the French Revolution of 1789 or that of 1848. Although at that moment he had not yet elaborated the concept of uneven and combined development, he already underlined the fact that in Russia the most advanced, capitalist forms of industrialization *in the world* could be found in combination with the most backward feudal, agrarian structures. Russia's privilege of backwardness had allowed the country, in conjunction with foreign capital, to establish the most developed factories and the most modern urban proletariat. Because of its character as a young but extremely modern working class, the Russian proletariat was in a position to lead a national coalition of subaltern actors against both czarism and imperialist capitalism (see Alexander and Bassiouny 2014: 30–1). Less optimistic than Lenin about the directive capacities of the peasantry, Trotsky devised only a supporting role for the smallholding farmers in a struggle led by the proletariat (Trotsky 2005). The spontaneous emergence of soviets (workers' and soldiers' councils) during the 1905 Revolution had already empirically shown the hegemonic abilities of the proletariat. Moreover, it had revealed that a struggle for political emancipation led by the working class would uninterruptedly morph into a struggle for social emancipation (see Chapter 4). In this regard, the revolution would become permanent (Townshend 1996: 64–5).

It was not only within the confines of Russian society that the revolution was to become permanent – or better, perhaps, uninterrupted. On the contrary, Mensheviks, Bolsheviks, and Trotsky agreed that complete social emancipation was impossible in the context of Russia's limited economic base and that this would require material support from a West European proletarian revolution. In fact, in 'The Class Struggles in France' (1850), Marx had already stressed the hard, material limits to a revolutionary struggle restricted to France's national boundaries, because the nation's 'relations of production are conditioned by ... foreign trade ..., by her position on the world market and the laws thereof' (Marx 1978: 56). France's relative underdevelopment, in comparison to 'the despot of the world market, England' (Marx 1978: 56) had turned the industrial bourgeoisie into a weak political actor, subordinated to finance capital. The globalization of capital and the forging of a world market had created a global arena for the class struggle. The French proletariat could not achieve its own emancipation without turning their domestic class struggle into a 'world war' that penetrated the centre of global capital accumulation: 'Accomplishment begins only when, through the world war, the proletariat is pushed to the fore in the nation which dominates the world market, to the forefront in England' (Marx 1978: 117).

However, precisely *because of* the integration of the various national economies into capitalism as a global system, Russia was not doomed to bide its time until the West was ready to revolt. Marx had mused that '[v]iolent outbreaks must naturally occur rather in the extremities of the bourgeois body than in its heart, since the possibility of adjustment is greater here than there' (Marx 1978: 134). Similarly, Gramsci claimed that 'in periods of crisis it is the weakest and most marginal sector which reacts first' (Gramsci 1971: 93; Q19§26); and Lenin formulated his famous aphorism that 'the chain is no stronger than its weakest link' (Lenin 1964c: 519–20). The First World War revealed the organic crisis of capitalism in the form of a geopolitical crisis of imperialism. The weakness of Russian capitalism and the strength of its proletariat meant that the Russian proletariat, instead of tail-ending the process of world revolution, would constitute its international vanguard.

The czarist state had not yet emancipated itself as an abstract entity from the economic sphere and direct coercion remained an important means of surplus extraction. Unlike in the Western liberal democracies, political and civil societies were not fully differentiated, leading to an immediate integration, in a primordial form, of the political and social struggle. Because capital was more primitively (and thus explicitly) organized than the state, the state 'as a more visibly centralized and universal class-enemy, has served as a focus for mass-struggle' (Wood

2012: 29). Labour relations were mediated by state coercion rather than hegemonic consent, creating a situation 'in which every form and expression of the labour movement is forbidden, in which the simplest strike is a political crime' (Luxemburg 1970: 190). As Gramsci suggested, whereas in Western Europe the mode of struggle had become a war of position, the conditions of Russian capitalism imposed a war of movement on the proletariat (see Chapter 4). The class struggle was punctuated by crises and sudden developmental jumps, such as the 1905 soviets, which rapidly organized the working class as a political entity against state power. In the context of czarist absolutism 'it must logically follow that every economic struggle will become a political one' (Luxemburg 1970: 190). A successful Russian war of movement – that is, one that resulted in the seizure of state power and the fall of czarism – would put the class struggle in the West on the offensive, making the revolution permanent on a world scale. Conversely, the geographical expansion of the proletarian revolution would scaffold the continuous process of socialist transformation in Russia after the conquest of power.

Without ever explicitly embracing Trotsky's 'theory of permanent revolution', Lenin accepted this proletarian strategy in his famous 'April Theses' during the revolutionary year of 1917. The slogan of 'All Power to the Soviets' rejected the democratic republic as the immediate end point of the Russian revolutionary movement, underlining the prefiguration of the 'dictatorship of the proletariat' in the spontaneous activity of the workers' and soldiers' councils. Lenin accepted the concept of an uninterrupted revolution through his contemplation of imperialism, concluding that the domination of international finance capital and aggressive geopolitics rendered the institution of a democratic bourgeois republic in Russia impossible (Townshend 1996: 67–9).

The passive-revolutionary displacement of popular initiative in the West, foreign military intervention, and civil war in Russia signalled the practical end of permanent revolution and the global war of manoeuvre. Isolated and forced on the defensive, the Communist Party of the Soviet Union attempted to build some form of socialist state. Under Stalin's influence, the Comintern advocated a return to the (Menshevik) two-stage strategy with regard to colonial and semi-colonial nations. Colonial worker parties had to support the progressive factions of their national bourgeois in waging a democratic struggle. This would open up a period of 'national capitalism' that would create the material conditions for a genuinely proletarian revolution. However, the disaster of the Chinese Revolution of 1927, when communists and trade unionists were slaughtered by their bourgeois allies of the Kuomintang, alarmed Trotsky (Davidson 2010; Townshend 1996: 97). Revisiting his theory of permanent revolution, he elaborated the concept of uneven and combined development, which affirmed the absolute impossibility of the national bourgeoisie's playing a progressive role in the age of monopoly capitalism. Whereas Comintern doctrine posited that the national bourgeoisie in colonial and semi-colonial countries was the natural ally of workers, farmers, and the petty bourgeoisie *because of* its subjugation and domination by international finance capital, Trotsky argued that this subordination had turned the colonial bourgeoisie into a weak and dependent class. In Gramscian language, the colonial bourgeoisie remained in a corporate state. Its accumulation strategy was primarily based on parasitic rentier activities rooted in landed property and commerce, which fettered industrialization. The idea was ridiculous that this national bourgeoisie would lead a class alliance to escape imperialism, develop the nation on a capitalist basis, and 'catch up' with the advanced countries, as this class was effectively the local form of appearance of imperialism.

Gramsci criticized Trotsky's development of Marx's concept of permanent revolution for being too abstract, literary, and intellectualistic, comparing it to Lenin's superior application

> in a form which adhered to actual, concrete, living history, adapted to the time and the place; as something that sprang from all the pores of the particular society which had to be transformed; as the alliance of two social groups [i.e. proletariat and peasantry] with the hegemony of the urban group. (Gramsci 1971: 84–5; Q19§28)

In general Gramsci's critique of Trotsky's concept of permanent revolution was unfair and misattributed (Thomas 2015: 295). In fact, Trotsky could not have formulated his theory of permanent revolution without investigating Russia's 'actual, concrete, living history' (see Davidson 2010). Yet Gramsci was correct to emphasize that the concrete problem of proletarian hegemony in a specific time and place could not be solved simply by the abstract formula of permanent revolution – in either its Marxian or Trotskyan formulations.[9] Lenin's 'April Theses' 'nationalized' the general tasks of the permanent revolution, and the slogans 'Peace, Bread, and Land' and later on 'All Power to the Soviets' discursively *constructed* the alliance between workers and peasants under the leadership of the first group. The concept of hegemony expanded and superseded the notion of permanent revolution (see Thomas 2015: 296, also see Chapter 4). Furthermore, whereas permanent revolution revealed the general possibility and strategy for socialist revolution to grow out of the democratic struggle, Trotsky did not contemplate its negative: passive revolution. In fact, the subsequent history of decolonization expressed the generalized *absence* of permanent revolution and the 1917 scenario.

Passive Revolution in Egypt

In the second half of the nineteenth century, Russian absolutism had attracted foreign capital in order to develop industries for military purposes, which, in turn, created a modern proletariat concentrated in large-scale factories. In Egypt, the weak absolutism of Muhammad Ali's successors and imperialist intervention blocked such an evolution. At the end of the nineteenth century, there was a gradual development towards waged labour, flowing from the slow penetration of foreign capital, which rooted itself in the pre-existing artisanal labour process. For example, the strike of Port Said coal heavers in 1882, who demanded a higher piece rate, revealed their hybrid nature as both 'wage workers subject to an essentially capitalist system of labor contracting' (Lockman 1994: 84) and artisanal labourers organized in precapitalist *tawaf'if*, which were overseen by *shuyukh*. Under the influence of capital the traditional guilds degenerated into labour contracting instruments (Chalcraft 2001: 114), which prompted new worker actions, this time against their own *shuyukh*.

By the end of the nineteenth century, an estimated 37 per cent of the rural workforce had become wage labourers (Chaichian 1988: 33). The concentration of landed property dispossessed smallholding peasants, but this process of primitive accumulation did not automatically result in a large-scale proletarianization of the population, as there were few factories that could absorb the surplus population.[10] Some dispossessed peasants ended up in the transport, communication, and services sector of the colonial state. In 1907 489,296 wage labourers worked in the colonial production and transport industries. By 1917 this number had increased to 639,929 (Ismael and al-Sa'id 1990: 15). Arguably these colonial workers were only formally subsumed under capital, as capital operating in the state sector did not qualitatively transform the labour process. Most landless farmers were driven to the cities, where they engaged in petty commodity production (Koptiuch 1996: 47), competing with traditional craftsmen.

The first Egyptian trade unions, such as the Manual Trades Workers' Union (MTWU), still embodied many precapitalist characteristics, such as the inclusion of non-wage labourers, property owners, and employers. Some trade unions refused members on the basis of their religion, nationality, or specific position within the occupational hierarchy. Many workers who were employed in the colonial enterprises were foreigners, living in their own, separate communities. For example, most cigarette rollers were Greek labourers, employed by Greek capitalists. Although their strike between December 1899 and February 1900 'involved several thousand skilled workers from many different workplaces, some of them quite large, who went on strike simultaneously and remained out for two months, suggesting a strong sense of solidarity and a capacity for effective organization' (Lockman 1994: 88), this was rather a particularist conflict within the Greek community than an exponent of the general struggle between labour and capital.

During the economic crisis of 1906–08 global prices of cotton dropped. Faced with decreasing profits, large landowners realized that cotton monoculture production posed risks. Allying themselves with domestic commercial capitalists, they began to invest in activities directed by low key money capital, such as loaning, real estate speculation, and intermediary trade. Landholders and merchant capitalists wanted to strengthen their position in the colonial historical bloc, which led to the formation of a nationalist movement and to a confrontation with the colonial state and international finance capital. The nationalist movement was led by conservative landlords and supported by *effendiyya*, peasants, and modern wage workers (Beinin 2001: 46–47, 72; Farah 2009: 28).

As in other colonial countries such as India and China, the First World War enabled the Egyptian nationalist movement to rally popular dissatisfaction for the cause of independence. After the war, the Egyptian *wafd* (delegation) led by the nationalist Saad Zaghlul (1859–1927) and supported by a popular campaign of civil disobedience and petitions, demanded independence. British repression of the movement in 1919 provoked a mass revolution. First the peasantry rose in a rural uprising, which was violently quelled by British military intervention. In the end, however, the nationalist movement was unable to rally the peasants behind its project, because their primary predicament was feudalism rather than imperialism. Like the Russian bourgeoisie before 1917, the Egyptian conservative landlords who led the nationalist movement were not interested in land reforms, which directly threatened their economic class base. The absence of peasants as a social force within the anti-imperialist hegemonic bloc would remain a weakness up until the Free Officers' coup. After the peasant insurrection the urban proletarian and *effendiyya* began to strike and demonstrate. This reflected a politicization and expansion of earlier wartime strikes, in which workers demanded higher wages and better working conditions (Beinin and Lockman 1987: 90). The political uprising was a means for workers to express their social grievances. Conversely, for the nationalist movement, social protests in the colonial industries and state apparatus became an instrument to politically undermine British domination. The mass movement forced the colonial masters to grant Egypt independence in 1922. The political system was transformed into a constitutional monarchy based on the Belgian model. Even though British imperialism relinquished its grip over the colonial state, it remained firmly in control of the Suez Canal and Egypt's defence, foreign affairs, minority policies, and the Sudan. Moreover, the new monarch, King Fuad (1868–1936), quickly reduced parliamentary powers and in exchange for military support, acted as the loyal guardian of British interests. The limited outcome of the 1919 revolution can be understood by deploying the criterion of passive revolution. Popular initiative from below was displaced not only by the reform from above of the British colonial state, but also by the conservative landlords who directed the nationalist movement. There was no Jacobin faction that pushed the movement to complete political emancipation: full national sovereignty, eradication of feudal relations, and a democratic republic. Instead of overthrowing and transforming the colonial historical bloc, the landowners merely renegotiated the relations of power to their advantage.

The new 'semi-colonial' bloc became an unstable mechanical unity in which no class fraction became hegemonic. The Egyptian bourgeoisie was torn between the interests of landed capital and its money-capitalist allies, and the opportunities for industrialization and expanded reproduction that opened up in the 1920s and 1930s. Representing the local form of imperialist rentier capital, Egyptian landlords would never move decisively against either British control or the dominance of landed property. The Egyptian monarchy used this paralysing contradiction between the fractions of national capital to strengthen its own position as the largest landowner and most powerful political actor. Nevertheless, Egyptian landed, commercial, and industrial capitalists were able to continue their leadership over the nationalist movement, consolidated in parties such as the National Party and the Wafd Party, because of the political weakness of subaltern actors.

The participation of workers as trade unionist actors in the 1919 revolution showed their potential as a social force, and it forged ties between their own organic intellectuals and the nationalist *effendiyya*. The *effendiyya* played an important role in assisting workers with the organization of new trade unions, but they also aimed to overwrite the emerging class consciousness with a nationalist narrative of anti-colonialism. The anti-imperialist coalition came naturally to most industrial workers, as their main antagonist was neither landed property nor national fractions of money capital, but *Western* capital in the direct, political appearance of the colonial state and the economic reality of foreign-owned factories. In general, the emergent trade unions recognized themselves politically through the 'chemical' mediation (see Chapter 4) of non-proletarian class forces such as (petty) bourgeois nationalists. Nationalists offered workers the promise of an organic passage to their variant of bourgeois society through the curtailing of monarchical power and the establishment of national industries that would not exploit labour. Because of the 'external' appearance of capital, exploitation by capitalist production could be primarily represented in terms of *cultural* alienation and uprooting instead of *economic* surplus extraction. Advocates of national capitalism mobilized traditional notions of artisanal production, which reflected a hierarchical yet organic patron–client relation between 'producers', to legitimate their purely modern project of expanded reproduction. The nationalists' concept of 'worker' and 'capitalism' was amorphous and undeveloped, reflecting the still gelatinous composition of the Egyptian working class and the lack of large-scale private industries owned by Egyptian capitalists. It was not the social position within the ensemble of production relations, but the material form of labour, that determined if a person was considered a worker or not. Likewise, a critique of capitalism was reduced to a critique of foreign domination, because the nationalists themselves had little experience with the capitalist mode of production and its far-reaching social transformations (Beinin and Lockman 1987: 162).

Towards National Capitalism?

In 1920 nationalist landowners provided the capital for an independent Egyptian bank with the explicit goal of creating an indigenous industrial sector (Deeb 1976) that would diversify the landholders' sources of income and break the domination of foreign finance capital. Bank Misr (Egypt) concentrated its funds on low value-added cotton production, establishing industries such as the Misr Spinning and Weaving Company in Mahalla al-Kubra, which had become the largest industrial complex in the Middle East by the end of the Second World War. Political developments such as the 1936 Anglo-Egyptian Treaty and the abolition of capitulations in 1937 allowed the Egyptian state to implement protectionist measures in order to shield its economy from foreign competition and pursue a policy of import substitution industrialization (ISI). The crisis of the 1930s reduced European commodity exports to the Middle East and expanded the market for domestic firms (Beinin and Lockman 1987: 257). At the same time, the crisis increased Western capital exports, as British and French capitalists were more inclined to invest outside Europe because of falling profits in their domestic markets (Clawson 1978: 19).

The development of 'national capitalism' went hand in hand with the development of the Egyptian workers' movement, which had emerged stronger out of the revolutionary year of 1919, encompassing 89 trade unions in Cairo, Alexandria, and the Suez Canal Zone (Beinin and Lockman 1987: 124). The nationalism of the National Party and the Wafd was increasingly challenged by socialist ideas. Before and during the First World War Egyptian students who returned from Europe brought with them socialist concepts and methods of struggle, but only in 1921 was the Egyptian Socialist Party (ESP) formally established. Within a year the ESP formally embraced Bolshevism, and, reborn as the Communist Party of Egypt (CPE), became a member of the Comintern. Initially the CPE was principally anti-capitalist, rejecting an alliance with bourgeois nationalist forces. However, the Fourth Congress of the Comintern in 1923 encouraged communist parties in colonial countries to participate in national liberation movements, even if they were dominated by bourgeois class fractions. For Egypt, this marked the embrace of a two-stage theory of revolution: first communists had to cooperate with nationalists in order to get rid of foreign domination, and only then could they fight for socialism. The 'first wave of communism' was short-lived. In 1924 a spontaneous strike movement in Alexandria, supported but not organized by the fading National Party and the young CPE, was violently crushed by a Wafd government. CPE leaders were arrested and the communist movement collapsed. Attempts were made to revive it but, due to the liquidation of its vanguard and the continued state repression of its activists, communism as a political force only resurfaced during the Second World War.

The eradication of the CPE cleared the way for an uncontested Wafd leadership over the workers' movement. After 1924 the party aimed to subsume the independent trade unions under its direct paternalistic control in a General Federation of Labour Unions (GFLU) (Ismael and al-Sa'id 1990: 28–9). Workers accepted the Wafd's hegemony on condition that the party would be able to alleviate their immediate economic problems. In particular, they accepted the Wafd's claim that fighting Britain's continued domination was the nation's priority, since it was mostly British troops who quelled strikes and labour protests (Beinin and Lockman 1987: 135–7).

The development of Egyptian-owned industries and their modern forms of exploitation began to alienate the workers from 'their' bourgeoisie. The pro-capitalist policies of the Wafd and its moderate opposition against the monarchy and British influence created cracks in the nationalist bloc. Between 1930 and 1935 the mediation of the Wafd was replaced by the patronage of Prince Abbas Ibrahim Halim, a great-grandson of Muhammad Ali and a cousin of King Fuad. Halim gathered the trade unions in the National Federation of Trade Unions in Egypt (NFTUE). To counterbalance the influence of the Wafd and secure the NFTUE as a personal base of power, the prince encouraged workers instead of non-proletarian elements to lead the movement. In reality the NFTUE remained under strict control of its princely patron. Nevertheless, for the workers' movement Abbas Halim's patronage represented an important transition towards autonomy from the Wafd (Beinin and Lockman 1987: 210–215).

In 1936 King Fuad died and was succeeded by his son Faruq. The Wafd returned to power and negotiated the Anglo-Egyptian Treaty, which granted Egypt increased independence – except for a continued presence of British troops in the Suez Canal Zone. This episode was both the high point and the beginning of the end for the Wafd as a political force. Not only did Britain and the King systematically undermine its rule; from 1936 onwards its leadership over the national–popular counter-bloc was eroded from within by the emergence of an independent workers' movement, as well as the rise of the Muslim Brotherhood and of extreme nationalist or fascist groups such as Young Egypt.

In 1928 the young teacher Hassan al-Banna established the Society of Muslim Brothers or al-Ikhwan al-Muslimun. The class base of the Society was composed of traditional urban artisans and petty merchants, as well as layers of the modern effendiyya (Ayubi 1991: 171). The society was involved in education, charity, the building of mosques, sports, the organization of healthcare and welfare, media, and politics. Its associations articulated a hybrid social form between modern civil society and traditional community life. On the one hand, the Brotherhood upheld a utopian vision of the Islamic past as an organic alternative to foreign capitalism (al-Ghobashy 2005: 376); on the other, it organized its members along modern meritocratic lines (Lia 1998: 60–71, 98–104). Unlike its ideology, its political practice was oriented less towards a utopian notion of the past than a modernist view of the future. The militancy of its anti-colonial discourse surpassed that of the secular Wafd, which was held back by its leadership of large landholders. The political programme of the Brotherhood demanded a state-led economy, nationalization of key industries, an 'Islamic' financial system – which would guarantee interest-free loans for Egypt's budding industrial development – and social reforms, such as a minimum wage for civil servants and unemployment benefits (Mitchell 1993: 7–19). However, the Ikhwan rejected the autonomy of the workers' movement and only supported strikes in foreign-owned companies. The workers' social problems had to be solved through the tripartite corporatism of state, employers, and employees (Ayubi 1991: 174). This stance towards organized labour combined both a traditional 'guild' outlook of vertical integration of the interests of 'masters' and 'craftsmen' and a modern notion of the defence of the 'national good'.

Yet workers would no longer wait to address their economic problems until the colonial question was resolved. Inspired by mass strikes in Europe, they began to strike themselves. Confronted with an increasingly independent and militant workers' movement, the Wafd changed tactics in the second half of the 1930s to maintain its leadership. Its hegemony 'was based not on patriotism or the need for national unity but on purely pragmatic grounds' (Beinin and Lockman 1987: 224). In exchange for the workers' vote the Wafd would concede, step by step, to their economic demands. The position of workers within the nationalist movement was reconfigured; they now appeared as a more or less independent ally of the bourgeoisie. From 1937 onwards, autonomous trade unions aimed to create a new labour federation that was independent of the state. They established the General Federation of Labour Unions in the Kingdom of Egypt (GFLUKE), which was the first fully independent trade union federation in Egyptian history. Trade unionism finally began to overcome the corporate condition of the Egyptian working class. From the spontaneous activity of the workers' struggle a self-concept of wage labourers as a class emerged – even though many of its members were still artisans and petty producers. Ironically, at this point trade unionism already showed signs of becoming a future obstacle to the further development of the workers' movement. Governed by pragmatism, trade union leaders were not interested in politics as such, and were ready to strike a deal with any party as long as it suited their short-term goals. Moreover, the GFLUKE was never legalized, and the outbreak of the Second World War granted the state the opportunity to repress the federation (Beinin and Lockman 1987: 234–241).

Organic Crisis

With the rise of Bank Misr it appeared that Egypt's 'privilege of backwardness' was catapulting the country into the small circle of 'advanced' nations. However, Misr Industries was unable to transform the Egyptian economy. Firstly, the 'privilege of backwardness' only applies when a society is able to use the most advanced forms available in order to skip the intermediate stages of development. In Egypt the imported machines were already outdated, which rendered its industry less productive and more labour intensive than its international competitors. Moreover, the low level of wages paid to workers gave them no incentive for increasing efficiency. The full subordination of workers to the authority of management was deemed more important than their productivity.

Secondly, Bank Misr was not strong enough to compete with foreign capital. Even though 'indigenous' Egyptian capitalists played an important role in the industrialization process of the 1930s and 1940s, foreign and *mutamassir* capital remained the chief protagonists of capitalist development. Their industries were better established and they often enjoyed a monopoly position in the domestic market. Since Egyptian rural landowners and commercial capitalists remained sceptical about investing in industrial production, Bank Misr entered into joint ventures with British enterprises in the late 1930s (Clawson 1978: 20). Consequently, Bank Misr's 'national character' was subordinated to foreign capital (Deeb 1976: 79). The largest share of Egyptian capital was still controlled by landlords and directed towards the foreign and *mutamassir*-dominated cotton market.

Thirdly, the Second World War encouraged industrial production while it reoriented industries towards the needs and demands of foreign markets. In 1942 British troops intervened against King Faruq – who behaved increasingly sympathetically towards Nazi Germany to counterbalance British influence in Egypt – and, ironically, they brought a Wafd government to power. By 1948, more than half a million workers were employed in the new war industries (Chaichian 1988: 33). The end of the war lowered foreign demand and plunged Egyptian industries into crisis, causing high rates of unemployment and raising the cost of living. Landowners were even more inclined to invest in their profitable landholdings rather than in risky industrial projects.

Furthermore, industrial unemployment decreased, not only due to the end of wartime demand, but also because of the increased mechanization of industries and the concentration of the workforce in a few large factories. The industries could not absorb the exodus of rural labourers, who ended up in the service and petty trading sectors. Uneven industrialization resulted in a diverse labour population with

> at one end of the spectrum, a large number of workers employed in very small enterprises producing in labor-intensive and capital-poor conditions where the distinction between employer and employee was often not very sharp, and at the other end, a large, and what is more important, growing number of workers in large-scale mass production industries. (Beinin and Lockman 1987: 265)

As the war economy needed a stable and docile workforce, Britain had favoured a (temporary) politics of co-optation and concession towards overseas workers' movements. For the first time in Egyptian history, trade unions were legalized. Trade union *federations*, however, remained outlawed, crippling the capacity of workers to overcome their fragmentation into different workplaces and industrial sectors. Circumventing the law, the Wafd organized its own 'Clubs' and 'Fronts', which gathered together unions from various companies. However, after the Wafd left power in 1944, its role in the workers' movement ended for good. Trade unionists began to experiment with politicized national organs of their own, such as the Workers' Committee for National Liberation (WCNL) in 1945.

The emergence of a fully independent workers' movement was reciprocally connected to the rebirth of communism in Egypt. In the second half of the 1930s, communist ideas had been reintroduced by Italian and Greek migrants and Jewish intellectuals (Ismael and al-Sa'id 1990: 32–3). From the 1940s onwards, this 'second wave of communism' granted the proletarian struggle a political perspective and bridged the gap between a layer of radicalized nationalist *effendiyya* and workers. Between 1942 and 1952, the political 'party' of the workers, in its broad sense, was represented by various organizations, of which the most influential were the Communist Party of Egypt, the People's Liberation Group, Iskra, the Egyptian Movement for National Liberation (EMNL), and New Dawn. Apart from personal and sectarian infighting, there were important organizational, tactical, and strategic differences with regard to the degree of centralization of the movement, the role of students and intellectuals, and the nature of the Egyptian working class and bourgeoisie.

The failure of national capitalists to industrialize the economy, and the consolidation of the power of domestic commercial capitalists, large estate holders, the Palace, and foreign financial capital, revealed that Egypt in the first half of the twentieth century was not a social formation moving gradually and naturally towards 'full' capitalism, but an unstable combination of national capitalist and precapitalist forms subordinated to international monopoly capital. British imperialist intervention continuously reinforced the position of landed property, the monarchy, and petty money capital vis-à-vis fledgling domestic industrial capital. Instead of simply 'dissolving' precapitalist relations, capitalism added a new layer of social contradictions to Egyptian society. Up until the early 1950s, powerful landlords were still able to block any attempt at land distribution among the small peasants. In general, landowners were reluctant to free resources from agriculture, especially the profitable production of cotton, and channel it into industrial initiatives, which, after all, could not compete with Western monopoly capital. Some of them did engage, hesitantly, in the building of an Egyptian industrial base, and could be perceived as a kind of 'national bourgeoisie', but, in the end, there was no fundamental differentiation between landed, financial, commercial, and industrial interests, nor was there a clear break between national, foreign, and *mutamassir* capital (Clawson 1978: 21). The Egyptian industrial bourgeoisie had not developed itself as a political force, but remained a fragmented, amorphous collection of economic actors, subjugated to conservative landlords and imperialist finance capital (Farah 2009: 31).

The *effendiyya*, for their part, longed for national sovereignty and economic modernization, but they did not constitute a social force on their own. Disappointed with the Wafd-led nationalist movement, they turned increasingly to other subaltern groups, such as the emerging workers' movement, as a means of emancipating themselves from colonialism. Especially with the weakening of British and French imperialist power after the Second World War (Hanieh 2013: 21), workers, supported by communists, left-nationalists, and, sometimes Muslim Brothers organized a series of economic and political strikes and protests, which spawned nationwide political bodies such as the National Committee for Workers and Students (NCWS). The coalescence of the workers' and nationalist movement constructed a new and more radical national–popular counter-bloc with the trade unions and the communist and left-nationalist *effendiyya* as its 'hard core' and the Brotherhood as its sometime ally.

However, the counter-bloc was not able to defeat the coalition between the Palace and Britain. The vacillating support of the Muslim Brotherhood for the emancipation of the subaltern classes undermined the national–popular alliance. More importantly, the workers' movement remained isolated from the peasantry and lacked a unified leadership with a clear class analysis (Beinin and Lockman 1987: 455). Even in the early 1950s, the Egyptian working class as a whole was still inexperienced and unorganized in comparison with its vanguard of textile workers. Workers were not able to develop a cohesive trade union movement, let alone a political apparatus, in less than a decade. Furthermore, the communist movement failed to support the development of proletarian hegemony within the counter-bloc. Understanding the Egyptian predicament from the perspective of Menshevik–Stalinist two-stage theory, they 'consistently subordinated class struggle to the anti-imperialist national struggle' (Beinin 1996: 254). The direct tasks of the epoch were national liberation and the bourgeois revolution, led by an alliance between workers and the 'progressive national bourgeoisie' against imperialist monopoly capital and feudal landowners. Despite the peasants' historical participation in the revolution of 1919, they were discarded as possible class allies in the national-democratic revolution – perceived as a backward group that generated the social basis of the reactionary monarchy. Political emancipation from imperialism and feudalism would create the framework for an accumulation strategy that favoured 'productive' (as opposed to rentier), 'national' (as opposed to foreign), and 'industrial' (as opposed to agricultural) capitalism.

Up to 1952, strikes, protests, riots, and insurrections destabilized the colonial historical bloc. The end of the Second World War had opened up the territory of the class struggle for a war of movement. The oppositional forces were able to disorganize state power, but they were incapable of building a successful counter-hegemony, let alone of acquiring state power for themselves. The Palace's increasing use of coercive state power and reliance on direct British military support revealed its weakness in the face of popular revolt from below. In a true Caesarist manner, the stalemate was forcefully resolved by the intervention of a third party: the Free Officers' movement.

Passive Revolution With or Against Imperialism

Lenin had written 'Imperialism' in the midst of the First World War, and the pamphlet strongly reverberated with the cataclysmic consequences of the concentration and financialization of capital on a global scale. However, the successful isolation of the Russian Revolution and the passive-revolutionary stabilization of Western nations after the war ensured that both world revolution and the barbaric collapse of civilization were avoided. Still, in the 1930s the economic downturn and the threat of a new world war shattered the illusion of a newfound stability. Instead of a sudden collapse, the death agony of capitalism appeared as a drawn-out process. The concept of uneven and combined development disclosed the complexity of class and state power in the imperialist epoch. National capital in the colonial world could not develop in the same way as in the advanced nations because capital, in its developed, international, financial, monopolist, that is, imperialist form, *was already there*. The paradigm shift that saw national underdevelopment as the logical consequence of global capitalist development also included a rejection of a tragic understanding of the colonial revolution. The reactionary character of global capitalism had become absolute: therefore, as a general prospect bourgeois revolution and development on a capitalist basis was no longer a possibility in developing nations. The proletariat had to take a leading role in the national liberation movements, pushing them towards socialist revolution (Davidson 2012: 432). As a critique of Stalinist two-stage theory, permanent revolution had liberated the world's working classes from 'waiting out' their time and playing second fiddle to an imaginary progressive bourgeoisie that had to accomplish some predetermined historical task. On the contrary, as capitalism was to break at its weakest link, the colonial proletariat played a crucial, vanguard role in initiating the world revolution. Because capitalism as a whole had already developed the necessary productive forces for the transition to socialism, the limits that a 'national' material base posed to the social emancipation of colonial subaltern groups would be overcome by solidarity from victorious worker states in the advanced nations – turning the 'privilege of backwardness' into a reality.

In Trotsky's version, the concept of permanent revolution no longer represented the abstract elasticity of every democratic struggle waged by the proletariat to grow into a fight for social emancipation, but it became an inherent element of capitalist development itself. Yet the correct *general* observation of the possibility of permanent revolution in the imperialist epoch failed to solve the riddle of hegemony for the *specific* territories of the class struggle. Gramsci had strongly condemned the theory for being 'a generic forecast presented as dogma, and which demolishes itself by not in fact coming true' (Gramsci 1971: 241; Q14§68). This harsh judgment overlooked Trotsky's warning that '[a] backward colonial or semi-colonial country, the proletariat of which is insufficiently prepared to unite the peasantry and take power, is thereby incapable of bringing the democratic revolution to its conclusion' (Trotsky 2005: 263). The theory of permanent revolution did not illuminate the inevitable march of history; it merely highlighted the conditions for the only possible progressive outcome of the colonial class struggle. Evidently, this meant that the national-democratic revolution would fail if the working class was unable to develop itself as a political force and exert hegemony over the other subaltern actors.

Deploying the interpretative criterion of passive revolution, colonialism presented a capitalist revolution from above that was, however, necessarily incomplete. Apart from creating new capitalist relations, imperialism blocked local processes of proletarianization and capital formation, sustaining or even artificially creating 'traditional' subaltern and dominant classes and ethnic or religious groups, which often functioned as subordinated partners for international finance capital. In the Egyptian case, British imperialist intervention supported the position of conservative landlords and their local money-capitalist allies and sustained the existence of the precapitalist peasant masses and urban *artisanat*. This dynamic threw up material obstacles for the formation of a popular will and initiative.

Nevertheless, the capacity of national elites to push back imperialist forces and develop the productive forces differed wildly from nation to nation. Trotsky recognized that in some cases the national bourgeoisie was able to become hegemonic by pushing back imperialist domination (with various degrees of success) and securing some form of effective political and economic autonomy (Davidson 2012: 433). In this scenario, Jacobin intellectuals often played a key role in pushing forward the agenda of the 'bourgeois revolution'. Inter-imperialist rivalry created opportunities for savvy national elites to develop the productive forces, thereby prolonging capitalism's life. The Meiji Revolution/Restoration in Japan (1868–1912) showed that it was possible for a non-Western state to make use of the 'privilege of backwardness' and develop the productive forces, even without the presence of a 'progressive bourgeoisie'. Here capitalism was successfully constituted by a vanguard samurai stratum, which had been gradually separated from their traditional tributary means of surplus extraction due to processes of commercialization and primitive accumulation. The economic base of this declassed aristocratic layer shifted to state office-holding, transforming the samurai into a bureaucratic caste, which instrumentalized the state apparatus to reconstitute the historical bloc to their advantage. Alarmed by Western imperialist encroachment in the region, especially the subordination of China, Japan came to realize the necessity and possibility of importing advanced technologies and production methods and industrialization before it was too late from a world-historical perspective of capitalist development and imperialist subjugation (Allinson and Anievas 2010).

In Russia, the strong absolutist state survived – until the revolution, that is – because it successfully subjugated industry to the monopolist demands of military production. Popular initiative was displaced by the top-down abolition of serfdom in 1861 – which, however, increased rural unrest in the long term – state coercion, and cosmetic constitutional and political changes, such as the establishment of the Duma after the 1905 Revolution. A restricted capitalist transformation from above was achieved, aided by foreign capital injections, while maintaining independence from international finance and state intervention. Nonetheless, military performance during the Russo-Japanese War (1904–05) and the First World War revealed the inadequacy of Russia's economic base. The military defeat of the imperialist-backed czarist forces during the Russian Civil War (1917–22) created the necessary space for development independent from imperialism. Stalinist forced collectivization and industrialization from 1928 onwards could be conceived of as a second moment of transformation from above, responding to a crisis of the New Economic Policy (NEP). Soviet bureaucracy fully replaced the popular initiative, which had been steadily substituted and pacified since the 1917 revolution.

Developments in Turkey and Iran presented other trajectories. Although these nations were never formally colonized, they were dominated by foreign interests, and their modernization efforts were blocked, particularly as a result of the struggle for power between Britain and Russia. The Young Turks led by Mustafa Kemal Atatürk (1881–1938) turned the crisis and collapse of the Ottoman Empire into an opportunity to establish a modern nation, renegotiating the relation between national capital and imperialism. Similarly to the Russian case, the Young Turks were able to push back imperialism by militarily defeating the Western-supported Sultanate. The Kemalist transformation from above fulfilled all the 'historical tasks' of the bourgeois revolution, but in a Bonapartist way, without a bourgeoisie leading a popular revolt from below (Achcar 2013: 89). The Sultanate was replaced by a modern, secular, and fully independent republic. The prefigurative dynamic of permanent revolution was displaced by an authoritarian political emancipation from above, granting civil rights, equality of the sexes, universal suffrage, etc. The new military and bureaucratic elite substituted its state power for the absent bourgeoisie's class power, implementing land reform and stimulating capital accumulation through state-led industrialization and banking.

Although the geopolitical battle for influence over Persia[11] between the Russian and the British Empires had prevented the colonization of the nation, their intervention actively blocked its development.[12] The coalition between imperialism and the Shah of the ruling Qadjar dynasty brought discontented urban merchants, traditionalist *ulama*,[13] and liberal reformists together in an anti-imperialist alliance. The defeat of Russia in the Russo-Japanese war and the subsequent revolution in 1905 led to the Constitutional Revolution in Iran (1905–11), led by moderate opposition forces, which demanded a constitutional monarchy and democratic reform. However, the Shah, supported by Russian and British troops, violently defeated the revolutionaries, thereby indicating that a moderate solution to Persia's political and economic problems was impossible in the age of imperialism. During the First World War Russia and Britain occupied Persia. The fall of the czarist empire encouraged the formation of trade unions, communist parties and guerrilla movements in the region. Britain and the United States supported the coup of the Persian minister of war, Reza Khan, in 1921, seeing in him a potential strongman who could suppress the communist threat (Behrooz

1999). In 1923 Reza Khan dethroned the last Qadjar Shah, supported by the *ulama* and large landholders, on the condition that Reza Khan would create a constitutional monarchy instead of a radical 'Kemalist' secular republic. Nevertheless, the new Pahlavi Shah based his project of transformation from above on the Turkish model, but without any substantial concessions towards democratic reform and civil and social rights. Unlike Turkey, Persia remained much more dependent on foreign capital, for example through the Anglo-Persian Oil Company, and its industrialization efforts could not establish an industrial base. Similarly to Egypt, Reza Shah's flirtation with Nazi-Germany to counterbalance British imperialism resulted in its occupation during the Second World War and the forced abdication of the monarch (Keddie 1981: 109–12).

In the cases of Japan, Russia, Turkey, and Iran, revolutions from above shielded late-developing nations against imperialism, with varying degrees of success. Their trajectories illustrate that a conceptualization of passive revolution as a clearly delineated *type* of modernization – instead of an interpretative criterion – runs into contradictions. Both the imperialist and anti-imperialist constitution of capitalism displayed 'passive-revolutionary' characteristics as they materially and politically displaced popular initiative. In Japan rapid capitalist transformation was the outcome of the agility of a conservative class fraction that was losing its traditional sources of income and power. Here it was a precapitalist declassed elite that captured and became the state apparatus, substituting its agency for the non-existing 'progressive bourgeoisie'. Ironically, the comfortable power position of czarist absolutism restricted such a transformation process in Russia, leading to a revolutionary crisis. In Turkey the crisis of the Ottoman Empire was appropriated by a radical nationalist stratum against both imperialist and conservative forces. Here the agency of the 'progressive bourgeoisie' was emulated by a group of junior officers – setting a historical precedent for many decolonization movements after the Second World War. Reza Shah's authoritarian modernization project most clearly displayed the counter-revolutionary essence of these transformations from above, as it was directly and explicitly oriented against communist uprisings in the wake of the Russian Revolution. Finding himself in a much weaker position than Atatürk, both domestically and geopolitically, the Shah's anti-communist stance allowed him to shift Persia's status from a protectorate to a subordinated junior partner of imperialism. This dynamic anticipated the relations of many postcolonial nations during the Cold War.

Lastly, Egypt's trajectory differed in important ways from the aforementioned cases. Samir Amin has suggested that, without imperialist aggression, the contradictions of the nineteenth-century modernist

Egyptian project would probably have been overcome in a manner similar to that adopted by Japan (Amin 2011). Although this claim cannot be verified, Amin might be reading too much into the modernization efforts of Muhammad Ali and his successors, which did not reflect a development towards capitalism or bourgeois society. In any case, colonialism *did* subjugate Egyptian society, as I have explained above. Whereas the Russian Revolution of 1905 and the Iranian Constitutional Revolution of 1905–11 were forcefully repressed, the Egyptian national-democratic revolution of 1919 ended in a pyrrhic victory against British imperialism, stopping short of completing the struggle for national independence, land reform, and democracy. Unable to crush the uprising, the British Empire negotiated an outcome with the conservative and liberal leaders of the nationalist movement, which left their core interests intact. From a popular revolution against imperialism, the 1919 movement turned into a national capitalist alliance with foreign capital. The incomplete revolution led to a weak and openly contradictory historical bloc. In order to become really independent from imperialism, Egypt had to modernize its economy. In order to modernize its economy, it needed capital accumulation rooted in expanded reproduction: industrialization and a process of real subsumption of labour under capital. However, rural and commercial elites were loath to direct investments away from their profitable rentier activities, which drove Egypt's industries back into the arms of foreign capital, reinforcing economic dependency. The incomplete revolution of 1919 had saddled the nation with a British-backed monarchy, which blocked any serious attempt of the nationalist movement to substitute itself for the missing progressive bourgeoisie – a nationalist movement that was itself riddled with contradictions because of its conservative leadership.

It is crucial to conceive of the individual trajectories of Russia, Turkey, Iran, and Egypt as part of the same particular epoch of capitalist development. Despite important differences that underline their historical uniqueness, which created divergent outcomes, these nations shared the same world-historical conditions. The two decades between the First and the Second World War signalled the breakdown of the old imperialist bloc and the emergence of a new Fordist and bipolar world order that would reconfigure these conditions, allowing postcolonial states new ways to develop in spite of global capitalism (see Hanieh 2013: 21–2).

6. Lineages of Egyptian Caesarism

The Spectre of Nasserism

On Wednesday 9 February 2011, in the face of renewed mass protests and emerging strikes in the whole of Egypt the newly appointed vice president Omar Suleiman warned of the possibility of a coup if the uprising continued. He emphasized that the demands of an end to the regime and the immediate resignation of the president were out of the question. However, protesters remained adamant in demanding the instant removal of Mubarak. The next day, faced with the stubborn continuation of protests the Armed Forces made their entrance in the revolutionary process under the opaque form of the 'Supreme Council of Armed Forces' (SCAF). The SCAF consisted of the Defence Minister, the Chief of Staff, and other high-ranking officers representing all military services, districts, and departments. In an ominous 'Communiqué no. 1', the SCAF reassured the protesters that they were in control of the situation and that all their legitimate demands would be met. The mere fact that the SCAF convened independently of the president was proof that a 'silent coup' was taking place. Although Mubarak had not yet formally resigned, he had been sidelined and political decision making at the top level had, in practice, already shifted to the military (Kandil 2012: 227). There was a growing consensus among different capitalist class fractions and foreign allies, such as the United States, that Mubarak's days were numbered and that the military was the only stable sector of the state apparatus able to contain the revolutionary flood (Amar 2011). State television radically changed its tone and coverage, showing the masses in Tahrir Square and accusing former ministers of corruption. Rumours spread that Mubarak would be announcing his resignation in the evening, or at least a transfer of power to vice president Omar Suleiman. Triumph mixed with anxiety gripped the demonstrators in Tahrir as the prospect of Mubarak's removal from power was tainted with fear of a military coup.

Despite the critical attitude of organized activists vis-à-vis the role of the Armed Forces, the broad masses cautiously welcomed the intervention of the military, embracing and kissing soldiers and conscripts, giving them flowers, food, and drink, talking and discussing with them, and demanding 'that our brothers in the national armed forces clearly define their stance by either lining up with the real legitimacy provided by millions of Egyptians on strike on the streets, or standing in the camp of the regime that has killed our people, terrorized them and stole from them' (Guardian Live Blog, 31 January 2011). Opposition figures such as Mohammed el-Baradei called upon the army to 'save the country now' or it 'will explode' (Guardian Live Blog, 10 February 2011).

At around 10.45 p.m., Hosni Mubarak addressed the nation. He repeated his commitment not to participate in presidential elections and he promised the eventual abolition of emergency law. Yet he did not step down as president. In Tahrir anticipation turned into anger as demonstrators waved their shoes at the giant screen where the president's speech was projected. Groups of protesters marched towards the state television headquarters at Maspero and towards the presidential palace. In Alexandria thousands of people rallied to the military base. The 6 April Youth Movement called for 'an all-out general strike' on Friday (Guardian Live Blog, 11 February 2011).

On Friday morning 11 February, the SCAF, in a second communiqué, again reassured the protesters that it would supervise a democratic transition, but it remained silent on the fate of the president. In the afternoon, Egyptian streets buzzed with the news brought by state television that a new 'statement from the presidency' was to be expected in the evening. At 6 p.m., a surprisingly brief declaration followed, given by the vice president: 'In these difficult circumstances that the country is passing through, president Hosni Mubarak has decided to leave the position of the presidency. He has commissioned the armed forces council to direct the issues of the state' (Guardian Live Blog, 11 February 2011). The accumulated anger and anxiety of the Egyptian masses suddenly metamorphosed into exhilaration and joy. At around 8.30 p.m., in its third communiqué, the SCAF acknowledged the resignation of Mubarak as president and committed itself to supervising a transition of power. The political intervention of the military was positively received among many activists and protesters. Youth activist Wael Ghonim, for example, declared in a tweet: 'The military statement is great. I trust our Egyptian Army' (Guardian Live Blog, 11 February 2011). President Obama praised the Egyptian Armed Forces as well: 'The military has served patriotically and responsibly as a caretaker to the state and will now have to ensure a transition that is credible in the eyes of the Egyptian people' (Guardian Live Blog, 11 February 2011).

The idea of the Armed Forces as a potential revolutionary ally was not only the product of a simple naivety of the masses towards the real interests of the military, or, conversely, a calculated pragmatism not to confront the armed bodies of the state, but it also represented deeply entrenched historical expectations of the army as a national and popular force of change. This lineage was firmly rooted in the Nasserist experience of the 1950s and 1960s, which still resonated in contemporary Egyptian politics. Fragments of Nasserist ideology were entrenched within popular common-sense notions about social justice, relations between 'state' and 'economy', and anti-imperialism. For many Egyptian workers and farmers, the historical figure of Gamal Abd al-Nasser remained an icon of liberation because of his domestic redistributive and social welfare politics and his prestigious role in the non-aligned movement.

In the eyes of leftist political activists and intellectuals, however, the Nasserist heritage was much more ambiguous. The novelist Alaa al-Aswany offered an intuitive glimpse of the contradictions that operated at the core of the Nasserist project:

many Egyptians had, for the first time, the opportunity to enjoy a good education, healthcare, food, because of Nasser's revolution ... However, we shouldn't forget that the current dictatorship and regime is based on Nasser. Everything: the security state, the control system, the elections ... everything is based on this regime. The irony is that he established a dictatorship while he didn't need it. Nasser was supported to the extent that in any free elections he would have easily gained a majority. That was not the case with the presidents who came after him. He was the one who built the dictatorship machine. (Personal communication with Alaa al-Aswany, 26 November 2010)

In academic analyses of Nasserism as early as the 1960s and 1970s, the military was presented as a relatively progressive, transformative force (for example Hurewitz 1969; Vatikiotis, 1972). Unlike the conservative ruling elites, the military, and its leading petty-bourgeois stratum in particular (see, for example, Halpern 1963), appeared as a modern agent that could act as a substitute for the absent progressive national bourgeoisie. From the 1970s onwards, the developmental and democratic failures of the 'Arab socialist' states provoked a critique of these perspectives (Picard 1990: 198–9). Some of these analyses even rejected the transformative capacity of the military, regarding 'praetorian' coups as forms of pre-modern continuity rather than modernist change (for example Perlmutter 1974). Others recognized the (failed) modernization efforts of the regime, but denied any progressive character of the military dictatorship, citing its violent and authoritarian politics against workers and farmers (for example Beinin 2013b).

In order to understand these contradictions, authors operating within a Gramscian tradition have categorized the Nasserist intervention as a form of passive revolution (for example Cox 1987: 210; al-Shakry 2012). However, as I argue below, as a mere 'regime label' passive revolution creates more problems than it solves: by itself, it cannot explain in a satisfactory manner the complex interdependency between popular masses and state elites, nor the transformative shift from Nasser to Sadat and Mubarak. Thus Gramsci's notion of Caesarism appears as an additional, yet indispensable, conceptual tool for understanding the chemical dialectic between subaltern actors and ruling groups.

Escaping Colonialism

A spontaneous popular insurrection on 25 January 1952 in Cairo led to a mass repression of trade union and communist leaders. Whereas the state's violent coercion successfully weakened the proletarian vanguard of the national–popular alliance, it also revealed its own feeble grasp over Egypt's gelatinous civil society. Sections of the Egyptian police and military had also joined the counter-hegemonic mobilization. The 25 January insurrection heralded the practical end of the rule of the Palace, but there was no social force that could fill the power vacuum. Central state power was disorganized, but not conquered, let alone transformed. The political void lasted for six months until, on 23 July 1952, the Free Officers of the Revolutionary Command Council (RCC), led by Colonel Gamal Abd al-Nasser, appeared on the political scene as a *deus ex machina*. The RCC organized a coup, cutting the Gordian knot that the national–popular movement had tied and couldn't unravel.

Most members of the RCC came from a petty-bourgeois background (Richards and Waterbury 2008: 127) and their goals coincided with the demands of the national–popular bloc. Once in power they improvised a 'classic' programme of political emancipation in the context of colonialism: a democratic republic, social justice, abolition of feudalism, establishment of a strong national army, and full independence and sovereignty for Egypt (al-Khafaji 2004: 199). The RCC understood the main predicament for the nation's underdevelopment and subordination to Britain in terms of the twin evils of imperialism and feudalism. In general, the military intervention was welcomed by oppositional forces. The Muslim Brotherhood's Supreme Guide al-Hudaybi welcomed the coup as a means for solving social and political instability, while rank-and-file Ikhwan saw the RCC as the harbinger of decolonization.

After the coup a power struggle within the military clique ensued, which was expressed in terms of the character of the new national-popular bloc. General Muhammad Naguib, who was chosen by the RCC as head of state because of his seniority and prestige, aimed to reduce the military intervention to a minimum and advocated the establishment of bourgeois democracy and free-market policies (Kandil 2012: 27). Nasser, however, claimed that this withdrawal represented a return to the societal stalemate. Only the transformation of the national–popular project into a strong, homogeneous, and centralized state could overcome Egypt's predicaments. In 1953 the new government banned all parties except for the Brotherhood, which remained loyal to the RCC. The Ikhwan were asked to join the Nasser-led 'Liberation Rally', and as a token of goodwill al-Hudaybi dissolved the Society's paramilitary secret apparatus and kicked its leaders out of the organization. During the open power struggle between Nasser and Naguib in late 1953 and 1954, the Brotherhood first sided with Naguib, but then switched to the Nasser camp. In exchange for its support, the Brotherhood demanded an Islamic constitution, democratic institutions, freedom of press, and an end to emergency law. As Nasser was not inclined to share power, a number of Ikhwan members secretively founded a new paramilitary cell which tried to assassinate the president on 26 October 1954. The attempt failed, but it gave Nasser a perfect alibi to eliminate the Muslim Brotherhood as a competitor for power.

Ironically, in the first two years of the new regime it was Naguib, not Nasser, who appeared as the 'charismatic' leader, drawing legitimacy and prestige from his *personal* relation with the masses.[1] Nasser on the other hand began to build a *state apparatus* that *organized* his leadership, creating ministries of intelligence, security, and propaganda, establishing loyal cells in the military and trade unions, and launching political projects such as the Liberation Rally. Moreover, presenting himself as a potential strongman in the region he secured the support of the United States, whereas Naguib failed to win their trust (Kandil 2012: 29). The direct outcome of the power struggle remained highly contingent, as Nasser barely survived two spontaneous mutinies, respectively of the artillery in January 1953 and the cavalry in March 1954, backed by mass street protests in favour of Naguib (Kandil 2012: 30–35). Against the largely spontaneous mass demonstrations of Naguib, Nasser mobilized his own political apparatus: the Liberation Rally and reliable trade union leaders who organized strikes, paralysing the country. The strike of the Cairo transport workers in particular 'was a decisive contribution to the RCC's ability to turn back the tide of popular opinion, consolidate the power of 'Abd al-Nasir, and confirm the continuation of military rule' (Beinin and Lockman 1987: 440).

Immediately after the coup Nasser began to limit and counterbalance the autonomous power of the military – embodied in such independent figures as the charismatic chief of staff Abd al-Hakim Amer – within the ensemble of state structures through the development of the existing security apparatus (Kandil 2012: 18). Nasser did not want to establish an explicitly military regime but a populist dictatorship centred around his persona and safeguarded by the Armed Forces. Although he tried to develop a political apparatus, first in the form of the Liberation Rally and later through the Arab Socialist Union (ASU), these institutions could not counterbalance the powerful military. The military became a 'state within a state', consisting of various contending power structures – the army, air defence, air force, navy, intelligence services, Republican Guard, Ministry of Defence, etc. – which were each ruled by their generals as small fiefdoms. Nasser had to rely increasingly on the security apparatus as a counterweight to the generals – especially Amer (Kandil 2012: 41–2). This uncomfortable equilibrium created a state that represented a peculiar hybrid between a military and police dictatorship.

In order to overcome feudalism, Egypt had to be industrialized. In order to industrialize, the nation had to be able to overcome its subaltern position within the international state system and the world economy. Full national sovereignty was the key to overcoming Egypt's predicament. Although an agreement in 1954 between Egypt and Britain to demilitarize and evacuate the Suez Canal region and revert control of the canal to the Egyptian state stipulated a phased and conditional withdrawal of troops and personnel, Nasser would have to achieve national sovereignty much more quickly if he wanted to consolidate his prestige as leader of the national–popular bloc. In addition, he perceived the creation of Israel in 1948 as a direct threat against Egyptian and Arab sovereignty. As a directive force, the Free Officers had to prove that they were able to defend the country against British and Israeli imperialist forces. The emerging bipolar world order offered Nasser a way to achieve these goals. Both the United States and the USSR sought strong allies in the region against each other. Nasser aimed to achieve a balance between the two superpowers, creating the necessary geopolitical space for national sovereignty (Gaddis 1997: 167–72).

At first Nasser hoped to buy arms from the United States to start building a modern military. At the time this was a logical move as Nasser had been supported by the US state department and the CIA even before the coup of 1952 (Kandil 2012: 15, 20). However, his strong anti-Zionist stance blocked any possibility of US Congress approving the sale of military material to Egypt. Nasser then turned to the USSR, which sold him weapons through the Czech arms deal in 1955. The following year the United States retaliated by withdrawing its financial support for the Aswan Dam project. Nasser immediately reacted with the nationalization of the Suez Canal. A tripartite British, French, and Israeli force invaded Egypt in October 1956 to neutralize what they had come to perceive as a fundamental danger to their interests in the region. The Egyptian army was routed. However, diplomatic and financial pressure by the United States, along with military threats by the Soviet Union, forced the invaders to withdraw their forces. Even though the Egyptian military had been defeated, Nasser emerged victorious from the conflict, strengthening national sovereignty, the prestige of Egypt in the Arab world, and his own position within the regime at home.

As early as September 1952 the new regime undertook a number of important rural reforms in its war against feudalism. Land size was capped to 200 feddans[2] per owner and 300 feddans per family. Subsequent land reforms in 1961, 1963, and 1969 redistributed some 12 per cent of cultivable lands among landless and near-landless farmers. Rents were limited to seven times the land tax (Bush 2007: 1601). An agricultural minimum wage was implemented. Peasants gained the right of perpetual tenancy at controlled rents, which severely restricted the ownership rights of the feudal landlords. The position of landlords in the agricultural credit cooperatives – which supervised 'cropping patterns, input supplies, credit provision and marketing' (Bush 2007: 1601) – was replaced by state employees. This measure restricted the political influence of the landlords and formally excluded them as participants in the newly emerging Nasserist historical bloc (Aoude 1994). At no point was there a nationalization of lands. State intervention merely increased the productivity of lands, turning them over to private actors once they became profitable (Cooper 1983: 455). Expropriation, land reform, regulation of inputs and outputs of agricultural production, and rent control served three interconnected goals: (1) to weaken the class power of the monarchy and the large landholders; (2) to increase productivity in agriculture and to free capital for industrial development (Chaichian 1988: 35; Mitchell 2002: 226); (3) to control the economic activity of the small peasantry (Cooper 1983: 456). Still, the land reforms did not eradicate the political and economic role of landlords in the Egyptian social formation: 'Dispossessed landowners received compensation, private property persisted, large landowners found ways of retaining their land: there was ultimately very little fundamental shift in the balance of political and economic power' (Bush 2007: 1601). While the small peasantry became directly dependent on the state, large landholders became its objective allies (Cooper 1983: 456).

With regard to industrial development the state's rationale was purely political (Ayubi 1992: 92) and served to strengthen national sovereignty – an economic means for 'catching up' with the Western nations (Chaichian 1988: 35). At first the state merely acted as the midwife of 'spontaneous' industrial development by private domestic and foreign actors. Roughly from 1954 until 1960 state power diligently defended the interests of private industrial capital (Johnson 1973: 4). The government encouraged domestic and foreign industrial investments by lowering corporate taxes and relaxing protectionist measures. By establishing public–private committees that guided national development, the state cast itself in the role of impartial facilitator (Aoude 1994). However, neither domestic nor foreign capitalists were interested in industrialization. Between 1950 and 1956 private investments dropped by 300 per cent (Farah 2009: 33). Step by step the state itself was forced to take the economic initiative: 'In 1952–1953, 72 per cent of gross capital formation took place in the private sector. By 1959–1960, the state was responsible for 74 per cent of gross capital formation' (Beinin 1989: 79).

Geopolitically motivated foreign aid and economic assistance on the one hand, and the contingent sequestration of private assets on the other, allocated the capital and expertise necessary for industrialization to the state, which became the primary economic actor, substituting state power for absent bourgeois class power (Achcar 2013: 90). In 1959 the First Five-Year Plan for the whole economy was formulated. The Plan acknowledged an already existing reality as it established the public sector as the dominant industrial producer and investor. The Egyptian textile sector spearheaded an ISI-policy, which was expected to create a domestic demand for spinning and weaving machinery, which, in turn, would stimulate the local production of iron and steel. Between 1952 and 1960 the number of wage labourers working in manufacture increased from 260,052 to 321,083 – more than half of whom were employed in the textile industry (Beinin 1989: 77).

A bourgeois anti-Nasserist revolt in Syria, the disinclination of the private sector to support the Five-Year Plan, and a conspiracy between high-ranking officers and private capitalists to oust Nasser led to the socialist decrees of 1961, through which, at once, large-scale industry, banking, insurance, foreign trade, utilities, marine transport, airlines, and many hotels and department stores were nationalized (Aoude 1994). Instead of a preconceived plan, the increasing role of the state and the expansion of the public sector was an unintended, but logical, outcome of the reluctance of domestic capital groups to support Nasser's industrialization project and the restructuring of geopolitics after the Second World War. The 'socialist' decrees qualitatively deepened the intervention and direction of the political state in the economic structure, and explicitly connected this policy to that of the Soviet geopolitical bloc. Moreover, the 'socialist' turn of the Nasserist bloc also entailed a more profound integration of subaltern groups, especially industrial workers, into the authoritarian-turned national–popular bloc. This integration was expressed in the key regime concept of 'democratic cooperative socialism', which represented first and foremost Egyptian and Arab unity, from which all other political and economic ideological notions, such as egalitarianism and social justice, were derived (Akhavi 1975).

Displacing Popular Initiative

Under the slogan of 'Unity, Order, and Labour' the working class was integrated into the Nasserist bloc, in a way that obliterated its autonomous agency. After less than a month in power, the RCC government violently repressed a strike at Kafr al-Dawwar, hanging two worker leaders (Beinin and Lockman 1987: 418). Nasserist hegemony over the workers' movement was secured by coercive consent: through a combination of unilateral and far-reaching social reforms and the liquidation or transformism of the class's organic intellectuals. Strikes and independent worker actions were prohibited, but from 1957 onwards proletarian bargaining power was secured by the state-controlled General Federation of Egyptian Trade Unions (GFETU). Historian Anne Alexander summarized the dual hegemonic role of the Nasserist unions in civil and political society:

[A]s organs of social control they channelled benefits such as access to workplace-based social welfare schemes to workers and worked hand in glove with state employers to enforce 'social peace' within the workplace. As organs of political control they acted as an electoral machine for the ruling party, controlling nominations for the 50 percent of seats in parliament which were reserved for 'workers and peasants', and a mechanism for mobilising a stage army of apparently loyal regime supporters whenever the regime felt it needed to make a show of its 'mass base'. Consistent with both of these roles the trade union bureaucracy acted ruthlessly in concert with the repressive apparatus of the state to crush workers' attempts to organise collective action and build their own independent organisations. (Alexander 2012: 111)

Unilateral concessions towards the workers' social conditions softened class contradictions in the industrial sphere. In exchange for syndical and political passivity, the workers gained social reforms and rights such as a 42-hour working week, higher wages, social security, free healthcare, protection against arbitrary dismissal, and education (Clément 2009: 103). Even in the private sector, the government enforced minimum wage standards and protective laws (Posusney 1996: 218). In the public sector the introduction of workers' participation or co-management had the objective of integrating the working class in the national project, softening class contradictions, and raising productivity. In reality it was participation without the right to debate or disagree. Industrial power relations did not change and the trade union leadership and the workers' representatives were integrated into the state bureaucracy (Bayat 1993: 68–74).

The reluctance of the bourgeoisie to take up its expected role in the industrialization process and the rapprochement with the Soviet Union strengthened corporatist structures and inspired an increasingly radical anti-imperialist and socialistic rhetoric. The agent of 'Arab socialism' was, in theory, the 'alliance of working forces', consisting of peasants, wage workers, urban intellectuals and professionals, national capitalists, and the military. In practice the popular masses were the object of authoritarian regime policies instead of an independent political subject. Despite the improved living conditions and social status of 'the industrial worker' in Egyptian society, the working class was reduced to a corporate, subaltern position in the Nasserist bloc.

As a new and unexpected phenomenon, the Nasserist coup and the formation of an authoritarian national–popular bloc sowed confusion among the Egyptian left. The largest communist organization, the Democratic Movement for National Liberation (DMNL) supported the Free Officers in 1952, seeing them as an anti-imperialist force (Beinin and Lockman 1987: 427). The government's subsequent violent crackdown on communist activists pushed the movement into the opposition camp. Unilaterally declared labour reforms in December 1952, and the transformism of trade unionist leaders, however, weakened the class base of communist and leftist nationalist political activists, which had united in the National Democratic Front (NDF). Nasser deployed the subsumed trade unions as a social force in the streets against the popular demonstrations that called for a democratization of the regime (see above).

In 1952 Nasser had been supported by the United States, who saw in him an Egyptian Atatürk who could replace 'Egypt's archaic and corrupt monarchy before the increasing radicalization of Egyptian workers and peasants drove the country into the arms of communism' (Kandil 2012: 24). By 1956 the Nasserist regime was distancing itself from the United States and was moving towards a position of 'non-alignment'. Almost all communist factions agreed to support Nasser's project. There was a clear tendency among communists to subordinate the struggle for democracy and socialism to the formation of a 'popular front' against imperialism. The only substantial political difference between nationalists and communists was the latter's emphasis on the vanguard role of the working class. However, a conflict between Nasser and the Iraqi communists in 1958 created a division within the Egyptian communist movement, with a majority taking the side of their Iraqi comrades (Beinin and Lockman 1987: 580–1).

The 'socialist turn' from 1960 onwards was devised by Nasser as a political instrument to counterbalance the influence of the military and the old, pre-1952 elites (see Ayubi 1992: 94). Changes in the political apparatus, such as the formation of the Arab Socialist Union (ASU) in 1962, the foundation of a Marxist cadre school (Egyptian Socialist Youth) in 1965, and the removal of pro-capitalist ministers from government, accompanied socialistic economic initiatives and improved relations with the Soviet Union (Johnson 1973: 4). When in 1964 communist prisoners were released, the two biggest communist organizations voluntarily dissolved themselves into the ASU (Beinin and Lockman 1987: 583–4). Communist 'auto-transformism' not only reinforced Nasser's hegemony, it also offered him a new layer of political personnel to consolidate his state.

Deflected Permanent Revolution?

Events in Egypt and the colonial world at large showed that the rules of the old imperialist epoch no longer applied. In the late 1930s Trotsky had framed the rise of Fascism and Nazism, the economic depression, and the signs of impending war as the 'death agony' of capitalism. Capitalism had ceased, once and for all, to be a progressive force, able to develop the productive forces. The next world war would lead to the collapse of social democracy and Stalinism, replacing both by either world socialist revolution or global Fascism (Davidson 2012: 430). However, Stalinism and social democracy emerged strengthened out of the world war. In less than a decade, the Soviet Union became a superpower, gathering a number of client states around its socialistic empire, while Western welfare states pledged their allegiance to the United States. Although some followers of Trotsky wrestled for decades with the cognitive dissonance between Trotsky's 'predictions' and the unfolding reality, other Marxists tried to make sense of the new situation. For example, in the British Revolutionary Communist Party (RCP) figures such as Ted Grant (1913–2006) and Tony Cliff (1917–2000) criticized the political line of the Fourth International (FI).[3]

The FI claimed that the epoch of imperialism and Fascism had rendered bourgeois democracy impossible and that therefore the post-war states by default were a form of Bonapartism. In contradistinction, Grant posited in 1945 that the post-war period was already displaying a reinvigoration of Western democracies under the aegis of US imperialism, which, essentially, represented a 'counter-revolution in a democratic form'. Despite Grant's appeal to Trotskyite orthodoxy, the assertion that the bourgeoisie was able to recreate the conditions for its power in a seemingly progressive manner was something of a theoretical novelty. Faced with the prospect of popular revolt after the world war 'the task of Anglo-American imperialism to restore "order" to Europe, to establish the rule of capital, assumes the shape of complicated and dexterous manoeuvres' (Grant 1989: 102). In other words, the West European bourgeoisie had to be agile and careful, retreat tactically, make some concessions to the working class, while maintaining the overall initiative of political and economic reform. Conversely, the establishment of Soviet puppet regimes in Eastern Europe, which were eventually forced to implement a planned economy and the one-party system, reflected a counter-revolution in a socialistic guise.[4] Relatively progressive transformations were implemented to pre-empt popular revolution. Yet at the time Grant underestimated the duration and depth of these reforms, expecting the dynamic of permanent revolution to be merely *delayed* as capital regained its composure (Grant 1989: 88–133; 340).[5] However, the democratic or pseudo-socialist reconstitution of the European states was able to displace popular initiative in a structural (that is, Fordist) way by developing the productive forces, forging new class alliances, co-opting trade unions and workers' parties, and rearticulating hegemonic projects (see Chapter 3).

Grant claimed that the delay of a socialist revolution in the advanced capitalist nations and the continued development of the productive forces in the colonial and post-colonial nations 'has meant that *the development of the permanent revolution in these underdeveloped countries has taken a distorted pattern*' (Grant 1989: 312). Tony Cliff rejected even more categorically Trotsky's presumption that the colonial revolution would *necessarily* take on the form a permanent revolution. Cliff accepted Trotsky's claim that the colonial bourgeoisie came too late on the scene of global capitalist development to play an independent part. However, he pointed out that the colonial workers' movements were not necessarily militant or revolutionary: 'While the conservative, cowardly nature of a late-developing bourgeoisie ... is an absolute law, the revolutionary character of the young working class ... is neither absolute nor inevitable' (Cliff 2000: 44). Because of stunted economic development colonial workers were often inexperienced and uneducated, remaining socially entangled with the countryside, their organizations led by non-proletarian actors and dependent on state intervention. These material conditions were reinforced by the absence of political bodies (that is, communist parties) that actively tried to develop proletarian hegemony. Witnessing the new states that were born in the process of decolonization, especially the Chinese and the Cuban revolutions, he posited that the absence of *both* a progressive bourgeoisie and a revolutionary proletariat did not necessarily impede colonial countries in throwing off the imperialist yoke and developing the productive forces (Cliff 1963).

In China the bourgeois Kuomintang government was militarily defeated by a peasant army led by a communist party without any social base among industrial workers, who remained passive in the face of communist victory. Similarly, the Cuban Revolution happened without any initiative from the working class, and was the result of a guerrilla struggle waged by petty-bourgeois forces, mainly supported by impoverished landless peasants. In both China and Cuba the new revolutionary governments initially emphasized that their conquest of power did not entail a transition to socialism, but a liberation from feudalism and imperialism, creating the conditions for national capitalism. Colonialism and dependency were defeated by effectively pro-capitalist nationalist rebellions. According to Cliff, this was possible because of an active peasantry, the reconfiguration of post-war geopolitical relations of power into a bipolar world order, and the role of the state and the intelligentsia (Cliff 1963). These developments *deflected* the process of permanent revolution.

Cliff posited: 'It is one of the tricks of history that when an historical task faces society, and the class that traditionally carries it out is absent, some other group of people, quite often a state power, implements it' (Cliff 2000: 45).[6] This observation strongly echoes Gramsci's notion of Caesarism as the intervention of a 'third party', which substitutes its agency for that of the contending classes to solve a societal stalemate. Cliff suggested that intellectuals could develop into a more or less independent stratum, if left unchecked by the organized workers' movement. Often this represented the only 'national' social group, the bearer of a shared culture and defender of the common good of the nation against narrow sectional interests. Insightfully Davidson (2010) underlined that the colonial intelligentsia resembled much more the radical Jacobins of 1789 than the cowardly liberals of the 1848 revolutions. Because of systemic underdevelopment the intellectuals remained largely unemployed, unable to mobilize their capacities for the development of the nation. Unlike the dependent national bourgeois, they did not share a material interest with imperialism or landed property. However, they also considered themselves as elevated above the uneducated masses, which they desired to emancipate by leading them from above. This social psychology made the intelligentsia favourable towards authoritarian and state-led projects of modernization. When intellectuals led national liberation movements, the outcome was not a distortion but a deflection of permanent revolution by a state capitalist outcome.[7] The strategic consequences of deflected permanent revolution were important. The development of capitalism under state capitalist regimes meant that the class struggle in the postcolonial world lost its peculiar, 'combined' character, turning into the 'classic' conflict between proletariat and national bourgeoisie (Cliff 1963).[8]

Often the active intellectual stratum was not a civil or guerrilla group, but a military one (Davidson 2012: 462–3; Zeilig 2010). Grant observed that in cases such as Burma, Egypt, Iraq, Syria, and Ethiopia it was junior officers who conquered the state apparatus, using military power to subjugate (sections of) the national bourgeoisie and foreign capital, and develop the economy 'from above' (Grant 1989: 317–9). Junior officers were obviously *able* to play a Caesarist role by substituting military for civil–political power, but, more importantly, they were often *willing* because they saw themselves as the only group that represented the national good. Their education in modern European-styled military academies stimulated a national consciousness, pride, and patriotism, which came into conflict with the reality of foreign supremacy, economic backwardness, and the political collaboration of traditional elites with imperialism (see Kandil 2012: 9–10). They combined an aversion towards the decadence of the old ruling classes and the passivity of the bourgeoisie with a distrust of working-class militancy, which threatened national security and development.

Cliff's appraisal of the independence of the *particularly colonial* intelligentsia raises questions about the character of 'intellectuals' in *general*. Davidson wondered: 'was the class fraction it describes a new development in the history of capitalism? Are the leaders or ideologues of the "deflected" revolutions so very different from those who led the bourgeois revolutions between 1789 and 1848?' (Davidson 2012: 463). Gramsci's concept of organic and traditional intellectuals allows for a more sophisticated understanding of the relation between class and 'intelligentsia' (see Chapter 2). With regard to the French Revolution, the petty-bourgeois layers that formed the Jacobin vanguard functioned as the organic personnel of the bourgeois class. In the German case, the traditional *Junkers* were gradually replaced as a ruling class by their transformation into state personnel. In both cases their role as personnel was based on their effective social *separation* from the bourgeois class. This separation allowed them to appear as transcending narrow class interests and defending the national, common good – even though they remained 'chemically' connected to the bourgeois class. This chemical connection could become unstable when the personnel moved too much ahead of their class, as was the case with the Jacobins, leading to their eventual isolation and replacement by more conservative elements; or when it tail-ended its class, as was the case with the conservative *Junkers*, which, for example, led to a confrontation between Bismarck and Emperor Wilhelm II on the question of anti-socialist legislation in 1890.

This general observation on the nature of the 'intelligentsia' becomes more complicated in the context of colonialism. Modern intellectuals such as lawyers, journalists, artists, teachers, engineers, officers, etc., were the product of both blocked, 'indigenous' modernization efforts and imperialist-driven development, manning the colonial and semi-colonial state apparatus and industries. Their formation was entwined with the imperialist formation of capital in their countries, which threw them onto the stage of national leadership while pulling away the supports from under its independent political platform. The colonial intelligentsia was inherently no more independent than its Western historical predecessors. However, the corporate condition of 'its' national bourgeoisie and the weight of imperialist domination rendered a more explicit autonomy both possible and necessary. Gramsci reminded us that

> when the impetus of progress is not tightly linked to a vast local economic development which is artificially limited and repressed, but is instead the reflection of international developments which transmit their ideological currents to the periphery – currents born on the basis of the productive development of the more advanced countries – then the group which is the bearer of the new ideas is not the economic group but the intellectual stratum, and the conception of the State advocated by them changes aspect; it is conceived of as something in itself, as a rational absolute ... [S]ince the State is the concrete form of a productive world and since the intellectuals are the social element from which the governing personnel is drawn, the intellectual who is not firmly anchored to a strong economic group will tend to present the State as an absolute. (Gramsci 1971: 116–7; Q10ii§61)

Cliff alluded to state power as a force that implemented radical change, but he did not connect this agency to the character of the colonial intelligentsia. In the above passage, Gramsci suggested that the unevenness between local and global development may lead to cultural inertia and political passivity of the domestic ruling class, but to initiative by a more cosmopolitan intellectual stratum. The intelligentsia may begin to detach itself from its constituent class and its 'autonomy' is reflected in the state that it constructs. This autonomy should not be understood in essentialist but in relational terms – as the *elasticity* of organic intellectuals towards their constituent class. However, there is an elastic limit to representation: at a certain point, in order to remain a directive force, intellectuals have to sink roots in a new class, or become an isolated caste (see Grant 1989: 342).

Thus the struggle between the Kuomintang and the Chinese Communist Party (CCP) appears as a conflict between a moderate and radical layer of petty-bourgeois intellectuals, both originally representing their feeble national bourgeoisie. Grant claimed that the CCP was not able to fuse with the national bourgeoisie and 'manoeuvred between the classes, at one time resting on the "national" bourgeoisie, or the peasants, and at others on the working class' (Grant 1989: 307).[9] As the route to classical capitalist development was blocked, the CCP had to accumulate capital through the nationalization of lands and industries. The choice of the Communist intelligentsia for a 'state capitalist' solution to the problem of capital accumulation seems less determined by an a priori authoritarian predisposition (Cliff) or attraction to 'a ready-made Bonapartist model' (Grant), than the political result of the chemical relation with its popular class base. Put simply, albeit organized in an authoritarian, coercive, and inorganic way, in order to become and remain hegemonic, petty-bourgeois intellectuals had to represent workers' and peasants' interests.

Caesarism Beyond Passive Revolution

The Caesarism constitutive of the process of deflected permanent revolution defies Gramsci's dichotomy between 'progressive' and 'reactionary' Caesarism. Looking at structural outcomes, from a strictly national perspective the process is qualitative and progressive as it develops societies beyond the boundaries set by domestic and imperialist capital – a 'functional equivalent' of the bourgeois revolution in the Global South (Davidson 2010). Ironically, the concept of deflected permanent revolution thus appears as a critical version of the Stalinist doctrine of the 'non-capitalist path to development'. In Egypt, the Nasserist regime forcefully abolished feudalism and imperialism, implementing political and social reforms that even went beyond the traditional 'tasks' of the bourgeois revolution. In this regard the historical meaning of Nasserism was much closer to the 'classic' Caesarism of Napoleon I than to the modern Caesarism of Mussolini. Nasser's 'Arab socialism' proved to be the most efficient way to transform lingering precapitalist social forms into capitalist relations of production (see Ayubi 1992: 94). The rationale of Nasserist 'state capitalism' was the inverse of the historical logic of capital in Western Europe. In Egypt, the goal of national development was pursued through the means of state-led capital accumulation, whereas in Western Europe the development of the productive forces had been a by-product of profit-driven private accumulation. State-led industrialization, construction, and land reclamation projects absorbed the surplus population from the countryside and turned peasants into modern wage labourers. Between 1961 and 1967 the propertyless workforce increased from 6 to 7.3 million (Chaichian 1988: 39). This process of formal subsumption of labour under capital (the expansion of wage labour) was complemented with a real subsumption of labour under capital: the transformation and modernization of the labour process and the methods of production themselves due to the influx of new sources of capital and technical expertise.

Nonetheless, from a world-historical point of view, deflected permanent revolution did not overcome the limits of the capitalist mode of production and merely reconfigured existing historical blocs in line with the contemporary form of capitalism. For the West, passive revolution functioned as a historical criterion to interpret transformations from above, first in the epoch of the constitution of capitalism and then in the ages of its reconstitution in imperialist and Fordist forms. With regard to the Global South, passive revolution has to comprehend capitalist constitution within an already ongoing process of capitalist reconstitution. Imperialism never properly constituted the capitalist mode of production, let alone bourgeois society, in the Global South (see Chapter 5). The defeat or collapse of the old European powers, the geopolitical competition between the United States and the USSR, the sustained post-war economic boom, and the absence of a revolutionary proletariat created new opportunities and imperatives for postcolonial nations to continue capitalist development *immediately in its new Fordist form*. The formation of postcolonial states was greatly accelerated by the emerging geopolitical bipolar world order after the Second World War, which forced radical liberation movements into the camp of the Soviet Union, and more conservative countries into the arms of the United States. Just as international finance capital and European imperialist state power shaped the colonial historical blocs, so did US or Soviet military, political, economic, and ideological assistance become a constituent factor of the base and superstructures of postcolonial nations: 'the drive for renewal may be caused by the combination of progressive forces which in themselves are scanty and inadequate ... with an international situation favourable to their expansion and victory' (Gramsci 1971: 116; Q10ii§61).

The postcolonial 'developmental states' reflected the general global consensus of a Fordist accumulation strategy, as variants of either the

Western 'welfare' state or Stalinist state capitalist archetypes. In general, between 1950 and 1975 postcolonial countries enjoyed a high economic growth, realized behind protective tariffs and by planned industrialization, coercive control over labour, and state regulation of industrial and financial capital (Kiely 2005: 52–3). ISI emerged as the logical accumulation strategy that expressed the developmental rationale of the nationalist historical blocs. Shielding the home market from foreign imports would direct local capital to the domestic production of these goods, initiating a 'normal' process of capitalist expanded reproduction. Moreover, the availability and consumption of ISI-produced goods would bind the subaltern classes materially to the ruling classes. In this regard, ISI was not only a technical accumulation strategy, but also one of the hegemonic pillars of class rule (Hesketh 2010: 391–3). International institutions such as the IMF, World Bank, and GATT actively disseminated Fordist principles, regulated global capital flows, and offered 'developing' countries some breathing room to deal with foreign competition (Kiely 2005: 53; Simon 2010: 432). Consequently, national development was as much the outcome of domestic class initiative and the internal transformation of the economic base, as it was caused by the intervention of US and Soviet power and the import of capital and political projects. Trotsky's vision of socialist advanced nations helping to transform 'backward' countries came true, but in a cynical, distorted version of two empires sponsoring their client states and moulding them into a broken mirror of their own historical bloc.

The ambiguity of deflected permanent revolution as both a revolutionary and a restorative process was also determined by the class base of Caesarism. In Chapter 4, I rejected the strategic possibility of a modern progressive Caesarism – a Caesarism that accomplishes the project of social emancipation in the absence of a hegemonic working class. However, from an analytical point of view, the Caesarism constitutive of deflected permanent revolution was progressive when the leading stratum based itself explicitly on the subaltern masses, especially poor peasants and workers, using their class power to defeat the domestic ruling classes and imperialism. In Egypt the Free Officers' coup took the side of the fledgling national–popular bloc against British colonialism. This was reflected in the 'national-democratic' programme of the RCC and the subsequent policies of land reform, welfare, and education, which favoured the subaltern classes. Although the Free Officers had delivered the death blow to the old colonial bloc by using military force, they could and would not base their rule solely on coercion. In order to offer the masses an organic passage to the state, the regime had to create the terrain of a modern civil society. The absorption of the existing, underdeveloped modern civil society, together with lingering premodern social forms, into an expanding and developing political society also entailed the massification of these structures and practices. The political state created mass trade unions, professional syndicates, public companies, universities and schools, women's, youths', and children's organizations, cultural clubs, peasant associations, and so on; drawing, for the first time in Egypt's history, the majority of the population into the activity of a – tightly state-controlled – mass civil society (see Ayubi 1992: 98). The progressive, Jacobin character of the Nasserist state attracted intellectuals from diverse class backgrounds to its authoritarian project. This recalls Gramsci's claim that:

> the intellectuals of the historically (and concretely) progressive class, in the given conditions, exercise such a power of attraction that, in the last analysis, they end up by subjugating the intellectuals of the other social groups; they thereby create a system of solidarity between all the intellectuals, with bonds of a psychological nature (vanity, etc.) and often of a caste character (technico-juridical, corporate, etc.). This phenomenon manifests itself 'spontaneously' in the historical periods in which the given social group is really progressive – i.e. really causes the whole society to move forward, not merely satisfying its own existential requirements, but continuously augmenting its cadres for the conquest of ever new spheres of economic and productive activity. (Gramsci 1971: 60; Q19§24)

Just as the colonial era had produced the *effendiyya*, the expansion of modern education under Nasserism created a fresh layer of intellectuals who were embedded within the nationalist project. The rule of the military and security clique was not only based upon coercion, but also on its prestige and its economic and political direction of the Egyptian social formation. The elastic connection of the petty-bourgeois officers with the elusive progressive Egyptian bourgeoisie and US capital snapped when these forces were unwilling to invest in the developmental and military project of the regime. Gradually the class base of the regime was expanded to include farmers and workers. The Nasserist project included an ethico-political dimension, expressed in its populist, nationalist, 'nonaligned', and eventually 'Arab socialist' ideology, which mobilized and inspired the masses. For a while, it seemed that the Nasserist regime could organize an (authoritarian form of) organic passage for the population to the new state.

Nevertheless, despite its relatively progressive and qualitative character, from the perspective of self-emancipation the Nasserist era was a throwback compared to the decades before. The Free Officers' coup captured central state power before the masses had matured into a political subject that could conquer state power. Their Caesarist intervention 'deflected' the revolutionary process, and substituted its own authoritarian direction for the embryonic hegemony of the subaltern alliance. Nasserism was essentially reactionary, for it replaced organic subaltern prefiguration by a chemical state. Here its political significance becomes analogous to that of Fascism, as independent working-class associations were destroyed and labour was subsumed directly under capital in the command economy of the totalitarian state. State intervention softened the economic predicament in the workplace by improving the immediate living conditions of Egyptian wage workers. The expanding public sector confronted workers in the production process directly as the state and not as capital, thereby transforming the economic relation between workers and management into a patron–client relation: '[M]aintaining an image of national harmony and worker satisfaction seem to be far more important to Egypt's rulers than minimizing financial concessions' (Posusney 1996: 216). At the same time, independent organizations of the working class were destroyed by the Nasserist state and replaced by corporatist structures. Recalcitrant worker leaders and communists were detained, political and trade union organizations outlawed. Organic subaltern intellectuals were absorbed by an extension of the state (see Hanieh 2013: 26).

Whereas the concept of 'passive revolution' evokes the image of a weak or restricted hegemony, Nasserist Caesarism became rooted in a strong hegemony, based on the consent of broad layers of the population. The concept of Caesarism denotes not only the 'instrumentality' of passive revolution in the Global South (Cox 1987: 192), for its meaning, at least in its progressive form, cannot fully be subsumed by a revolution from above that displaces popular initiative. Although Nasser represented anything but a Modern Prince, his rise to power on the waves of insurrections and mass strikes necessarily transformed him into a popular Bonaparte. While the subaltern classes were politically subordinated to the military dictatorship, the regime itself was heir to the class forces that generated it. Nasserism was the elastic product of revolutionary, popular mobilization and the dictatorship could not easily abandon its subaltern clients without, at the same time, forfeiting its hegemonic base.

Organic Crisis

Despite its hegemony, the popular–authoritarian historical bloc that Nasser created was an inherently unstable and contradictory ensemble.

Firstly, there was a contradiction between the class nature of the regime and its state capitalist logic of accumulation. The state had to achieve a balance between securing political consent from its popular base and allocating sufficient resources for its project of modernization: the state's expansive 'populist consumption policy' stood in contradiction to the 'investment demands of developmentalism' (Cooper 1979: 482–3). At a certain point, the ISI strategy had to be transformed into an export-led growth path or the state would face a balance-of-payments crisis (Ayubi 1992: 99). This necessitated competitive industries, which required the import of capital goods and an economic rationale of labour discipline, high productivity, and low wages. This logic conflicted with the interests of its subaltern base: workers demanded full employment, workers' control (or at least real participation), reductions in working hours, and high wages (see Hanieh 2013: 26). As the state claimed to be the expression of the 'alliance of working forces' workers became frustrated when, with the best of intentions, they tried to appropriate and mobilize its bureaucratic organs (Bayat 1993: 70–4). Suddenly they realized that their goals were not identical with, but rather were opposed to the means of mediation the state provided. From 1965 onwards, it became obvious that the system could not sustain both capital-intensive indus-trialization and high levels of consumption (Beinin and Lockman 1987: 459). While the First Five-Year Plan was a success (Achcar 2013: 64), growth rates almost halved during the Second Five-Year Plan (1965–70) (Farah 1986: 98). Industrial productivity was fettered by a high ratio of variable capital (caused by job security and guaranteed employment in the face of a population boom), rising fixed costs, and under-capacity. The regime remained reluctant to cut consumption after a brief and much contested experiment in 1965 (Farah 1986: 98–9). However, the defeat of Egypt in the Six Day War in 1967 set hard limits to the 'populist consumption policy': prices and taxes were increased, the workweek was increased from 42 to 48 hours without compensation, forced savings were deducted from monthly wages, and paid holidays were cancelled (Posusney 1996: 219).

Secondly, the partial and authoritarian statification of the economy generated a tendency towards *private* capital accumulation and a 'self-privatization' of the public sector (see Achcar 2013: 119). Egypt's economy was never fully nationalized, and pockets of private accumulation continued to exist in agriculture, trade, and some industrial sectors. Although the rural ruling class had lost lands, it was able to continue its domination of the countryside through traditional networks and the new government cooperatives. Moreover, the new ruling stratum of state bureaucrats was primarily composed of the sons of rural elites (Kandil

2012: 64). Because domestic trade was left relatively free and prices of consumer goods were only influenced through subsidies, commercial capitalists flourished (Cooper 1979: 499). The industrial bourgeoisie developed new activities to accumulate capital, especially as middlemen or subcontractors for the government (see Cooper 1983: 458). Without the full liquidation of the private sector, the growth of the public sector stimulated a proportional expansion of the subcontracting companies (al-Khafaji 2004: 247).

Thirdly, without any democratic supervision over the economy, the powerful state bureaucracy adopted more and more the consciousness and agency of an independent ruling class, treating the 'public' sector as its own property (Farah 2009: 36, 76). However, as a bureaucracy cannot reproduce itself legally as a private class it has to find footholds outside the 'public' sphere to safeguard its private interests (Richards and Waterbury 2008: 207–9). Nasserist state capitalism was unstable because in the long run it had 'an inherent tendency to divert resources to private hands ... and therefore it paved the road for economic liberalization irrespective of the intentions of its political leaders' (al-Khafaji 2004: 241). This tendency was reinforced by the appointment of former owners of private companies, such as construction mogul Osman Ahmed Osman, as managers of public companies. Fractions of state capital developed into private capitalist groups, and private capitalists (re)captured state power.

After the costly military intervention in Yemen (1963–67) and especially the disastrous Six Day War with Israel (1967) the political optimism of the Nasserist epoch was transformed into cynicism. Israel (and its emerging conservative partner Saudi Arabia) had functioned as the bridgehead of the US counter-revolution in the region (Kandil 2012: 94–5). The dream of 'Arab socialism' was shattered and the state had lost its ethico-political dimension. The organic crisis forced the leading stratum within the Nasserist bloc to change its accumulation strategy and the composition of its class alliances (Ayubi 1992: 99–100). Even though a democratization of the state was out of the question for the ruling clique, at the end of the 1960s there was a debate on the manner in which the economic crisis might be solved. One faction proposed reinforcing the authoritarian national–popular bloc by a further radicalization of the 'socialist' aspect of the regime, that is, the full nationalization and statification of the economy. This strategy of accumulation was opposed by those who wished to strengthen private actors through the liberalization of trade, the privatization of public companies, and the attraction of foreign investment (Beattie 2000: 12). These included wealthy landlords, industrial capitalists who had become managers of public companies, bureaucratic state elites that had emerged during the Nasserist era, high-ranking army officers, and commercial capitalists who wanted to expand their activities.

In any case, the Nasserist bloc was, in Gramsci's words: '"saturated": it not only does not expand – it starts to disintegrate; it not only does not assimilate new elements, it loses part of itself (or at least its losses are enormously more numerous than its assimilations)' (Gramsci 1971: 260; Q8§2). This remark followed Marx's observation that 'Society is saved just as often as the circle of its rulers contracts, as a more exclusive interest is maintained against a wider one' (Marx 1979a: 111–2). The governing stratum reduced its social base to the state apparatus, the bureaucratic and technocratic middle classes, and the army. To secure the support of these groups, import policy was changed, granting these groups expanded access to luxury consumer goods. Moreover, the first denationalizations were carried through in mid-1968, and licenses for private production quadrupled between 1967 and 1969. Incentives were given to the rural bourgeoisie to increase agricultural production (Cooper 1979: 484–8).

Through the influential and charismatic figure of Field Marshal Amer, the military had been able to continue its domination of domestic security until the Six Day War of 1967. Nasser used Amer's fall and the tainted prestige of the Armed Forces to reduce the army's authority to purely military matters. From 1967 onwards, the balance of power shifted from the Ministry of Defence to the Ministry of Interior (Kandil 2012: 92–3). To compensate for the military's retreat to the barracks and to counterbalance its power, the president created *Al-Amn al-Markazi*, the (General Security and) Central Security Forces (CSF) (Springborg 2009: 10). In addition, the civil *Amn al-Dawla*, the General Investigations Department (GID), was charged with internal repression.[10] Whereas the CSF was established as a direct and straightforward coercive state instrument to assault and disperse mass protests and strikes, the GID engaged in the selective detainment and torture of activists and political leaders.

When Nasser died in 1970, Egypt stood already at the threshold of an upturn of the class struggle. The military defeat of 1967 is often perceived as the harbinger of the downfall of Arab nationalism and its subsequent substitution by political Islam. Indeed, the Six Day War provoked an ideological crisis, but not the automatic victory of Islamism. On the contrary, it led to a huge popular mass movement, which lasted until the general uprising in 1977 (Farah 1986: 22–4). As early as February 1968 workers in Helwan went on strike against the light sentences received by the Egyptian officers who were considered responsible for the 1967 defeat. Workers from other workplaces and students from all Cairo's universities joined their protest (Anderson 2011). In November, students organized actions against education reform plans and in favour of an expansion of political freedoms, occupying Alexandria University. In 1969 mass meetings organized by leftists in Helwan gathered some 4,000 or 5,000 workers discussing political and economic issues (Posusney 1996: 220). The rising mass movement from below would come into conflict with neoliberal transformations from above.

Infitah and Class Struggle

When Anwar al-Sadat (1918–81) became president in 1970, he was deemed a transitional figure by the military and security ruling strata. Nevertheless the new president was able to strengthen his position by maintaining a balance between the powerful groups. With proof of an ASU conspiracy to remove him from the presidency and after ensuring he had Soviet support, Sadat started a top-down 'Corrective Revolution' between 1971 and 1972 that cleansed the political state apparatus of Nasserists who opposed his rule (Kandil 2012: 105–8). Sadat obtained a swift victory over the bureaucratic left, which failed to mobilize the masses to save its skin (Aoude 1994; Farah 1986: 27). In 1976 the ASU was split up into 'left', 'centre', and 'right' 'platforms', which later became independent parties. In 1977–78 Sadat created the National Democratic Party (NDP), which became the ruling party of Egypt. The new course was presented as a democratic revolution bringing 'supremacy of law, the state of institutions, the establishment of freedoms, and respect for the constitution' (Tucker 1978: 6). However, the multi-party system was merely a democratic façade for Sadat's personal dictatorship (Aoude 1994).

Sadat's 'counter-revolution in democratic form' legitimized the reduction and reconfiguration of the position of the military in the historical bloc, which had already begun under Nasser. The Egyptian state turned into a largely civil dictatorship of the police and the bureaucracy. After the Camp David negotiations of 1978, the Armed Forces also lost their military function within the new bloc, as from now on the United States would protect Egypt's sovereignty (Kandil 2012: 156–7). To appease the officers, Sadat granted them economic concessions. Facing budget cuts the Armed Forces began to diversify their income sources, engaging with manufacturing of weapons and civil consumer goods, agriculture, land reclamation, construction, and services. Consequently, the military–industrial complex became a more or less autonomous fraction of state capital (Alexander and Bassiouny 2014: 9, 55–6). By the mid-1990s half of its production was oriented towards the civil sector (Abdelrahman 2014: 22). From Caesarist overlords, the generals were transformed into petty capitalists, whose mediocre surpluses were artificially shielded from private and public competition: 'They have been granted concessions to run shopping malls in Egypt, develop gated cities in the desert and beach resorts on the coasts. And they are encouraged to sit around in cheap social clubs' (Amar 2012: 85).

Despite being sidelined as the active governing stratum, the Armed Forces remained the backbone of state power, reappearing in the streets to save the regime during the episodes of the 'bread riots' in 1977, the CSF conscripts' uprising in 1986, and, of course, in 2011 (Achcar 2013: 184–5).

Whereas workers and peasants had constituted the distorted class base of Nasserism, Sadat leaned heavily on private capital groups in order to 'solve' the problems of Egypt's economic base. The new president supported the market-oriented strategy of private capital accumulation and continued the process of economic liberalization and privatization that had already begun under Nasser in the late 1960s. This required a reconfiguration of the class alliances. Only two months after Nasser's death, large landowners were able to reclaim some of their sequestered lands (Kandil 2012: 160). Agricultural rents were raised for the first time since 1952 (Bush 2007: 1603). Private companies were legally protected against nationalization, public–private enterprises were regulated as private instead of public companies, and a number of 'free economic zones' were created that offered beneficial labour and tax conditions to foreign investors. As the global economic downturn began to affect the Egyptian economy the president announced in 1974 the *Infitah* (Open Door Policy), a programme of economic and political liberalization and reintegration in the capitalist world market, aimed at attracting foreign investment. The Infitah was accompanied by huge loans from the Arab oil states, the United States, and the International Monetary Fund (IMF), which demanded that the Egyptian state devalue the pound and cut subsidies on basic consumer goods. The Infitah initiated a new strategy of accumulation that reoriented Egypt's domestic economic structure along a neoliberal path, anticipating changes in the global economy (see Cox 1987: 219–44). Together with Pinochet's Chile, Sadat's Egypt pioneered the worldwide neoliberal shift in the Global South (Beinin 1999: 21; Callinicos 2011).

Sadat's counter-reforms persuaded many Muslim Brothers who had migrated to the Gulf countries during the Nasser era to return to Egypt, bringing with them petrodollars and social-conservative values. In the 1970s the Brotherhood had become an elite organization of a few hundred activists with strong ties to Saudi Arabia – the state that had become, together with Israel and the Shah's Iran, the main stronghold of US imperialism and counter-revolution in the region (Hanieh 2013: 27).

Brothers active in the liberalized financial and service sectors became a rising 'Islamic' business class, which rejected Western moral and cultural values, but embraced a free-market capitalist economy. By the 1980s the rising private sector was controlled by 18 families, of which eight had ties to the Brotherhood. About 40 per cent of all private economic ventures were connected with Ikhwan interests (Naguib 2009: 163). Because of its support for the Infitah and its enmity towards the left, the new Brotherhood gained the tacit approval of the Sadat regime. Together with state bureaucrats, military officers, and Infitah nouveaux riches the Brotherhood became a crucial vassal of Sadat's new hegemonic project (Naguib 2009: 162–3).

The Islamic bourgeoisie could not have become a social force without the mass support of Islamist students who came from rural areas and small towns (Farah 1986: 34–35). Thanks to state support, clientelism, violence, intimidation, a strong moral vision, and the failure of the left the Islamist student movement grew quickly (Beinin 2005a: 119). At the end of the 1970s *al-Gama'at al-Islamiyyat* (literally, 'the Islamic associations') had taken over the domination of the left on university campuses (Naguib 2009: 163–4). The withdrawal of the state from public services opened up new possibilities for the Islamists to expand their influence among the urban poor and impoverished middle classes. Rich Ikhwan patrons established their own charity organizations. Through the patron–client relations of these foundations the Islamic bourgeoisie was able to mobilize layers of the lower-middle classes, the 'lumpenin-telligentsia',[11] and the urban poor. Due to their exclusion from Sadat's emerging bloc, students and professionals from the South in particular were attracted to radical forms of Islamism. Once they had benefited from Nasser's land reform and free education; now, when they migrated to the cities, they lacked employment and social networks (Ates 2005: 137). Ironically, petrodollars and Infitah money financed the private Islamic welfare policies that had become necessary due to Sadat's privat-ization and liberalization politics, of which the Brotherhood bourgeoisie was the main beneficiary. Islamism came to represent the ideology of both those who were included in, and those who were excluded from Sadat's new hegemonic bloc.

As the Egyptian bourgeoisie was too weak to force an Israeli retreat from the Sinai, Sadat had to court the United States in order to solve the important question of the occupied lands. A reorientation of foreign policy, away from the Soviet Union and towards the United States, was a crucial addition to Sadat's domestic political realignment. The October War of 1973 improved Sadat's nationalist credentials and prestige and allowed him to negotiate a separate peace with Israel, switch sides in the bipolar world order, and become a loyal client state of the United States. The cost of the war was paid with new loans from the United States, Europe, and the Gulf, which demanded that Egypt sever ties with Moscow in return for their aid. Consequently, Sadat annulled the Soviet–Egypt Friendship Treaty in 1976 (Hanieh 2013: 31).

Sadat's breakdown of the Nasserist bloc along neoliberal lines signalled a strengthening of the position of both private and state capital fractions vis-à-vis labour. His capitalist offensive interpellated a strong reaction on the part of subaltern groups, especially the workers' and students' movements. The collapse of popular hegemony disconnected intellectuals and subaltern groups from the state: 'As soon as the dominant social group has exhausted its function, the ideological bloc tends to crumble away; then "spontaneity" may be replaced by "constraint" in ever less disguised and indirect forms, culminating in outright police measures and coups d'état' (Gramsci 1971: 60–1; Q19§24). From 1968 to 1973 the student movement formed the nucleus of the opposition movement, reflecting the global wave of revolt of May 1968. After the October War and the implementation of the Infitah, general living conditions deteriorated and as universities struggled to function normally political student activities collapsed (Anderson 2011). Economic malaise and labour unrest shifted the centre of gravity of the protests to the factories and workers' communities. Due to the success of Nasserist hegemony, workers had remained relatively passive during the 1950s and 1960s, but in the 1970s they started to move when their economic predicament worsened and the national–popular bloc collapsed. Privatization and liberalization of state companies, coupled with high inflation rates – an average of 25 to 30 per cent per annum – led to a process of deindustrialization (Kandil 2012: 161), an increase in unemployment – from 2.2 per cent in 1960 to 11 per cent in 1986 – and a decrease in real wages (Farah 2009: 39–41). A first wave of labour protests took place in 1971 and in 1972, primarily directed against the slow erosion of wages. The restoration of wage levels in 1972 and the October War in 1973 temporarily halted the strike activities, which were resumed in the autumn of 1974. Between 1975 and 1977 workers protested against the Infitah, which they perceived as an assault on the rights and concessions they had gained under Nasser (Posusney 1996: 220–2). In 1975 a series of clashes took place between workers and the police in urban areas and between evicted peasants and the security forces in the countryside. Students joined in the protests and marched on the People's Council, demanding democracy and the right to assembly, strike, demonstrate, and organize political parties (Lachine 1977: 4–5). Social and political demands were made at the same time.

In the public sector workers had kept their old leaders and preserved collective memories of the struggles of the 1940s and 1950s, which meant that they did not have to build their movement entirely from scratch. Meanwhile, the Egyptian left was reorganizing itself as a political force. During the second half of the 1970s and throughout the 1980s two parties encompassed the majority of leftist activists: Tagammu and the Egyptian Communist Party (ECP). From its inception, Tagammu had been a construct of the regime as it moved towards a controlled multi-party system. Tagammu was established in 1975 as the left wing of the ASU and turned into a full party in 1976. When Tagammu sided with the mass movement after the January riots of 1975, issuing declarations in favour of the right to strike and political freedoms, it was accused by Sadat of being a cover for illegal communists. Some 200 of its members were arrested (Lachine 1977: 5). In the same year when the Tagammu 'platform' was created, communists of various backgrounds closed ranks and founded the underground Egyptian Communist Party (ECP). ECP members succeeded in acquiring influential positions within the Tagammu apparatus. The ECP was itself a heterogeneous organization with various tendencies expressing the unresolved discussions that had dominated the Egyptian communist movement since the Second World War. Its membership consisted of the old cadres from the 1940s and 1950s and young militants, who had emerged from the post-1967 student movements (Farag 1999).

The implementation of IMF austerity measures resulted in price hikes, which provoked the spontaneous 'bread riots' of January 18–19 in Cairo in 1977 – the joint zenith of the neoliberal and subaltern war of movement. Industrial workers in Helwan struck and demonstrated in Tahrir Square. Leftist students joined workers in their protests, which quickly spread through the whole country, from Aswan to Alexandria. Even though the movement had started as a protest about everyday economic grievances, it soon raised demands of democracy and social justice (Beinin 1996: 250). Sadat's regime was shocked by the uprising and quickly restored the subsidies on basic consumer goods in order to disperse the spontaneous protests. The government denied the spontaneous nature of the insurrection and blamed 'secret communist organizations' for organizing the 'riots'. Sadat mobilized the police, security forces, and the army on the streets to stem the pre-revolutionary tide. Once the masses were demobilized, the state implemented a zero tolerance policy for street politics. Leftist newspapers were shut down and socialist, communist, and Nasserist leaders – especially those active in the workers' movement – were imprisoned (Posusney 1996: 237). New laws restricted mass political action and mandated life sentences for participation in demonstrations (Farag 2007).

That the masses could be quickly demobilized was due to the organizational and ideological weakness of the proletarian and national–popular organizations. Even though there was almost feverish political activity among workers and leftist activists during this decade, it was impossible in such a short period of time for the working class to develop itself, on its own, from its shattered, corporate condition into an independent hegemonic force (Beinin 1996: 261). The autonomous political expression of the working class had been eradicated during the Nasserist era and had to be forged in the struggle itself. This was complicated by the lack of understanding of leftists of the character of their opponents and their own tasks in the struggle. At the beginning of Sadat's reign, many leftists believed that his coming to power signalled a leftist shift in Egyptian politics. Even after the president's 'Corrective Revolution', communists still had illusions about Sadat's continuation of Nasser's national–popular bloc and only hesitantly (if at all) supported the workers' strikes in 1971 and 1972 (Beinin 1996: 256–7). The October War of 1973 postponed any critical reflection of the Marxist intelligentsia on the right-wing reconfiguration of the Nasserist historical bloc until the declaration of Infitah in late 1974. The left was shocked by Sadat's 'betrayal' of the Nasserist project. In the next few years, workers' actions were supported, but '[o]nce again, workers' struggles were represented by the Left as a component of the nationalist project, a front in the battle for economic self-determination' (Beinin 1996: 258). The left's organizational weakness, paternalist attitude towards the working class, and political myopia left it unprepared for a leading role in either the strike movements of 1975 and 1976 or the insurrection of 1977. Leftists were primarily occupied with issues of imperialism, Zionism, and national development, while the political consciousness of workers began with their concrete, everyday economic grievances and worries. The fact that most leftists courted the illusive 'national bourgeoisie' as allies in their anti-imperialist struggle did not help their rapprochement with the workers (Tucker 1978: 7). In short, the lack of a shared political project and language between leftists and workers blocked the organic formation of a counter-hegemonic alliance that offered solutions for the emancipation of workers and other subaltern groups.

The regime's fear of a repetition of the 'bread riots' slowed down the process of liberalization and privatization (Bayat 1993: 76–8). Although the spontaneous opposition had not been able to present itself as a counter-hegemonic force and transform the neoliberal bloc, it succeeded in turning Sadat's capitalist offensive into a more gradual and cautious transformation. Contingent changes in the Egyptian economic structure because of regional developments – especially the influx of rents and migration of labour to the Gulf countries – created room for a more molecular and gradual process of neoliberal reform (see Ayubi 1992: 100). The restoration of real wages combined with a targeted attack on militant worker leaders prevented major industrial action between 1977 and 1981 (Posusney 1996: 222).

Meanwhile, the repression of the 1977 insurrection and the Camp David negotiations with Israel increasingly alienated the Islamists from their patron, the Sadat state (Farah 1986: 126). Conversely, Sadat distanced himself from his erstwhile Islamic discourse and claimed that the Islamist student associations were funded and supported from abroad. The confrontation between the state and the radical Islamist groups, on the one hand, and the powerful example of the Iranian Revolution of 1979 on the other, led to a radicalization of Islamist groups. In 1981, at the yearly October War parade, four Islamists opened fire on Sadat, killing him.

Shades of Passive Revolution

The political trajectory of Egypt shows the nonsensicality of passive revolution as a specific, clearly delineated *type* of capitalist transition. The 1919 revolution, the 1952 Free Officers' coup, and Sadat's Infitah are not cosmetic iterations of basically the same phenomenon. Instead, what emerges is a cascade of qualitatively different passive revolutions, or, more correctly, a historical process for which the concept of passive revolution highlights the various forms in which the dynamic of permanent revolution is replaced by initiative from above. In the case of the 1919 revolution, popular initiative was displaced by the agility of British imperialism and the weakness of the Egyptian nationalist movement, which resulted in a 'bastard' bourgeois revolution that failed to solve the economic and political contradictions of Egypt's modernity. The 1952 'coup-revolution' presented a fundamentally different picture. Here permanent revolution was deflected, not by the craftiness of imperialism or domestic ruling groups, but by a 'third party'. Nasserism started as bourgeois Caesarism, substituting its military agency for that of the absent progressive bourgeoisie, but, because of internal and external imperatives, it increasingly became popular Caesarism. Although the reconfiguration of the historical bloc was directed from above in an authoritarian and coercive manner, it was nonetheless broadly supported by the subaltern groups, who conceived of the Nasserist regime as a particular 'Arab' organic passage to modernity.

Caesarism appears as a necessary conceptual addition to passive revolution in order to understand the ambiguity and complexity of the Nasserist episode. In contrast, Sadat's reconstitution of the Nasserist bloc was unambiguously counter-revolutionary, both in content and in form. Although he presented his reforms as a democratic revolution, thereby attempting to appropriate subaltern democratic demands, he did not succeed in creating a stable hegemony, based on a broad class alliance. Nasser's qualitative, progressive Caesarism turned into a reactionary dictatorship that merely served as the gestational carrier for new rentier capitalist groups.

Sadat's Infitah was meant to move the main burden of industrial development from the state to the private sector by activating domestic capital groups and attracting foreign investment. However, the privatization and liberalization process did not reinforce the position of industrial capital, but that of domestic and foreign commercial and financial capitalists. Despite a high economic growth of 8 per cent between 1975 and 1982, foreign investment was meagre and almost solely directed towards the development of tourism and the new private financial sector. In 1982 only 20 per cent of total investments went into manufacturing activities (al-Khafaji 2004: 278). Commercial capitalists were not interested in revolutionizing production, but followed the principle of 'buying cheap, selling dear' through trade and speculation, and by controlling local markets, real estate, and petty production units. They were able to function as mediators between foreign capital and local markets. Together with commercial capitalists, large landowners engaged in speculative activities, for the combination of high rental income and real estate property granted higher revenues. Due to their monopoly position and technological and infrastructural superiority, foreign industries were more competitive than their Egyptian counterparts. In the emerging free-trade regime their advantages increased. Due to a lack of labour-saving techniques and technological investments, along with the undesirability of a higher rate of exploitation, the integration of Egypt in US-dominated global circuits of capital rendered its economy even more dependent on foreign capital, aid, and imports.

Despite the failure of the ISI-model, the end of state-led industrialization, and the collapse of the Nasserist consensus, the public sector continued to expand until the mid-1980s and the regime was able to sustain its redistributive polices (Richards and Waterbury 2008: 190). State capitalism had given up its industrializing ambitions, but it was able to prolong its life-form through the accumulation of rents. From the second half of the 1970s, a steady stream of revenues from migrant workers' remittances from the Gulf region, foreign loans and aid, tariffs of the Suez Canal, oil, gas, and tourism, compensated the loss of income from the productive sectors. In practice, it was not the 'liberated' capital accumulation of the private sector, but state-controlled rent accumulation and distribution that became the economic backbone of Sadat's historical bloc. This 'rentier capitalism' served the interests of both 'public' bureaucrats and private capitalists: rents were accumulated and distributed centrally through the state on the basis of patron–client relations, while private capital entered the rent distribution process through subcontracting and the black market (Farah 1986: 115). In addition, a sizeable part of rents that escaped direct state control were absorbed by the Islamic banks and investment companies, fuelling the economic activities of the rising Islamic bourgeoisie (Mitchell 2002: 278).

In the 1960s the economic structure of the state had played a relatively progressive role in developing the means of production. The political society had subsumed the capitalist classes under its developmentalist project. From the 1970s onwards, the form of state capitalism remained, but its content was turned inside out. The state bureaucracy and Infitah bourgeoisie subsumed the state under their project of private rent accumulation. Neoliberal policies did not 'roll back' the state in favour of the market, but they instrumentalized state power according to the interests of the new ruling alliance. The cynical, direct patronage of the state replaced Nasserist leadership and prestige as the main pillar of the rulers' hegemony.

After the assassination of Sadat in 1981, his successor, Hosni Mubarak, leant on the rentier economic structure as a material scaffold for a transformism of the political opposition. Political prisoners were released, civil rights such as freedom of the press and of association were restored – to a degree – and in 1984 parliamentary elections were held. Relations with other Arabic nations, which had soured over the separate peace with Israel, were improved. This political 'détente' was not a process of 'democratization from above', but a tactical retreat of the dictatorship, leaving limited spaces open in civil and political society for contentious politics that remained subordinated to regime interests. Via the prolongation of emergency law, the state held civil society in a tight grip, banning strikes, demonstrations, and critical newspapers, and introducing military courts to deal with recalcitrant political opposition (see Marfleet 2011). The rules of the new democratic game were set by the government and the NDP. Elections were manipulated and voters were systematically bought or intimidated. The Political Party Committee systematically blocked the legalization of important political trends such as the Muslim Brothers, and it monitored and supervised parties even after their recognition. However, as long as the legal and illegal, secular and Islamist oppositions played along, they were tolerated.

Between 1976 and 1981, Tagammu had waged a fierce opposition against the Sadat state, building a membership of between 125,000 and 160,000 members (Tucker 1978: 7). Although Tagammu and the Egyptian left in general intervened in the 1977 insurrectionary movement, they were not able to organize, structure, and direct the masses against the power of the state. Some leftist leaders drew pessimistic conclusions about the potential of street politics to change the status quo. From 1984 onwards Tagammu participated in parliamentary elections, but this once mass party of the left with strong ties to the industrial working class only received a few per cent of the national vote. Government rigging was only one cause of the electoral defeat. Tagammu had acquired the right to compete in elections and to operate freely in the national political sphere in exchange for a moratorium on street politics. Without the ability to mobilize its traditional mass base, the party was cut off from its organic electorate. Ironically, whereas the absence of mass street politics convinced the leftist leadership that democratization had to come through negotiations with the regime, its reluctance to mobilize subaltern actors deprived them of any effective bargaining tool vis-à-vis the state (Howeidy 2006).

The cautious and molecular transformation of the Nasserist bloc in the first years of Mubarak's presidency was rendered possible because of the unexpected influx of rents, which stalled the need for a hard confrontation with labour, as happened in other nations in the Global South. Arguably, new loans and an increase in rentier income delayed the effects of the 'Volcker Shock'[12] for Egypt until the end of the 1980s. A mounting fiscal crisis from the second half of the 1980s onwards revealed the shaky economic base of the regime, forcing the Mubarak state on the offensive in order to restore rates of rentier income and profits. This class offensive created the foundations for the mass movements that eventually toppled Mubarak in 2011.

7. The 25 January Revolution

The Neoliberal Offensive

Until the mid-1980s the rentier economy supplied the Egyptian ruling classes with sufficient financial leeway to appease the popular classes. However, the collapse of oil prices diminished the influx of petrodollars from the Gulf region, and high inflation depressed real wages. A section within the Egyptian ruling class called for a far-reaching process of liberalization and privatization to fight rising inflation and to restore the rate of profit. Due to the fall in real wages and the threat of neoliberal reform, workers increased collective action from 1984 onwards. The actions of the workers' movement were primarily defensive and apolitical, aimed at achieving simple social demands and restoring their strong bargaining position vis-à-vis the state. Ideologically workers remained embedded in the Nasserist consensus, affirming their loyalty to the state by 'work-ins', 'during which management is ejected or ignored but workers continue running the factory on their own', rather than by 'work stoppages' (Posusney 1996: 223). As long as the state was able to fulfil its paternalist obligations, the illusion of populist politics could continue. Because of direct, 'vertical' state mediation – and violent repression – of labour conflicts through the GFETU and the police, there was little solidarity between factories in the same sector, let alone between different sections of the working class (Alexander 2012). The GFETU was caught between its loyalty to the Mubarak regime and its role as guardian of the Nasserist social reforms (Bayat 1993: 77–8). Nevertheless, the obstinacy of the labour bureaucracy, combined with grassroots working-class actions, slowed down the process of neoliberal reform.

Despite the injection of IMF-sponsored 'stabilization packages', at the end of the 1980s national debt rose to more than 38 billion USD in foreign obligations and the budgetary deficit increased to over 20 per cent (Richards and Waterbury 2008: 225). The Gulf War of 1991 led to the return of migrant workers to Egypt, who flooded the domestic labour market. It also resulted in the collapse of tourism, compounding the state's fiscal crisis, which was prompted by the regime's inability to pay back its military debts (Mitchell 2002: 276) and compounded by the liquidation of the Islamic investment bank sector (Roccu 2012: 123). Lastly, for the United States, the fall of Stalinism decreased the value of Egypt's geopolitical or 'mercenary' rent (see Achcar 2013: 73): that is, the price in loans and financial and military aid for its alliance with the Western bloc. Its geopolitical supremacy secured, US imperialism sought to integrate the economies of client nations such as Egypt in a more profoundly neoliberal way in the world market, reconstituting their labour markets as cheap reservoirs for US capital (see Hanieh 2013: 36–7; 59). The dry spell in traditional sources of rent income, combined with the reluctance of the state and private capital groups to invest in the productivity of agriculture and industry, left the Egyptian regime with only three options: finding new sources of external rent, increasing the rate of exploitation of labour (absolute surplus extraction), or the dispossession of public assets.

The Mubarak regime turned to the IMF and World Bank to save the economy from imminent bankruptcy (Farah 2009: 41). In 1991 Egypt accepted an Economic Reform and Structural Adjustment Programme (ERSAP) inspired by the neoliberal paradigm of the Washington consensus (Bush 2007: 1599). Whereas the Egyptian government had largely resisted the proposed economic reforms that came along with previous stabilization packages, now it embraced neoliberal recipes in order to implement far-reaching transformations of the economic base (Roccu 2012: 112). The IMF loan allowed the government to 'solve' the financial crisis of 1990–91 with a massive capital injection in the banking sector of 5.5 per cent of GDP and an additional fiscal exemption worth 10 per cent of GDP (Mitchell 2002: 279). In exchange, the ERSAP aimed to contain and decrease foreign debt and inflation, by cutting state subsidies on consumer goods, privatizing public companies, divesting state-owned shares in joint-venture banks, liberalizing markets and prices, freezing wages, commercializing agricultural lands, and implementing a flat tax. Neoliberal, 'market-oriented' reform became the discursive instrumentality of an increasingly narrow capitalist oligarchy that desired to restore the rate of profit (Abdelrahman 2014: 10).

The liberalization of agricultural prices and markets had already begun in 1987. The Egyptian government promoted 'a US farm-type model of extensive capital-intensive agriculture driven by market liberalisation, export-led growth and tenure reform' (Bush 2007: 1604). The underlying rationale of liberalization was that rising prices of agricultural produce would attract capital to invest in rural production. The state regarded landowners as willing allies in the realization of the free-trade policies of the IMF, which promoted cash crop production. As in the colonial era, the economic interests of large-scale landholders were tied to those of foreign capital groups, leading to the formation of a new agrarian bourgeoisie (Hanieh 2013: 88–9).

The Mubarak state abrogated Nasser's Agrarian Reform Law of 1952, granting former landowners the right to reclaim the lands that their families had lost during the redistribution policies of the 1950s and 1960s. After a five-year transition period, a New Tenancy Law came into effect in 1997: from then onwards, land rents were governed by market prices instead of the former fixed rent system. Rents increased by as much as 400 per cent (Bush 2007: 1606). In addition, landowners started to drive tenants from their land (Beinin 2001: 164). A majority of lands became fully owned by the landed elite and embedded in a modern capitalist system of cash-paid tenancies, allowing the landlords to accumulate capital at an accelerated rate (Bush 2009: 88–90). The livelihoods of some 5 million Egyptians were endangered by the New Tenancy Law as neoliberal reform in the countryside brought about a rise in land rents, the concentration of landholdings, and rural violence; landowners sent police troops and thugs to chase farmers from their lands.[1] The fragmented forms of resistance against the neoliberal land reforms organized by landless or small landholding farmers were violently repressed (Bush 2000, 239). By the mid-1990s, half of the rural population lived in poverty, an increase of 10 per cent in comparison to 1990 (Mitchell 1999: 463). By 2007 the neoliberal offensive in the countryside had resulted in '119 deaths, 846 injuries and 1409 arrests' (Bush 2007: 1606).

In the industrial sector, neoliberal reform began to dismantle the vertically integrated manufacturing sector, which had been the historical product of ISI strategies. Facing increasing global competition from cheaper East Asian commodities – produced with even lower wages – the public manufacturing sector needed more investments. Nevertheless, state companies were deliberately put at a disadvantage vis-à-vis private enterprises in order to force their bankruptcy and subsequent privatization. A new Ministry of Investments was established, which became the primary executor of the privatization process. Selling shares of state-owned enterprises on the Cairo stock market created an economic mini-boom in 1996–97. The state earned 1.5 billion USD from these privatizations. Public holding companies remained the largest shareholders in many of the privatized enterprises. Some privatized firms were sold to public banks. State holding companies set up private corporations or joint ventures. State elites became investors in large private-sector enterprises or used state power to favour their friends and families in the subcontracting sector, realizing huge profits (Mitchell 2002: 280–281). Between 1993 and 1999 over 100 factories passed into private hands (Beinin 2005b). By 2002 half of the public enterprises were privatized or liquidated (Richards and Waterbury 2008, 251). After 2004, a new cabinet headed by prime minister Ahmed Nazif stepped up the privatization and liberalization process. Corporate taxes were halved in 2005, from 40 to 20 per cent of earnings, whereas personal taxes were raised, especially those on housing. Private firms enjoyed the flat tax of 20 per cent while the public sector had to pay double (Farah 2009: 49–50). These aggressive policies resulted in an economic growth of between 5 and 7 per cent (Beinin 2009: 30). In 2008 the World Bank and the International Finance Corporation recognized Egypt as the 'World's Top Reformer' (Hanieh 2013: 52).

Economic growth partly reflected a neoliberal development of 'extended reproduction'. The growth path of large public-sector manufacturing units with strong traditions of state-supervised collective bargaining was replaced by the neoliberal model of smaller workplaces exploited by private capital, employing an often young workforce lacking class organization and experience. These units of production were located in new industrial cities such as 10th of Ramadan City, 6th of October City, Sadat City, etc. (Alexander and Bassiouny 2014: 76).

Conversely, privatization and liberalization represented a new form of the existing rentier strategy of accumulation, but now driven by the active dispossession of public assets and by an increase of absolute surplus extraction. State factories were sold far beneath their actual value (Farah 2009: 49–50). It was a myth that public-sector companies were unprofitable: 'In 1989/90, on the eve of the reforms, 260 out of 314 non-financial state-owned enterprises were profitable and only 54 were making losses' (Mitchell 1999: 458). Selling these valuable productive assets, however, resulted in quick and easy (yet unsustainable) profits, both for private actors and the state. The rate of exploitation in the industrial public sector was driven up as real wages dropped by 8 per cent between 1990 and 1996 (Mitchell 2002: 280; 286). Privatization often led to mass firing of workers, with the aim of increasing productivity. As in the countryside, neoliberal reform in the industries did not encourage investment. The process of dispossession did not enhance the rate of capital accumulation, but increased surplus extraction in the form of rents. Capital was directed to the construction of real estate, the production of luxury goods, and grand schemes such as the *Toshka* irrigation project, rather than invested in export-oriented industrial production (Mitchell 1999: 457). Public services were outsourced to the private and often informal sector: 'Tuk-tuks and microbus services save the state having to provide mass transport systems for the poor, just as private lessons are primarily a subsidy from working-class and poor parents to make up for teachers' low pay' (Alexander and Bassiouny 2014: 93).

Cutting back on public services, subsidies, and wages decreased the purchasing power of the workforce. In 1998 it was estimated that 70 per cent of the workers in the private sector lived in poverty (see Farah 2009: 44). The destruction of employment in the public sector was not compensated by new jobs in the private sector. In general, unemployment between 1998 and 2006 did not increase, as people either engaged in subsistence production, or joined the informal sector, which was often characterized by low wages and adverse working conditions. Rising food prices, exacerbated by the 2007–08 global financial crisis, put further pressure on the purchasing power of the majority of the population (Hanieh 2013: 146).

The Mechanical State

The neoliberal strategy of accumulation initiated a new era of intensified class confrontation and increased authoritarianism, since it required not only changes in the economic structure, but also a corresponding political reconfiguration of the historical bloc: that is, the exclusion of subaltern forces and the subduing of subordinate fractions of the capitalist class (see Abdelrahman 2014: 16–20). Neoliberal reform represented a global capitalist offensive, not only by rolling back 'Fordist' and 'developmentalist' social gains, but also by undermining or even dismantling the democratic form of the bourgeois state. The constitution of authoritarian states or open dictatorships in countries such as Chile, South Korea, and Turkey was directly related to the transition to a neoliberal strategy of accumulation. Adam Hanieh observed with insight that in Tunisia, Ben Ali's coup in 1987 'marked the real commencement of neoliberalism' (Hanieh 2013: 64).

Standing squarely behind private capitalists and landlords, the Mubarak state undermined the traditional patron–client relations between the subaltern groups and the ruling classes. In political society, direct state control over elections and parliament was increased. The electoral law was changed to the disadvantage of the Brotherhood, which, together with most other opposition parties, boycotted the 1990 parliamentary elections. The state tightened its grip over civil society as well. When the Brotherhood obtained majorities in the doctors', journalists', and bar associations, the government put all professional syndicates under direct state supervision (Abdalla 1993). From 1995 onwards, Ikhwan activists, student leaders, and members of parliament were systematically arrested, intimidated, detained, and tortured. In addition, journalists and human rights activists were increasingly brought before court and tried. In 1999 the government decreed that to operate legally in Egypt all NGO-type organizations must reapply for licences. NGOs that engaged in political activities were banned (Mitchell 1999: 456).

The state presented its coercive political project as a necessary anti-Islamist and anti-terrorist alliance in order to incorporate Western governments and frightened secular nationalist, liberal, and leftist intellectuals in its hegemony. The war against the Islamists was strongly articulated in the domain of cultural politics, with secular intellectuals and parties playing the part of the state's enlightened allies against the dark forces of religious reaction. The government integrated intellectuals into its project by (re)building and (re)financing cultural institutions such as the Cairo Book Fair,[2] the Cairo Opera, and the Alexandria Library, and by opening up new money streams and platforms for writers and artists: 'Thus, within a decade, the state went from being one of the chief obstacles to cultural production, to one of its chief protectors and subsidizers' (Colla 2011). This anti-Islamist alliance between regime and subordinated 'secular' opposition forces would resurface after the 2011 uprising.

The neoliberal reconstitution of the historical bloc also reconfigured relations of power between the ruling groups. Since the 1970s, the political power of the Armed Forces within the Egyptian state had decreased. Through military aid, the United States helped to transform the military in a docile and reliable state structure that functioned as a guardian of the status quo. However, the financial and military dependence on the United States also created feelings of resentment among nationalist officers towards their foreign donors (Amar 2012). Moreover, the position of the military in Egyptian society was crumbling, while the NDP and the Interior Ministry emerged as the primary structures of state power. In 1986, under the leadership of Major General Abd al-Halim Abu Ghazala the Armed Forces had graciously saved the Mubarak regime from a CSF conscripts' uprising. This was to be the last 'national' act of the military until 2011, as Mubarak cleverly pre-empted the formation of charismatic military leaders in the following two decades (Kandil 2012: 179–81).

On the eve of the 25 January Revolution, the Interior Ministry controlled all aspects of law enforcement, criminal investigations and repression through its various departments: State Security Investigations Sector (SSIS), Public Security, Municipal Police, Special Police, General Security and Central Security Forces (CSF), Traffic Police, Tourism and Antiquities Police, and so on. In the 2000s the civil security apparatus counted a staggering total of 2 million affiliates, which meant that roughly one in 40 Egyptians was associated in one way or another with the police. The numbers of the 'ordinary' police forces grew from 150,000 in 1974 to more than 1 million in 2002 (Kandil 2012: 194). The hated

SSIS or *Amn al-Dawla* numbered some 3,000 officers (Kandil 2011), who infiltrated, controlled, and terrorized political opposition groups and thus constituted the first line of defence of the state, preventing protest movements rather than containing them. When political or social protest did emerge, the CSF, which had grown to a body of 450,000 conscripts, rivalling the number of military troops, was mobilized to quickly and brutally subdue it (Kandil 2012: 194). The *Amn al-Markazi* was equipped with armed personnel carriers (APCs), rubber bullets, water cannons, and tear gas canisters. From the end of the 1980s onwards, the CSF enjoyed the support of informal plainclothes police, or *baltageyya*: 'a million and a half ... hired thugs or informers without uniform or ranks, often people with a criminal record who had cut deals with the authorities' (Kandil 2011). The *baltageyya*'s job was to intimidate voters, beat up, abuse and rape criminal suspects and political activists, break up demonstrations, etc. (Abdelrahman 2014: 19–20). In contradistinction to the military, the CSF and the plainclothes police were an apolitical, disloyal, and undisciplined force. Because of their low morale and morality, this blunt instrument was only effective if it could be mobilized in great numbers, surrounding and overrunning any opposition (Khalil 2012: 39). Failure to execute this simple tactic would result in demoralization and retreat, as eventually happened during the uprising on 28 January 2011. Apart from the direct and centrally coordinated repression by the SSIS and CSF, the terror through which the state governed was also rooted in everyday, decentralized, and local forms of violence. Police forces engaged in independent activities of exploitation, oppression, and domination of ordinary civilians, drug running, the organizing of protection rackets, and other criminal activities (Amar 2012).

Furthermore, in the 1990s and 2000s the *economic* power of the Armed Forces was overshadowed by the rise of neoliberal businessmen surrounding the president's son Gamal Mubarak, who were perceived by the generals as 'crony capitalists' and greedy plunderers of the nation's wealth – even though military state capital constituted as much a pillar of neoliberal reform as these parvenus (Alexander and Bassiouny 2014: 56). Kandil emphasized that the economic profits of the Armed Forces were modest compared to those of the 'civilian' state elites:

> [T]hey were given projects that would provide profits which could fund a decent life for officers: a car, a flat, a vacation house, and so on. But this is no economic empire on the scale the Turkish army has built up, for example. It is a much more modest enterprise. Military facilities are quite shabby compared with what is on offer in the wealthy districts of Cairo. Officers have not grossly enriched themselves. What

you gain in the army or air force pales in comparison to what you can get as a senior police officer or member of the ruling party. Under Mubarak, the Minister of the Interior stashed over $1 billion in his bank account. The Minister of Defence could not dream of that kind of money. (Kandil 2011)

Neoliberal reform in Egypt did not at all entail a 'retreat' of the state from the 'economic field', but a redirection of state power and resources towards an increased accretion of rents via an aggressive policy of dispossession, which only benefitted global capital and a small clique within the Egyptian ruling classes. The state lost its function and position as 'universal capitalist'. It no longer mediated between different fractions of capital (see Alexander and Bassiouny 2014: 4–5), instead becoming the obedient tool of a particular and select group of oligarchs around Mubarak who were closely connected to sources of foreign financial capital. The state also lost its semblance of representation of the interests of the subaltern classes. The chemical relation between state, ruling stratum, and society was increasingly replaced by a mechanical ensemble of classes (see Chapter 4). The increasing reliance on direct domination instead of political, cultural, or managerial leadership, and only a limited transformism of political opposition forces, provoked a growing resistance among the popular masses and even some factions of the bourgeoisie who were excluded from state power and its economic benefits.

The Process of Revolution

Since the 25 January uprising, many scholars have stressed that revolution cannot be reduced to a single event (for example Abdelrahman 2014; Alexander and Bassiouny 2014; Beinin 2013b), but that instead it constitutes a protracted process that consists of many events and moments (see Chapter 4). The Egyptian Revolution cannot be reduced to the 18 Days. This is an important insight, for the conceptual conflation of *thawra* (revolution) and *intifada* (insurrection) served the agenda of counter-revolutionary forces, which argued that after the mass mobilizations that caused the fall of Mubarak the 'revolution' was finished and the masses could leave politics in the capable hands of professionals. Moreover, revolution is a temporally, socio-geographically, and politically *uneven* process. Popular initiative moves forward and backward, in gradual steps and sudden leaps, in reaction to victories, defeats, hopes and (dis)illusions, which characterize the pace and direction of revolution as punctuated and non-linear. Within the revolution, discrete – often spatially bounded – groups move ahead of or behind the whole of the movement, creating a temporal differentiation *within* the process. Furthermore, different social and/or geographical groups are faced with different obstacles, learn collectively through different experiences, and advance different slogans, programmes, and aims throughout the process. The unevenness of revolution means that the development of the popular masses into a social force can become accelerated, if the vanguard succeeds in bringing the whole movement up to its speed, or retarded, if static or slow-moving elements fetter progress.

From an objectivist perspective (see Chapter 4) revolutions are defined *post factum* by their outcomes. However, activists who find themselves in the middle of the revolutionary process don't have the luxury of hindsight and have to take a subjectivist point of view. From the subjectivist angle, the process of revolution consists of three phases. Firstly, a drawn-out prehistory of the molecular accumulation of movements and collective actions that lead up to a 'revolutionary situation'. Yet the self-conscious conceptualization of revolution begins in its second phase, marked by open insurrection and the entrance of the masses as active forces in the streets. The confusion between revolution and uprising flows from the fact that the actors only become conscious of their activity as a revolution in the middle of the process. Revolution is not created by the event of the mass uprising, which constitutes the (crucial) *transition* towards a massification and explicitation of already existing activities of resistance (De Smet 2014d). The third phase is the unwinding of the revolutionary process, when the insurgents have to establish their own state and hegemony after the destruction of the old state power.

In Egypt, the long duration of revolution and counter-revolution spanned several decades, creating different revolutionary movements that were disassembled and reassembled in response to reconfigurations of the Egyptian historical bloc. The last forward thrust of this historical ebb and flow entailed the resurgence of politics 'from below' in the decade before 25 January 2011. The rise of Islamist movements and a reluctance to 'go back to the streets' in the 1990s drove the leaders of leftist parties such as Tagammu and the ECP even further into the arms of the regime. After the repression of the 1977 insurrection the prospect of mass mobilization had been greeted with cynicism by party leaders: in the 1990s and 2000s, with Islamism on the rise, it was anticipated with dread – Tagammu chairman Rifaat al-Said claimed that the Brotherhood was the only organization capable of 'controlling' a mass movement (Farag 2007). By the year 2000, the integration of Tagammu's leaders into the Mubarak consensus had reduced the active cadre of this historical party of the left, once counting some 200,000 members, to a few hundred. The party lost its traditional influence in the universities, professional syndicates, and trade unions. When I spoke in 2009 to Husayn Abd al-Razek, a leader of the old guard in Tagammu, he admitted that 'for years, Tagammu took no initiatives whatsoever, people only sat in the party's headquarters and in the offices of the newspaper, discussing, not taking any action to the streets' (personal communication with H. Abd al-Razek, 12 April 2009).

However, in the 1980s leftist activists became increasingly dissatisfied with the transformism of Tagammu and the ECP by the state. At the end of the 1980s a group of young Marxists set up a reading group, criticizing the Stalinist traditions of the Egyptian communist movement. This informal political circle was in 1991 formally established as the Revolutionary Socialists (RS) (personal communication with M. Bassiouni, 12 October 2010). The rapprochement between Tagammu leaders and the Mubarak regime also alienated Nasserists and leftist nationalists. In 1992 they split from Tagammu and founded the Arab Democratic Nasserist Party (ADNP). In 1996 a group led by Hamdeen Sabahi left the ADNP, establishing the Karama (Dignity) party. Al-Karama oriented itself to street politics and participated in alliances with other political forces against the government. Other communists and leftists withdrew from the political arena altogether and engaged with movements from below through NGO-type organizations. Yussef Darwish and Kamal Abbas, for example, established in 1991 the Helwan-based Centre for Trade Union and Workers' Services (CTUWS), focusing on offering services, solidarity campaigns, and education to workers (Beinin and Hamalawy 2007). Within a few years the CTUWS was also active in other industrial areas, such as 10th of Ramadan City, Mahalla, and Nag Hammadi. The foundation of the CTUWS anticipated the rise of civil-democratic NGOs and human rights centres in the 1990s, of which the Hisham Mubarak Law Centre (HMLC) was one of the most influential. HMLC was established in 1999 to defend the rights of workers and political activists. The centre offered legal advice, contacts with the media, and support in court cases, as well as organizing seminars to raise awareness among workers of their labour rights. In the 2000s the centre's Cairo offices would host meetings of political committees, movements, and parties, such as 6 April and Tadamon (Solidarity), thereby becoming a hub of the democratic opposition in the next decade (personal communication with K. Ali, 13 October 2010).

The second half of the 1990s saw an increasing cooperation between leftist, Nasserist and Islamist groups at a grassroots level, especially in the Cairo and Ayn Shams universities. This cooperation tended to arise around a shared anti-imperialist and anti-Zionist agenda (Abdelrahman 2009: 42; Schwedler and Clark 2006: 10). Still, activists remained largely isolated from the subaltern masses. The real turning point for a resurgence of Egyptian 'politics from below' came with the Second Palestinian Intifada in the autumn of 2000. Students organized massive demonstrations in Cairo in support of the plight of the Palestinians – collective action 'from below' that ended two decades of political demobilization. Independent activists and some 20 NGOs established the Egyptian Popular Committee in Solidarity with the Palestinian Intifada (EPCSPI) (Howeidy 2005). The EPCSPI became a social and political network that, under pressure of international and domestic events, spawned new movements. It also became a platform for political discussion, coordination, and cooperation between leftist, Nasserist, and Islamist activists (Abdelrahman 2009: 42–4).

The war in Afghanistan in 2001 and the looming intervention in Iraq gave a new impetus to the movements. In January and February 2003 small rallies in Cairo and other cities protested against preparations for military intervention against Iraq, followed on 20 and 21 March by a mass protest of 20,000 Egyptians occupying Tahrir Square (Schwedler and Clark 2006: 10). This rally saliently signalled the return of mass politics to Egypt (Abdelrahman 2009: 43). Over the course of the following months, the anti-war and Palestinian solidarity movements began to tackle domestic issues. In September 2004, the 20 March Movement, the Muslim Brotherhood, the ECP, al-Karama, HMLC, and other organizations established the Popular Movement for Change with a slogan demanding free and democratic presidential elections. On 12 December the Popular Movement organized the first explicit anti-Mubarak demonstration. Although it mobilized only 300 to 400 activists, at the time the event constituted a landmark in Egyptian street politics for its bold criticism of the president (Howeidy 2005). On 21 February 2005 Kefaya (Enough) was established as a unitary movement of existing committees and campaigns.

Kefaya galvanized layers of the urban youth and created a momentum for contentious politics. Young and militant members of the Muslim Brotherhood were increasingly engaged with this civil-democratic movement, collaborating with leftist activists and progressive journalists from *al-Badil, al-Shorouk, al-Dostour*, and *al-Masry Al-Yawm*. The rise of internet activism further encouraged political discussion, the dissemination of information, and the mobilization of protest groups (Hirschkind 2011). The activists and networks that emerged from this civil-democratic movement would eventually become the organizers of the first, small-scale demonstrations on 25 January 2011 (Joya 2011: 369).

Yet in 2006 Kefaya appeared to be far from the spiritual and activist spark that would ignite a revolution some five years later. Firstly, the regime did not remain passive but actively countered the growing movement. At the beginning of the 2000s the government had attempted to co-opt the Palestinian solidarity campaign. As the protests grew in numbers and their goal shifted towards a criticism of domestic policies, the regime felt increasingly threatened. The CSF began to arrest hundreds of protesters and Muslim Brotherhood members and violently repressed peaceful Kefaya demonstrations. Moreover, the regime changed the constitution so that the president could be elected directly, pre-empting one of the chief demands of the civil-democratic movement. At the same time, it made sure that Mubarak would succeed himself as president. Secondly, as a loose movement, Kefaya lacked a real directional centre. It was scattered over bickering political families and prone to sectarian infighting. Thirdly, because it only expressed *political* demands, Kefaya remained largely confined to the social circles of students, intellectuals (in the non-Gramscian sense), urban professionals, and other middle-class groups (Mackel 2012: 21; Naguib 2011). The movement did not succeed in connecting its explicitly political, anti-Mubarak rhetoric with the social concerns of the working class, the poor, and the peasantry. Nevertheless, the state did not have time to rejoice in the collapse of the civil-democratic movement, as the demise of Kefaya was intersected by the rise of the workers' movement, which would pose an even greater challenge.

Diminishing bargaining power, the threat of privatization, increased exploitation, and repression of labour rights stimulated worker protests (Solidarity Center 2010: 47–55). At first, workers in the public sector called on the state to take up its traditional responsibility, using their tried tactic of the 'work-in' (see above). However, because of the neoliberal breakdown of Nasserist patron–client relations in the workplace, the 'work-in' had become an anachronism. Neither the management nor the government was interested in working–class displays of loyalty. While there were important and militant worker actions in the 1990s and early 2000s, the struggle of the textile workers of the Misr Spinning and Weaving Company in the Nile delta city of Mahalla al-Kubra can be seen as a turning point for the Egyptian working class, because of the scale, the intensity, the success, and the impact of the protests (see De Smet 2012, 2015). The industrial complex in Mahalla is of economic and symbolic importance to the whole Egyptian workers' movement. Since its foundation in 1927, Ghazl al-Mahalla has often acted as the vanguard of the working class, initiating important strikes and articulating the interests of the whole Egyptian working class (Beinin and Hamalawy 2007). Whenever Mahalla workers won an industrial victory, this led to a general upturn of industrial action in the whole of Egypt.

On 3 March 2006 prime minister Ahmed Nazif promised all public-sector manufacturing workers an increase in their annual bonus equal to a two-month wage. However, the Ghazl al-Mahalla management and the minister of labour refused to pay out the promised bonus. The workers refused their salaries and on 7 December at least 10,000 workers protested in front of the factory gates. When the security forces tried to shut down the factory the next morning, some 20,000 workers demonstrated. Their rally was joined by students and women from the urban community (Beinin and Hamalawy 2007). After four days the strikers were victorious, gaining a 45-day bonus and a promise that the factory would not be privatized. In the last week of September 2007 the workers of Mahalla went on strike again demanding a further increase in their bonuses and food allowances, a rise in the national minimum wage to 1,200 EGP, and the resignation of the management – and they were victorious (Mackell 2012: 23). The strike lasted for six days and ended in a victory for the workers, who gained a two-month bonus along with extra bonuses in January and June 2008 and January 2009. Additionally, they succeeded in impeaching the trade union leaders who were too close to the regime, and in reducing factory debt by one billion EGP. The strike spirit also took hold of workers in various other sectors and governorates, such as the cement industry in Tura and Helwan, Cairo subway drivers, bakers, and so on (Beinin and Hamalawy 2007). In contrast to the 1980s and 1990s, the strikes were not restricted to public-sector employees, but also encouraged workers in private companies to struggle for their rights (Beinin 2009: 38–9).

In February 2008, once more, some 20,000 workers and citizens took the streets of Mahalla. The factory had claimed a loss of 45 million EGP, despite a capital injection of 450 million EGP. On 6 April 2008, leftist worker leaders and activists planned a new strike. Some political groups, bloggers and intellectuals seized on the event to call for a political 'general strike' against the regime, without, however, organizing anything on the ground. A combination of repression and co-optation – the regime pledged to accede to some of the workers' demands – put pressure on the strike committee to cancel the strike. In the end, Mahalla workers and their families participated in street protests as citizens, shifting their demands to the high price of bread (Beinin 2011: 199). They were met by violence and the insurrection was quelled. While there were some symbolic solidarity actions in other cities, in general the adventurist call for a 'mass strike' was not heeded and the Mahalla uprising remained isolated (personal communication with S. Habib, 12 November 2010).

However, the Mahalla protests had initiated a new wave of workers' actions that did not simply subside after 6 April 2008, engulfing other workplaces and sectors and setting in motion a process of molecular change in the whole working class (personal communication with S. Barakat, 16 October 2010). A shared demand for a minimum wage united the Egyptian workers' movement – at least conceptually. Moreover, the movement found a new model for struggle and organization in the form of the Real Estate Tax Authority Union (RETAU), which even before the 25 January Revolution inspired other workers, such as teachers, health technicians, nurses, pensioners, etc., to create at least the seeds of their own independent trade unions. From 2009 onwards workers also increasingly protested in front of parliament, physically inserting their local strikes into the space of national politics. Two main economic demands emerged from the sit-ins: for a fair minimum wage, and for expanded rights for the temporarily employed (personal communication with K. Ali, 25 October 2010).

In conclusion, before the 25 January uprising there was already an independent and vibrant workers' movement in Egypt. Between 2004 and 2010 some 2 million workers had gone on strike (Clément 2011: 71). The organized workers' movement was the main force within a broad social movement gathering 'workers, farmers and almost everybody else' (Abdelrahman 2014: 52). Since the state had given up on its commitment to full employment, the steady decrease and proletarianization of the agricultural workforce was not compensated with an increase in industrial jobs. Whereas the contribution of manufacturing to GDP was higher in 2007 than in 1982, the number of workers in the industrial sector had declined (Alexander and Bassiouny 2014: 66–70). The formal and informal 'services' sector absorbed a large part of proletarianized labour. Apart from the proletarian class in its strict sense of those engaged in wage labour, other subaltern actors, such as dispossessed peasants,[3] street vendors, taxi drivers, the unemployed, housewives, and the urban poor, protested against the collapse of state services, diminishing purchasing power, and the breakdown of social rights, by occupying their land, blocking roads, vandalizing government buildings, and marching in the streets. Although these movements represented distinct social groups, they primarily mobilized on the basis of class demands and an agenda of social emancipation. They offered subaltern groups experience in organizing and protesting, self-educating and preparing them for the revolutionary uprising in 2011. Nevertheless, the ad hoc, local, and fragmentary character of their collective action meant that they could not play a hegemonic role in a subaltern bloc against the regime.

Mubarak's neoliberal offensive propelled workers and other subaltern actors into action, but at the same time the dictatorial character of the state restricted their capacity to organize themselves (Bassiouny and Omar 2008). The regime was not a passive obstacle, waiting to be overcome by the workers' movement, but an active force that continuously undermined its development. The crushed Mahalla uprising on 6 April 2008 served as a warning for the industrial core of workers not to challenge state power. At the same time it was a clear message that the workers' movement had to face the political character of its predicament – capital organized as state power – if it wanted to continue and complete its emancipatory struggle. An alliance with the civil-democratic movement was a necessary step in this process.

25 January

The generalization of discontent was accelerated in 2010 by events such as the murder of Khaled Said and the massive fraud of the November parliamentary elections. Khaled Said was an ordinary 28-year-old man from Alexandria who was brutally beaten to death by two policemen. After post-mortem pictures showing Said's battered face went viral on social media, the police's cover-up story that he had choked to death attempting to swallow a packet of hashish was revealed as a fabrication. The death of Said served as an example of the violent degeneration of the state that was supposed to protect the 'common good'. In addition to the centralized state attacks on political and human-rights activists, workers' and farmers' movements, local police officers habitually harassed, tortured, and extorted ordinary citizens (Amar 2011; Marfleet 2011). Moreover, the security apparatus had grown bolder in these attacks, not only dragging its victims to police stations and detention centres, but also terrorizing them openly in the public sphere – beating them in the streets, cafes, and workplaces (Abdelrahman 2014: 19). There was a growing indignation within the populace and an understanding that their oppression and exploitation by petty bureaucrats and administrators were only the local and everyday expressions of the corruption of the whole regime. The behaviour of the policemen who assaulted Khaled Said was not denounced because it was an aberration, but because it had become standard practice among state representatives. Terror had become the essence of the Mubarak state. The murder of Said spurred on middle-class youth to organize and protest against the police state, through Facebook groups such as 'We Are All Khaled Said', established by Google employee Wael Ghoneim, and '6th of April Youth Movement'.[4]

If the murder of Khaled Said served as an example of the rottenness of the system at the local level, the parliamentary elections of November 2010 became a symbol of the complete hubris of the rulers and their estrangement from society. Thanks to 'gerrymandering, intimidation, detention of opponents (especially Muslim Brotherhood members), old-fashioned [vote] rigging, physical violence – any and all means possible' (al-Bendary 2011), Mubarak's NDP secured 209 of the 211 seats in the first round of voting (BBC News, 7 December 2010). The Muslim Brotherhood, the biggest opposition force in parliament, almost magically lost all but one of its 88 seats. In the past, parliamentary elections had offered the regime an aura of legitimacy and a means for distributing favours and reinforcing patron–client relations with political and economic groups. Since the 1980s, one of the strengths of the Mubarak regime had been its ability to include and absorb political opposition forces. Now, the stubborn and disdainful rejection by the NDP's leaders of any meaningful concession for the opposition came, ironically, at a moment when the regime's overall hegemony was at a historical low point: 'The government's actions seemed rash, clumsy, and a little panicked. It simply wasn't the sort of thing a confident dictatorship does' (Khalil 2012: 103). The obsession of the inner NDP circle with the creation of an obedient parliament that would secure Gamal Mubarak's succession to power, combined with a supercilious and anxious refusal of any substantive democratic reform, spelled the end of the regime. The elections prompted huge protests in the Canal town of Suez, which anticipated the protests of 25 January 2011 and the vanguard role that this community would play throughout the insurrection (personal communication with S. Omar, 18 March 2011).

After an authoritarian reign of 24 years, on 14 January 2011 Tunisian president Zine al-Abidine Ben Ali was forced to resign and flee to Saudi Arabia. Weeks of largely peaceful mass protests had brought the dictatorship to its knees. Like other activists, Gihan Shabeen of the Socialist Renewal Current (SRC) emphasized the importance of Tunisia as a source of inspiration for the Egyptian revolution: 'Since twenty years ago we couldn't convince people that things would change through the people's power itself. Tunisia changed everything. We all saw on television how Egypt could change' (personal communication with G. Shabeen, 16 March 2011). The Tunisian example offered the Egyptian masses a glimpse of their own revolutionary potentiality (see Khalil 2012: 123). All that was needed was a spark that would allow this potentiality to develop into actuality. The 25 January protests became the catalyst of this revolutionary process.

An 'unlikely alliance of youth activists, political Islamists, industrial workers and hardcore football fans' (Shenker 2011a) felt confident to call on the Egyptian people to rise in protest on National Police Day, a national holiday on 25 January. The holiday had been established in

2010 and commemorated the Battle of Ismailia on 25 January 1952, when police officers had sided with the anti-colonial resistance against the British occupation forces. Ironically, the liberators of 1952 who were honoured on Police Day had become the loathed epitome of the oppressive state (al-Bendary 2011). As early as 2010, 6 April activists had organized a protest against the police (Khalil 2012: 122).

Mobilization towards the 'Day of Rage' was organized through grassroots organizations and virtual networks. In cyberspace, the two main mobilizing forces were the '6th of April Youth Movement' and the 'We Are All Khaled Said' Facebook networks. Whereas the Khaled Said group was the more popular one, the 6 April network still had some 70,000 members and a more political profile, including both social and democratic demands. 'We Are All Khaled Said' issued the call for a march against torture, corruption, poverty, and unemployment on 25 January, and the 6 April Movement quickly joined its initiative. Facebook users changed their profile pictures to indicate symbolic support for the protest. The call to protest from the new social media was strengthened by leftist e-zines such as *al-Badil* (The Alternative). Apart from these appeals by both the new and the traditional media, the mobilization of thousands of protesters was realized through the organizing activities of political movements.

There were four political tendencies that prepared for the Day of Rage, using the traditional means of face-to-face meetings of activists, distribution of pamphlets, and so on. The first tendency consisted of youths of the Muslim Brotherhood, who decided to join the demonstration against the wishes of the Society's leadership (Kandil 2011). The second group was made up of leftist activists: young members of traditional parties such as Tagammu and the ECP, and militants of new movements such as the RS and the SRC. The supporters of Muhammad al-Baradei and the National Association for Change (NAC) constituted a third faction, bringing together liberals, progressive Islamists, activists from the Democratic Front party, and middle-class professionals (Kandil 2011). In 2010 al-Baradei had become a rallying point for the civil-democratic movement, but his inability to connect with the masses and forge lasting political alliances with, for example, the Brotherhood, had marginalized the NAC by early 2011 (Khalil 2012: 115). A fourth group of those who organized the protests 'on the ground' was composed of human rights activists, some of whom also belonged to the new left or 6 April Movement umbrellas. For example, human-rights activist and 6 April member Asmaa Mahfouz distributed tens of thousands of leaflets in informal neighbourhoods in Cairo the day before the protests (Amar 2011).

A last and unlikely group of apolitical organizers was the 'Ultras', a movement of hardcore football fans that was formed in 2005. Like many other independent civil society groups, the Ultras had been repressed by the security forces, which tightly controlled football matches and stadiums. Before the first protests of 25 January, the Ultras reassured the demonstrators that they would protect them against the police (al-Werdani 2011).

The demands of the organizers reiterated the standard, minimal aims of the civil-democratic movement, focused on ending the emergency law and limiting the president's term. No one expected the demonstration to become a mass insurrection with revolutionary demands. It became such a success because 'it started from below, from the popular neighbourhoods' (personal communication with W. Tawfiq, 8 March 2011). The tactic of gathering in the more peripheral, working-class areas of Cairo and marching from there had been developed during the anti-war demonstrations of 2003 (personal communication with G. Shabeen, 16 March 2011). This enabled activists to assemble a critical mass of protesters before they arrived at Tahrir Square, as groups of only tens of demonstrators would easily be arrested by the police (Sowers 2012: 4). Moreover, through Twitter, Facebook, and snowball text messaging, organizers changed the original hour and place of the protests to around 10.30 a.m., outwitting the Ministry of Interior (Khalil 2012: 139).

The CSF were organized for a large-scale, but short-term and focused deployment, striking swift and hard at a single point of resistance and overwhelming protesters by sheer weight of numbers – as had happened in Mahalla on 6 April 2008. The arrogance of the Ministry of Interior had not prepared the CSF for massive street protests, which took the riot police by surprise (Kandil 2012: 236). As the numbers shifted in favour of the demonstrators, the CSF was no longer able simply to 'surround' and subdue protesters (Khalil 2012: 140–2). Already by noon it was clear to some participants that the massive demonstrations could be 'an opportunity to bring down the Mubarak regime' (Guardian Live Blog, 25 January 2011). Demonstrators began to chant the slogan of 'the people want the fall of the regime' (personal communication with H. Hassan, 7 March 2011). Protesters gathered on Tahrir Square, where they planned to make a stand against the riot police. During the late evening and night they were dispersed by the CSF, however (Khalil 2012: 149). Access to mobile phone networks and internet was gradually blocked. The protests in Cairo sparked off massive demonstrations in Alexandria and in major cities in the Delta, the Canal Zone, and Upper Egypt. In Suez the protests were brutally repressed in a fierce confrontation with the police.

From Demonstration to Uprising

The morning after 25 January downtown Cairo was empty of protesters. The Interior Ministry deployed thousands of riot police, blocking bridges and roads, and occupying strategic sites such as the Maspero television building and the NDP headquarters. Throughout the evening and the night, small rallies of a few hundred demonstrators were repeatedly charged and broken up by regular and plainclothes police only to regroup at another location and continue their protests (Khalil 2012: 149–53). Mobile-phone networks, internet services, and landlines were completely cut off. The websites of newspapers such as *al-Dostour* were taken down. Outside Cairo protests were often swiftly disbanded, but in the capital violent clashes between the police and the population ensued. Several civilians were killed and in retaliation protesters set fire to the police station and the local NDP headquarters (Guardian Live Blog, 27 January 2011).

The morning of Thursday 27 January saw a return of calm to Cairo, as most activists prepared for a massive mobilization after the Friday afternoon prayers. New spontaneous protests of hundreds of protesters took place in Suez, Ismailia, and Alexandria. Thursday also saw the formal entry of the Muslim Brotherhood into the protest movement, as Muhammad Morsi declared the participation of the Society in the demonstrations planned for Friday (Guardian Live Blog, 27 January 2011). In the evening Muhammad al-Baradei arrived in Cairo pledging his active participation in the Friday protests. Yet the fact that he had waited for three days since the first protests before returning to Egypt led to a good deal of criticism in the streets (Shenker 2011b).

The Friday of Anger, 28 January, became a pivotal moment for the revolution. The Egyptian regime took the call for renewed protests on the day seriously and prepared for the worst. From Thursday night on, all major ISPs were shut down and some 88 per cent of Egyptian internet connections were effectively blocked (Rashed 2011: 23). Security forces and plainclothes police were mobilized on a massive scale. As soon as the Friday prayers were finished, security forces launched a pre-emptive strike against (potential) protesters, using teargas, water cannons, and sound bombs. However, groups of protesters had assembled again in working-class neighbourhoods, from where they marched to Tahrir, attracting hundreds and even thousands of new participants to their demonstration (personal communication with W. Tawfiq, 8 March 2011). Moreover, this time, many activists were prepared for a confrontation with the police. Thousands of demonstrators started to clash with the police, not only in Cairo, but also in Alexandria, Beni Suef, Minya,

Asyut, Ismailia, Port Said, and al-Arish. In the Delta city of Mansura some 40,000 protesters destroyed the NDP headquarters. The NDP offices in Damietta followed suit. In Suez 80,000 citizens demonstrated, taking over the police station in the al-Arbain neighbourhood and freeing fellow protesters (personal communication with S. Omar, 18 March 2011). Security forces had to withdraw from the city (Al Jazeera Live Blog, 28 January 2011). In Alexandria too the police were defeated by mass mobilizations (Guardian Live Blog, 28 January 2011). Central Cairo, however, was turned into a battleground, divided between tens of thousands of protesters, who were trying to march to Tahrir Square, and the riot police, who were attempting to block roads and bridges and to disperse the demonstrators with tear gas and rubber bullets. The NDP headquarters near Tahrir was set on fire. A country-wide curfew was proclaimed, but it was largely ignored by the protesters. Throughout the afternoon, it became more and more clear that the Ministry of Interior was not able to stem the revolutionary tide, as Kandil noted: 'Coming together from different assembly points, and gathering steam as they marched towards Tahrir Square, crowds snowballing to some 80,000-strong were now ready to take on the police. Caught off-balance by the size and persistence of the demonstrators, the police were finally overwhelmed' (Kandil 2011). Sometime between 4 and 5 p.m. the police were defeated (Khalil 2012: 177; Rashed 2011: 23). The Friday of Anger was the moment when most people realized that they were in the process of 'making' a revolution (personal communication with M. Bassiouni, 17 March 2011). The radical demands of 'the people want the fall of the regime', 'leave, leave, Hosni Mubarak', and 'bread, freedom, and social justice' signified the explicit recognition of the masses that, during the past days, they had actually been waging a revolutionary struggle against the state.

Because of the defeat of the police and the CSF in the streets, Mubarak had to call on the army to restore order (Khalil 2012: 193). Tanks and APCs rolled into the centre of Alexandria, Cairo, and Suez, where they were welcomed by demonstrators who hoped that the army would side with them against the police. At this point, the Egyptian military did not intervene in the ongoing clashes between protesters and police. They did, however, disperse a group of protesters who tried to storm the Maspero state television building, sealed off access to parliament and cabinet buildings, and established control over Tahrir Square (personal communication with W. Tawifq, 8 March 2011). At around midnight President Mubarak appeared on Nile TV, declaring that he would fire the cabinet and appoint a new one on Saturday. In the same breath he warned Egyptians that he would not condone any more chaos in the streets. Even though the army called on the population to respect the curfew, thousands continued to protest throughout Saturday 29 January in Cairo, Alexandria, Ismailia, Suez, and Damanhur.

After the withdrawal of police forces from the streets, the revolutionary masses faced a new threat: criminal gangs, some of them escaped or released prisoners, and *baltageyya*, 'thugs' who terrorized neighbourhoods and looted houses, shops, and supermarkets (Stacher 2011a). These attacks were widely covered by state television and framed as a consequence of the anti-regime protests (Khalil 2012: 202). The state tried to undermine the legitimacy of the uprising by smothering it in a wave of orchestrated chaos. However, this obstacle became a springboard for the revolutionary movement. In the absence of law and order, popular collaborations established grassroots committees to protect families, homes, and neighbourhoods. Civil vigilante groups were improvised during the evening and night in order to protect neighbourhoods from the attackers. The people, in both popular and wealthy areas, organized themselves to maintain order. At around 5.30 p.m., Mubarak appointed intelligence chief Omar Suleiman as vice-president and Ahmed Shafiq, a former air force commander and civil aviation minister, as prime minister.[5] This move did not placate the masses, who continued their protests throughout the evening and the following day. Most banks, offices, and shopping malls remained closed.

At noon on Sunday 30 January, new tanks entered Tahrir Square, fortifying the salient military presence in the heart of the revolution where some 20,000 protesters were still gathered, chanting slogans against the president and the regime. On Monday 31 January most government offices, public companies, banks, schools, the stock market, and some private businesses remained closed. A group of 200 protesters had remained in Tahrir, occupying the square, while chanting and reading poetry. By the afternoon, the hard core of occupiers at Tahrir Square was again joined by tens of thousands of protesters, including women and children. In Alexandria, Mahalla al-Kubra, Tanta, Kafr al-Zayat, and Fayum the revolutionary mobilization continued as well, with thousands protesting. In Suez popular committees effectively controlled the city, organizing traffic and protecting neighbourhoods (Guardian Live Blog, 31 January 2011).

In the evening a surprising statement came from the army: it pledged not to shoot at civilians staging protests against the president, although it warned that it would not tolerate violence and chaos. Whereas the military, in general, exercised restraint in confronting the masses, it engaged in the systematic detention and torture of individual protesters (McGreal 2011). By the end of the second week of protests, some 10,000 people, especially, political and human rights activists, had been arrested in Cairo alone (Guardian Live Blog, 8 February 2011).

Vice-president Suleiman addressed the nation on state television, acknowledging the need to establish a dialogue with the opposition, reform the constitution, fight corruption, tackle unemployment, and investigate the November 2010 parliamentary elections. The speech was meant to co-opt the more moderate wing of the movement and isolate the more radical elements of the uprising from the rest of society. Suleiman's speech had little impact on the protests, and activists called for a *millioneya* or 'million-people march' on Tuesday. Friday was set as the deadline for Mubarak's departure; if he had not gone by then, they would march on the presidential palace in Heliopolis.

On the morning of Tuesday 1 February, the army closed main roads and train services to Cairo 'to prevent protesters from reaching mass protests today' (Guardian Live Blog, 1 February 2011). State television tried to frighten away protesters and ordered their employees to stage pro-Mubarak demonstrations. Nevertheless, tens of thousands of protesters made their way to Tahrir until more than one million people were occupying the square and its surrounding areas. Some activists began preparing for a continuous occupation. Huge protests also took place in Alexandria and provincial cities. Most people hoped that the massive scale and continuity of the demonstrations would be enough to force Mubarak to resign, as had happened in Tunisia with Ben Ali. At around 11 p.m. the president addressed the nation, promising not to run again for the presidency; this did not at all satisfy the disappointed crowd in Tahrir (Al Jazeera Live Blog, 1 February 2011). Outside Tahrir, however, the president's speech 'created a real sense of sympathy for Egypt's aging leader and this provided the pro-Mubarak camp with the momentum to maintain a strong counter-revolutionary movement for approximately one week after the speech' (Taha and Combs 2012: 83).

On Wednesday morning, some 20 pro-Mubarak supporters clashed with the 1,000 or so protesters who had remained at Tahrir Square. A few hours later a few thousand pro-Mubarak demonstrators gathered at the Mustafa Mahmud Mosque in Mohandiseen and near the Maspero television building, chanting slogans in support of the president. Meanwhile, the army issued a statement calling on the protesters to end their demonstrations as Mubarak had granted them important concessions. Internet services returned, Al Jazeera became available again, and the regime seemed bent on 'normalizing' economic life after a week of protests. At midday, thousands of organized Mubarak sympathizers battled their way into Tahrir.[6] The army stood by and allowed armed Mubarak supporters to enter the square.[7] Initially, the

Tahrir occupiers were able to form a human chain, pushing back the pro-Mubarak 'demonstrators' in a peaceful way. But then, by midday, the occupiers were suddenly attacked with rocks, machetes, razors, clubs, Molotov cocktails, and knives. In a bizarre scene, some pro-regime forces charged into the Tahrir occupiers mounted on horses and camels. Despite the assault of the *baltageyya*, the anti-regime forces held their ground. After 6 p.m. the protesters gained the upper hand and the thugs withdraw from the square. By midnight the 'Battle of the Camel' shifted towards the streets surrounding Tahrir and the area around the Egyptian Museum. Throughout the night the battle continued to rage, with pro-Mubarak snipers and gunmen terrorizing the protesters. Tensions ran high in Alexandria too, with supporters of the regime challenging the anti-Mubarak protesters.

On Thursday morning prime minister Shafiq, apologized for the violence in Tahrir and promised an investigation into the events. A meeting between Suleiman, Shafiq and opposition leaders was boycotted by most political forces, including the Muslim Brotherhood. Suleiman vacillated between describing the protesters as 'youth with genuine demands' and 'foreign infiltrators wishing to destabilize the nation' (Guardian Live Blog, 3 February 2011). The state media began to spread the rumour that there were Israeli spies among the foreigners in Egypt, leading to the harassment of foreign journalists and human rights activists. On the other hand, some cracks appeared in the state media as figures such as Shahira Amin from Nile TV resigned in protest at the regime violence: 'I quit my job because I don't want to be part of the state propaganda regime, I am with the people. I feel liberated and relieved. I have quit my job and joined the people in Tahrir Square' (Al Jazeera Live Blog, 3 February 2011).

On Friday 4 February protesters hoped to force an outcome in the stand-off through a mass mobilization after the midday prayers. The slow withdrawal of international support for Mubarak, combined with the president's expressed desire to stand down 'eventually' and their own victory in the Battle of the Camel, emboldened the revolutionary forces. In the morning people were already queuing in their thousands to get into the square. By around midday, hundreds of thousands were gathered in Tahrir, with Muslims, Copts, and Catholics praying together. The atmosphere in the square was defiant, but festive. An Al Jazeera reporter in Alexandria noted the bewilderment of people faced with the president's stubbornness: 'Some people are scratching their heads, wondering what more they need to do to make it clear to the president that they don't want him' (Al Jazeera Live Blog, 5 February 2011). Despite the rainy and relatively cold weather, rumours of a forced evacuation of Tahrir drew in thousands of anti-regime protesters on Saturday 5 February, strengthening the continuous occupation of the square. The government promised negotiations and did its best to steer the street back to 'normality'. On Sunday morning, 6 February, banks reopened for business. Protesters, however, tried to persuade civil servants working near Tahrir to strike and join the occupation. Omar Suleiman held a meeting with Muhammad al-Baradei, business tycoon Naguib Sawiris, and representatives of the Muslim Brotherhood, Wafd, Tagammu, and a number of youth groups. However, the negotiations yielded only vague promises. Throughout the night thousands continued to camp out in Tahrir.

On the afternoon of Monday 7 February, the regime promised public-sector employees an increase in salaries and pensions of 15 per cent. More concessions followed the next day, as Suleiman claimed to have a roadmap for the transition of power. He also promised that protesters would not be persecuted. Nevertheless, the following day saw the return of hundreds of thousands to Tahrir. Some were visiting the square for the first time. Cairo University professors and students joined the protesters. Extending the normal mid-term break, Egypt's schools and universities remained closed during the following week. The cracks in the state propaganda machinery seemed to widen, with journalists from the pro-regime *Rose al-Yusef* striking against their editor. Even a former minister of transport, Essam Sharaf, came to Tahrir Square.

Protests were not confined to Tahrir Square; demonstrations also took place near government buildings, the People's Assembly, and the Shura Council. Moreover, in Alexandria, thousands of people protested in front of the Ibrahim Mosque. In regional cities too, such as Ismailia, Asyut, and Mahalla al-Kubra, mass actions were organized. From 8 February onwards, Egyptian workers began to protest on a massive scale. In Suez, Port Said, and Ismailia, over 6,000 workers from the Suez Canal Company began an open-ended sit-in. Thousands of employees of Telecom Egypt started to protest as well, demanding a 10 per cent pay rise and the resignation of the top manager (Guardian Live Blog, 8 February 2011). In the New Valley area, some 500 kilometres south of Cairo, 3,000 protesters went on the streets and clashed with security forces. In Asyut, 8,000 people, a majority of them farmers, set up barricades of flaming palm trees, blocking the main highway and railway to Cairo, contesting bread shortages. Even in remote areas, such as the desert oasis of Kharga, protesters confronted the CSF, attacking government buildings and police headquarters, and demanding the resignation of the provincial security chief (Guardian Live Blog, 9 February 2011).

On Thursday 10 February the SCAF issued its first communiqué, claiming that the army was in control and that all legitimate demands of the protesters would be met. However, in a defiant speech later that night, Mubarak refused to step down, infuriating the masses who had gathered in Tahrir. In the whole of Egypt hundreds of thousands of people demonstrated, determined to stay in the streets until the president resigned. The next day at 6 p.m. Mubarak was removed from the presidency. On its Live Blog, Al Jazeera dryly remarked: 'No point any of our presenters trying to speak over the roar of Egyptians celebrating .... Mubarak steps down. Brought to you live on Al Jazeera' (Al Jazeera Live Blog, 11 February 2011).

The 'soft coup' ended the spontaneous, insurrectionary moment of the 25 January Revolution. However, the popular war of movement continued as the Egyptian streets, neighbourhoods, and workplaces remained a space for mass collective actions. At the same time, the revolutionary process was increasingly subsumed under waves of counter-revolution, epitomized by the second moment of popular mass mobilization, in June 2013, which firmly consolidated the reconfigured regime that was now back in power.

Tahrir as Prefiguration

The experience of the 25 January uprising reaffirmed Trotsky's subjectivist interpretation of revolution as 'the forcible entrance of the masses into the realm of rulership over their own destiny' (see Chapter 4). Although pre-existing political and social movements had prepared the groundwork for the insurrection, as soon as the masses entered the political field, the activity of protest acquired a qualitatively new and autonomous dynamic. Despite the importance of demonstrations and occupations in Alexandria, in provincial cities such as Suez and Mahalla, and in the countryside, the centre of gravity of the uprising was undeniably Tahrir Square (see De Smet 2014d). After the defeat of the police on Friday 28 January: 'Tahrir ... became the epicentre of a revolution. Protesters not only transformed it, they were themselves transformed by their presence in it. Tahrir became a revolutionary organism unto itself' (Khalil 2012: 5). Tahrir became almost synonymous with the 25 January Revolution, pushing forward the development of the entire struggle.

Tahrir was able to play a vanguard role because, firstly, it was 'a major transport hub surrounded by vital elements of the state apparatus: the parliament, several ministerial buildings, and the imposing Mogamma' (Rashed 2011: 23). Secondly, 'Liberation Square' referred to the 1919 revolutionary uprising against the British. Tahrir had become a favourite gathering place for celebrating national events (Shokr 2012: 41). In 2003 the square already functioned as the symbolic locale of political mobilization when demonstrators occupied it for ten hours in protest against the war in Iraq (Khalil 2012: 39). Thirdly, the 'realm of rulership' of the masses in Tahrir developed much faster than the revolution as a whole. The social space of the square developed 'from a rally site to a model for an alternative society' (Shokr 2012: 42).

The uprising started as a demonstration, directing a clear message towards those in power and a rallying call to potential supporters. The accumulation of anger, criticism, and resistance over the past years, the example projected by the Tunisian revolution, and the organization of marches from working-class neighbourhoods allowed activists to draw huge numbers of non-politicized citizens into showing their displeasure with the regime. When heavy street fights broke out between demonstrators and the CSF, protesters attempted to hold the square in order to make a stand against the riot police. At this point the occupation of Tahrir was merely an instrument to safeguard the demonstration against police brutality.

On Friday 28 January the masses returned to the streets on their day off. Traditional religious gatherings after the Friday midday prayers organically morphed into political mass demonstrations. The protesters were again confronted with the violence of the CSF and now demonstrations turned into huge street battles with the police. At this point the Gramscian military analogy between revolution and war of movement stopped being a mere resemblance and became the substance of the struggle. Using their overwhelming numbers and superior determination, the protesters were able to defeat the security apparatus in the streets. The revolutionaries physically conquered social spaces that were formerly controlled by the state. Occupation was no longer a mere means to protest against the state, for it expelled the state, creating the space for structures that developed organically from below. However, the masses were unable to liberate Cairo as a whole, and freed only pockets of the metropolitan city. The CSF was replaced by military troops who did not confront the protesters head-on, but preferred a literal war of position, digging 'urban trenches' around important state sites, such as parliament, the Maspero Radio and Television building, the presidential palace, the stock exchange, etc. (see Khalil 2012: 208).

A quick and dirty comparison to the experience of the Paris Commune (see Chapter 4) shows us that the 25 January uprising had the advantage of immediately constituting a national movement, so the vanguard at Tahrir could not be easily isolated and defeated. At the same time it had the disadvantage of not even locally overcoming and taking over state power, as the Communards were able to do in Paris. The occupiers created liberated zones, but they could not claim a more or less unified territory. They pushed back and disorganized state power, but they could not fully defeat it. They organized their own structures of self-governance, but they could not dismantle the existing state structures in the capital. If the uprising represented a nationwide war of movement, Tahrir reflected a war of position, the eye of the storm, as protesters were loath to confront the military and still hoped that Mubarak would leave of his own accord, as Ben Ali had done in Tunisia. Facing the state apparatus, occupiers dug their own trenches for a war of attrition with the regime.

The expulsion of existing state power from Tahrir transformed the square from an instrument of political emancipation into a *prefiguration* (see van de Sande 2013) of a free society: 'It is a real, actual, lived moment of the freedom and dignity that the pro-democracy movement demands' (Schielke 2011). In order to continue the occupation, housing in the form of tents was provided, blankets were distributed to overcome the chilly January nights, food and water were made available, and entertainment was arranged to keep the spirits of the occupiers high. Midan Tahrir was slowly transformed into a 'city of tents' (Guardian Live Blog, 6 February 2011). Even though the objective of the uprising, the overthrow of the Mubarak regime, remained grim, the liberating feeling among Tahrir occupiers that they could organize their own lives allowed for a 'festival of the oppressed and exploited' (see Lenin 1962). The occupation of Tahrir generated ways of enjoying life (see Rashed 2011), illustrated by 'the picnicking families, the raucous flag-wavers, the volunteer tea suppliers, the cheery human security cordons, the slumbering bodies curled up in the metal treads of the army's tanks, the pro-change graffiti that adorns every placard, every tent, every wall space in vision' (Guardian Live Blog, 8 February 2011). Many Egyptians experienced a greater authenticity of living, negating, albeit in a limited way, the realities of the oppressive regime.

The development of Tahrir was determined by the specific solutions it offered for overcoming the obstacles that were thrown into its path (see Bamyeh 2011). With every forward step in the struggle against the regime, Tahrir was itself transformed. It was from the masses themselves that there sprang, in Trotsky's words 'that leaping movement of ideas and passions which seems to the police mind a mere result of the activities of "demagogues"' (Trotsky 2001, 18). For example, the Battle of the Camel on Wednesday 2 February changed the square from a 'utopian street party' into 'Fortress Tahrir' (Khalil 2012: 243, 247). The borders of Tahrir changed into a continuous 'Front' (Rashed 2011: 25). A field hospital was erected in the centre of the square and a 'civil prison' was established. In the prison occupiers held captured plainclothes police officers and state security personnel in custody, not least to protect them from the wrath of other protesters (personal communication with W. Tawfiq, 8 March 2011).

The 'freed zone' was increasingly dubbed the 'Republic of Tahrir' by participants and observers alike (see Khalil 2012). As in the case of the Paris Commune, the spontaneous character of the mass movement did not prevent it from being organized. There was nothing disorganized about the committees that defended, cleaned, entertained, and governed Tahrir. If anything, they represented 'spontaneous order out of chaos' (Bamyeh 2011; Schielke 2011). Apart from the defence of the square, as outlined earlier, the occupiers had to create a daily life routine: securing food and shelter, treating the wounded, washing clothes, providing stations for charging mobile phones, building toilets, setting up nurseries for protesters' children, and so on (Keraitim and Mehrez 2012: 28). Doctors, engineers, and technicians supported the Republic of Tahrir with their expertise. Ultras shared their 'skills in banner writing, chanting, and the use of fireworks' (Keraitim and Mehrez 2012, 53) with other protesters. Political activists distributed leaflets with practical and tactical advice for demonstrators, for example what to do when being attacked by tear gas. Artists and actors joined the protests, and amateur cartoonists, musicians, and singers emerged from the activity of Tahrir itself (personal communication with M. Khaled, 25 March 2011). Stages were erected where anyone could speak, sing, act, recite, or play music (personal communication with M.Z. Murat, 30 March 2011). Classic songs of Fuad Negm and Shaykh Imam, such as 'I am the People' and 'I call on you' were sung and performed by protesters, alongside new and spontaneous creations (Antoon 2011). Catchy and humorous poems were composed in 'ammeyya, the Egyptian colloquial register. These cultural intellectuals not only provided entertainment, but also offered the semiotic means for the movement to comprehend its antagonist and itself. The art of the square was its material consciousness.

As a 'mini-state' besieged by the Mubarak regime, the square needed *directive* organs and practices of deliberation and decision. The intellectuals who provided leadership and direction to the movement consisted both of activists who had been a part of the political community before the revolution and of leaders who materialized spontaneously within the ranks of protesters. Political activists intervened in the movement with pamphlets and slogans, persuading protesters to stay in Tahrir when Mubarak pledged to fire the cabinet (personal communication with H. Hassan, 7 March 2011), putting forward concrete demands, and recommending instruments and methods to achieve the popular objectives. However, because of the vast numbers of protesters, the small groups of leftists were only able to give directive assistance in a fragmentary way and they were not at all able to lead the movement. Moreover, they were often the ones tail-ending the movement instead of moving ahead of it (personal communication with H. Fouad, 13 March 2011).

The development of Tahrir throughout the 18 Days illustrated the substance of revolution not only as the *expression* of an already-present popular will, but also as a *generative process* of self-emancipating practices and ideas. Revolution is not merely an instrument for accomplishing societal change: it is the movement itself towards a transformation of society. The future social formation is not an object external to the revolutionary process, lying in wait until the masses establish it 'at once', but it is immanent in the process of revolution itself. The forms of self-organization, democracy, and authentic living that arise during the mass mobilizations and protests are anticipations of a fully matured society based on the self-determination and self-governance of the people.

Political and Social Emancipation

The convergence of two processes led to the fall of Mubarak: the popular masses moving from Tahrir to parliament and the presidential palace, and the powerful entrance of workers as class actors in the revolution (personal communication with S. Omar, 18 March 2011). In Cairo, the standoff between the Republic of Tahrir and the state was heading towards a violent solution. Friday 5 February had been dubbed the Friday of Departure as an ultimatum to Mubarak. This episode expressed both the strength and the weakness of the revolutionary movement at that moment. Whereas the popular masses had been able to set their own concrete timetable and demands, they had not yet developed the means to enforce them. Tunisia's example of a successful revolution, which had been instructive in drawing in participants to the Egyptian uprising, now became a brake, as protesters hoped that Mubarak would, like Ben Ali, simply resign in the face of their mass demonstrations and occupations. State institutions were paralysed and disorganized due to the demonstrations and sit-ins, but they were not captured and transformed. As long as the main institutions, such as the Maspero television and radio building, parliament, the presidential palace, the army barracks, etc. were protected by the military, the state dug in, enduring the protests in the hope that the demonstrators' physical and mental constitution would quickly wear down. Revolutionary occupation, which had been the motor of the revolution in the previous days, now became a bottleneck for its further development.

Even on the first Friday, the Friday of Anger, 28 January, there were already activists who tried to rally and direct people towards occupying not only the largely symbolic location of Tahrir, but also 'real' sites of state power. During the Friday of Departure there was a renewed attempt to orient the masses towards a march on the presidential palace, but this call did not materialize. Conversely, the regime, after its disastrous attempts to repress the revolutionary uprising by force, was content to wage a war of attrition with the occupiers. Whereas the majority of protesters remained stuck in the strategy of occupation, from Tuesday 8 February onwards some participants tried to develop a 'second front' near the parliament and the presidential palace. Alexandria protesters sent a message to Tahrir that they should occupy the Maspero building (Schielke 2011). When in his speech on Thursday 10 February the president still refused to step down, out of the anger and confusion among the masses rose 'a feeling that people want to get on the move now. I can hear this chant: We'll go to the palace and tear him out' (Guardian Live Blog, 10 February 2011). The absence of a political centre that could direct the masses was temporarily compensated by songs and cartoons imagining the next step in the development of the revolution (De Smet 2015d; Gribbon and Hawas 2012: 104). However, the success of these semiotic stopgaps illustrated the weakness of the movement as a self-directing force. Without centralized organs of self-governance the popular movement towards political emancipation could easily be blocked and diffused by the 'soft coup' of the SCAF.

The second process that pressured the generals in removing Mubarak from office was the deepening of the revolution's social dimension by the participation of the working class. From the very beginning of the uprising the explicitly political movement contained a strong 'social soul' as the bulk of the protesters consisted of the urban popular masses, who demanded not only freedom, but bread and social justice too (Alexander and Bassiouny 2014: 12). As one of the many components of the amorphous 'people', wage labourers had joined unemployed youth, street vendors, small shopkeepers, housewives, taxi drivers, etc., in the uprising. The closure of companies, banks, and shops by the government during the first week and a half of the uprising locked workers out of their workplaces. In the streets, specific working-class demands were subsumed under the political goals of the movement. However, once the government had reopened businesses on 7 February, workers brought the insurrection back into their workplaces and started to strike or demonstrate as class actors. Their social demands were oriented not only towards the workplace, but also towards the whole class. These demands included the setting of a minimum wage, the employment of temporary workers, the return of privatized companies to the state, the reinstatement of workers fired for striking, and equal pay for workers (personal communication with F. Ramadan, 15 March 2011). Although workers often did not list the fall of the regime among their formal demands, they chanted the same radical slogans as the occupiers on Tahrir (al-Hamalawy 2011).

The decision of the government to reopen businesses was primarily aimed at insulating Egyptian society at large from the pockets of resistance. Yet, the regime's 'capital strike' was replaced with spontaneous workers' strikes that imported the uprising to workplaces in the whole country. Whereas the battle between the state and Tahrir had become a relatively static war of attrition, the strikes reignited the uprising as a popular war of movement (Alexander and Bassiouny 2014: 202). The awakening of the working class within the broad process of insurrection frightened the state and the ruling classes. Workers' strikes tipped the balance of power in the favour of the protesters. Reuters observed: 'If the strikes spread across the country, and paralyse key sectors, it could push Egypt's army to take sides, after trying to maintain an appearance of neutrality' (Guardian Live Blog, 10 February 2011). The strikes damaged not just the short-term interests of private capitalists, public companies, and military entrepreneurs; unlike the civil-democratic movement, the workers' movement posed a direct threat to the economic structure of the historical bloc.

It was the spectre of the development and growing interpenetration of political and social emancipation that frightened the SCAF into deposing Mubarak. If the substance of the 25 January Revolution was a war of movement against the neoliberal political and economic offensive, then it could only be completed by changing the domestic and transnational class alliances and accumulation strategy (Maher 2011). The political revolution could not succeed except by a reconfiguration of the economic structure, and the economic structure could not be transformed unless political power was captured and appropriated by the subaltern classes. The independent activity of the working class within the broad revolutionary process renders the unity of these two revolutionary tasks possible. Luxemburg astutely described the 'mass strike'[8] as 'the *method of motion of the proletarian mass*, the phenomenal form of the proletarian struggle in the revolution' (Luxemburg 1970: 182). Whereas the whole of the popular masses confronts capital in its concentrated but roundabout appearance as the state, the proletariat confronts capital directly at its many fragmented points of production, revealing in the process the class nature of the state as it comes to capital's aid. Following Luxemburg's interpretation permanent revolution is not only the linear growth of social emancipation from the conditions of political emancipation, but also a reciprocal, 'sideways' movement as the political and social struggles continuously 'fertilize' each other (Alexander and Bassiouny 2014: 13; Zemni, De Smet and Bogaert 2013):

> In a word: the economic struggle is the transmitter from one political center to another; the political struggle is the periodic fertilization of the soil for the economic struggle. Cause and effect here continually change places; and thus the economic and the political factor in the period of the mass strike, now widely removed, completely separated or even mutually exclusive, as the theoretical plan would have them, merely form the two interlacing sides of the proletarian class struggle in Russia. And *their unity* is precisely the mass strike. (Luxemburg 1970: 185)

Luxemburg described the mass strike as contemporaneous, objective unity between different instances of the political and social struggle. However, as Gramsci emphasized, permanent revolution has to be understood concretely as the formation of proletarian hegemony. In other words, what is needed is a hegemonic apparatus that actively and consciously integrates the different lines of development of the class struggle (De Smet 2015). In the Russian revolutions of 1905 and 1917 soviets – workers' and soldiers' councils – functioned as the apparatus that concretely connected the class struggle with the fight for democracy under the leadership of the working class, prefiguring the 'dictatorship of the proletariat' (see Alexander and Bassiouny 2014: 32). In Egypt, however, the popular movement lacked such a directive organ that could take decisions. In its early stages this had been an advantage: without a centre it was impossible for the state to defeat the masses by absorbing or liquidating their leadership. However, when the masses needed to strike a decisive blow against the regime the lack of a directive centre that showed them 'the shortest and most direct route to complete, absolute and decisive victory' (Lenin 1962: 113) locked the movement in a war of attrition. In order to transform the situation Tahrir had to turn itself inside out. Its revolutionary 'governance' had to be shared with neighbourhoods and workplaces all over Egypt. Tahrir had to become not only a prefiguration of an alternative society, but the hegemonic apparatus of the revolutionary movement, connecting itself to the struggles waged by the popular masses outside its borders, and transforming its concrete imaginary into national leadership.

From the beginning of the uprising, a continuous exchange had taken place between Tahrir and participants from other Cairo neighbourhoods and from provincial and even rural areas. In the square these 'delegations' enjoyed the freedom to debate the strategy of the movement and the future of Egypt. Farmers who were not able to return home when the regime closed the roads joined in the protests at Tahrir (El-Nour 2015: 203). When they returned to their own spaces, they transposed their participation in the self-governance of the square to these local sites of protests, sharing and diffusing the experience of Tahrir. However, these connections were anything but systematic and coherent.

In the square, representatives of the four independent unions decided to constitute the Egyptian Federation of Independent Trade Unions (EFITU) as a potential centre for the workers' movement (personal communication with K.A. Eita, 15 March 2011). They formulated a class programme that was based on demands that had emerged spontaneously from the strike movement since 2006, including a national minimum and maximum wage, the right to establish independent trade unions and the abolition of the GFETU, the right to strike and protest, the renationalization of privatized companies, the cleansing of the public sector of corrupt managers, improved healthcare, and the abolition of temporary contracts (personal communication with S. Omar, 18 March 2011). Independent trade unions, autonomous strike committees, and individual workers' leaders and leftist activists played a role in organizing strikes in solidarity with the insurrection. Perhaps if the Republic of Tahrir had been able to develop its own political organs trade union structures such as the EFITU would have played an important role in the formation of popular power. But even if this had been the case, the independent trade unions that had developed over the past years 'were too small in relation to the scale of the movement for their presence as an *organised* force to shape the overall outcome of the uprising, or even influence its direction much' (Alexander 2012: 113). There was no coordinated and concentrated collaboration between strikers, but only a de facto contemporaneity of worker protests. The trade unionist vanguard was but a drop in the ocean of thousands of spontaneously striking workers.

In order for the Egyptian revolution to become permanent, that is, to successfully integrate the moments of political and social emancipation, the popular masses would have to construct a means of exercising power, through which, in turn, the working class could establish its hegemony over the revolution. The failure to accomplish these two crucial political steps between 2011 and 2013 would eventually lead to the consolidation of the military-directed counter-revolution.

8. Revolution and Restoration

The 'Soft' Coup

When it became obvious that the masses would not accept an 'honorary' exit for the president, Mubarak had to be sacrificed on the altar of the counter-revolution. The best option for the survival of the Egyptian ruling classes was for the Armed Forces to place themselves at the head of the revolution and 'lead' it, in order to defeat it. CNN quoted an anonymous senior Egyptian official claiming that 'It's not a coup, it's a consensus' (Guardian Live Blog, 10 February 2011). The emerging consensus among Egypt's ruling classes and foreign allies, such as the United States, was that Mubarak's days were numbered and that the military was the only state structure able to contain the revolutionary flood. The interests of Egypt's military–industrial complex transcended the political survival of Mubarak and his dynasty – those interests were effectively national (Achcar 2013: 174). The confusion about the role of the Armed Forces in Egyptian society among many of the protesters, and the absence of a grassroots political centre, allowed the military leaders to step in and represent themselves as revolutionary arbiters or even leaders. On Sunday afternoon 13 February, in its fourth communiqué, the SCAF declared that parliament was dissolved and the constitution suspended and that it would run the country until presidential and parliamentary elections were held. It also called upon the population 'to head back to work, and stop the strikes that have disrupted Egypt's economy' (Al Jazeera Live Blog, 14 February 2011).

However, within the upper stratum of the Armed Forces there was a clash of interests. Whereas the high officers of the air force, military intelligence, and presidential guard were generally favoured by the Mubarak clique, others were less privileged (Amar 2012). In addition to the swings in the revolutionary atmosphere, the contradictory actions of soldiers and officers vis-à-vis the protesters – sometimes protecting them against the police and *baltageyya*, sometimes siding with the Interior Ministry against the demonstrators and occupiers – were determined by their discrete loyalties to particular departments and interest groups within the Armed Forces. When the 25 January protests turned into a general insurrection, a section of the generals was not inclined to save their main civil political and economic 'competitors' within the ruling stratum: the Interior Ministry, the NDP, and especially the capitalist clique around Gamal Mubarak. For the military elites the uprising was as much a *threat* as an *opportunity* to reconfigure the relations of power within the state to their advantage (Kandil 2012: 5). Therefore, they stood passively by when protesters burned down the NDP headquarters in Cairo (Amar 2012). To be clear: the generals were not against the neoliberal offensive in principle, but, apart from the danger of political destabilization it caused, they contested the fact that they did not sufficiently participate in the cannibalization of the public sector (Armbrust 2012).

The balance of power, which began to shift from the Ministry of Interior and the NDP to the Armed Forces after the first Friday of Anger, had now swung decisively in the favour of the military. Omar Suleiman's laconic statement that Mubarak had resigned not only signified the end of his presidency, it also established the SCAF as the sole supra-constitutional ruling power. The SCAF had to strike a careful balance between defending its own particular interests, and representing its intervention as a continuation of the revolution and a protection of the common good. Ironically, in 2011 the generals were able to emulate the Caesarist intervention of 1952 because of their forced retreat from political society since the 1970s, which inoculated the military from the popular criticisms of the escalated domination, oppression, and exploitation by the Mubarak state during the last two decades (see Alexander 2011). Simply put, unlike the Ministry of Interior, the NDP, and the business elites, the Armed Forces were not, in the eyes of the majority of protesters, one of the pillars of the Mubarak regime. On the contrary, in contradistinction to the civil institutions of the Mubarak regime, the Egyptian military had retained an aura of being a national and popular force.

The protesters were anxious when the Armed Forces entered the physical spaces of the uprising, since they recognized the decisive role the military was likely to play in the struggle against the Mubarak regime. They called on rank-and-file soldiers to join the revolution, but 'many were unaware of how stark the differences were between the interests of the soldiers and the generals' (Armbrust 2012: 119). The SCAF profited from this confusion about the character of the Armed Forces. Taking the lead in the revolutionary process seemed to be in accordance with the dominant sentiment among protesters that the soldiers were on their side. Conversely, the generals were pressured to act because the interpellation of 'the people and the army: one hand' started to affect the rank-and-file soldiers (personal communication with K. al-Balshy, 14 March 2011). The generals could not command their troops to open fire on the protesters because that would have broken the spell that conjured up the image of the Armed Forces as the defenders of the national popular interest. In order to halt the revolutionary process, the SCAF had to lead it, which, at face value, satisfied the expectations of both popular masses and soldiers (see Stacher 2011b).

The strength of the SCAF consisted mainly of the weakness of the national–popular counter-hegemony. The masses accepted the leadership of the SCAF because they had no directive centre and hegemonic apparatus of their own. The concrete figure of Mubarak had been a physical icon of everything that was structurally wrong with the Egyptian social formation, just as the iconicity of the mass protests represented the tangible substance of the national–popular revolution. Thousands of euphoric protesters remained overnight in the square to celebrate Mubarak's departure. On Saturday morning, however, the question arose as to whether the occupation of Tahrir should continue until there was more clarity about the promised transition to democracy. The hard core of occupiers argued that they should remain in Tahrir in order to pressure the SCAF for real reforms. In the past two weeks, the occupation of the square had proved to be an effective strategy for enforcing concessions from the regime. Tahrir was the soul of the revolution, and to abandon this liberated space would be to jeopardize the entire revolutionary process. Nevertheless, once the president had been removed the system was no longer immediately represented in a concentrated form, and its attributes – corruption, violence, authoritarianism, poverty, and so on – became disembodied and abstracted. The concretization of 'the regime' in thought required a thorough critique of the economic structure and the relations of domination and hegemony – a critique that would unmask the interests of the military, the Brotherhood, and other forces that claimed leadership in the ensuing struggle for hegemony. However, in the absence of a 'Modern Prince' of their own, the masses confused the military's substitutionism for revolutionary leadership, and the great majority returned to their homes (see Khalil 2012: 266).

People often expressed their confidence in their own collective agency to keep the SCAF in line and claimed that they could and would return to the streets when something did not work out as they wanted it to. Such statements highlighted the general rise in political consciousness that the uprising had stimulated. Although the SCAF governed, it was the people that had given the military a provisional mandate. The Tahrir mobilizations still had an effect after the fall of Mubarak. For example, protesters succeeded in putting enough pressure on the SCAF to fire the prime minister, Ahmed Shafiq, on 3 March and replace him with Essam Sharaf, who had a better standing with the masses because he had participated in the 25 January protests – even though he had served as minister of transportation in 2004 and 2005. Under pressure of the Tahrir occupiers, Sharaf reshuffled his cabinet, removing many figures who were perceived as being too close to the old regime. After March, Tahrir still welcomed tens of thousands of protesters and occupiers – for example during the Friday of Cleaning on 8 April 2011, the Second Friday of Anger on 27 May 2011, throughout July, on the Friday of Correcting the Path on 9 September 2011, and on the eve of the 2011 parliamentary and 2012 presidential elections. Those protesting were increasingly disappointed with the lack of real change and the counter-revolutionary role of the SCAF.

Yet without real structures that organized and concentrated popular power, revolutionary awareness became difficult to mobilize. As well as being a space for ritualistic protest, Tahrir Square was becoming a tourist site commemorating the revolutionary uprising, where T-shirts and souvenirs were sold – the emphasis now was more on the revolution's past than on its present or future (Gribbon and Hawas 2012: 135). Moreover, the separation of political consciousness from everyday practices of mass protest increasingly emptied the national–popular movement of its real content. The moment of general insurrection was dissolved back into its constituent parts. The past and present of the revolution were rewritten: some revolutionary actors, such as striking workers, were now excluded from those considered to have been genuine and crucial participants in the revolution. Right-wing nationalist, Islamist, liberal, and even some leftist forces rejected workers' protests for being *fi'awi* (factional), counter-revolutionary, and against the national interest (see Clément 2011; Sallam 2011b; Naguib 2011). Even independent media outlets such as *al-Masry al-Youm* portrayed the continuation of strikes in a negative light. This narrative also began to affect the ranks of non-proletarian revolutionary youth organizations and networks, which argued that

> those who are taking part in [the strikes] were classes with limited interests that primarily concerned them and weren't of concern to the rest of the classes in society, from their point of view. There was a situation of hostility between the workers and middle class youth. (Hamalawy, in Haddad 2011)[1]

The reframing of the 25 January uprising as a mere struggle for political democracy was also supported by US and European policy makers, who feared that the revolution would turn against the neoliberal restructuring of the Egyptian social formation. In fact, if 'authoritarianism' – understood as a freely floating political category without a class base

– was the main culprit, the revolution's demands could be reformulated as a plea for more free-market capitalism; that is, neoliberal reform (Hanieh 2013: 165–6).

Conversely, counter-revolutionary forces were included in the revolutionary narrative, hiding themselves, sometimes literally, behind the Egyptian flag. Mobinil and Vodaphone set up giant billboards in the national colors with the slogan 'We are all Egyptians'. Shops like Adidas painted their windows as Egyptian flags in order to prevent people from smashing them. The form of the national-popular revolution survived as a nationalist metanarrative, which could be easily appropriated by each of the political forces involved in the post-Mubarak hegemonic struggle.

Counter-Revolution in Democratic Form

Although thousands continued to protest and occupy Tahrir, the real masses, the millions who had poured into the streets during the uprising, returned to their homes after the Caesarist intervention, implicitly granting the SCAF a mandate for their emancipation. Once the bulk of the masses had been demobilized, the dictatorship regained the political initiative. The military elites were able to consolidate and improve their position within the ruling stratum at the expense of the capitalist groups close to Gamal Mubarak and the NDP elites. Their primary goals were protecting their military-economic assets and blocking civilian oversight over the defence budget (Hashim 2011: 109; Marshall and Stacher 2012). But the military had little interest in governing Egypt directly; firstly, because it was unfit to deal with domestic crowd control; secondly, because it was pressured by its Western allies into developing a civil façade (Achcar 2013: 236); and thirdly, because it was more suited to elevating itself above civil and political society, playing the part of arbiter between different political and economic factions of the ruling classes (Kandil 2011). The SCAF wanted to rule without governing (see Cook 2007) in order to insulate itself from the centrifugal forces of explicit politics. This recalls Gramsci's observation that

> [i]n certain situations it may happen that it suits better not to 'reveal' the army, not to have it cross the bounds of what is constitutional, not to introduce politics into the ranks, as the saying goes – so that the homogeneity between officers and other ranks is maintained, on a terrain of apparent neutrality and superiority to the factions; yet it is nonetheless the army, that is to say the General Staff and the officer

corps, which determines the new situation and dominates it. (Gramsci 1971: 212; Q13§23)

In order to present the state as an institution suitable for the modern democratic age the Armed Forces had to leave the streets and exercise their domination in a more mediated manner (see Fontana 2004: 189). Therefore, while the NDP was formally dissolved on 16 April 2011 by court order, the SCAF left the apparatus of the Interior Ministry largely intact (Khalil 2012: 302), because it remained a useful and necessary instrument of non-military coercion. Furthermore, the direct military Caesarism of the SCAF was expanded with a civil 'democratic transition' process, which was nothing other than a counter-revolution in the shape of military-supervised representative politics. Instead of representing a genuine process of revolutionary democratic change, elections and referenda were deployed by the 'transitional government' as weapons of restoration. Firstly, they narrowed the meaning and space of 'revolutionary politics' from spontaneous street and workplace protests to the limited and top-down controlled domain of the state. The concept of 'democracy' was realigned with the global common sense, which emphasized procedure, representation, and institutional formalism over organic processes of decision making from below. The focus on formal democratic practice served to sever the link between the struggle for democracy of the political opposition and urban middle classes and the social demands of workers, peasants, and the urban poor. Political activists were diverted from the more pressing task of reconnecting the vanguard with the masses. Secondly, elections atomized the general will that emerged on Tahrir into the fragmented wills of individual 'voters': the 'qualitative' majority in the streets was reduced to a 'quantitative' minority in the polling booths. The 'silent majority', which had not participated in the democratic experience of Tahrir and the popular committees, had not (yet) drawn the same revolutionary conclusions as the militant vanguard. Its convincing would take time, effort, and organization, which early elections did not allow for. Thirdly, by controlling the pace of elections and the agenda of referenda, new cleavages were created – especially the sectarian divide between 'secularists' and 'Islamists' – and certain political factions, such as the Brotherhood and the Salafists, were favoured at the expense of more revolutionary but less organized groups. Even though the Brotherhood and the Salafists profited from the sectarianization of the political debate in the short term, in the long run it became much more difficult for these forces to present themselves as the defenders of the national 'common good' (see Sallam 2011a). The stronger the Islamist factions became, the more the military leadership would be able to play up fears among secular liberal, nationalist, and 'old' leftist opposition forces about the danger of an imminent Islamization of society. Without the will or ability to mobilize an independent social base against the Islamists, secular parties had no option but to look to the Armed Forces for protection against the bigger 'threat' of Islamism. The Ikhwan bourgeoisie tried to take advantage of the situation to advance its own political and economic standing within the ensemble of dominating classes. To a certain extent the trajectory of the Muslim Brotherhood during the 25 January uprising reflected that of the military. The Society's leadership was anxious that it would suffer repression by the regime if it joined the 25 January protests, and suspicious of popular initiative and self-organization. Nevertheless it participated in the uprising because it was pushed by its enthusiastic youth membership (Alexander 2011: 544), and because it realized that the insurrection constituted an opportunity to swing the balance of power in its favour; but even with its formidable apparatus of relatively loyal, organized activists, the Brotherhood would not, and could not, *lead* the protests of millions (Bayat 2011; Sallam, Stacher, and Toensing 2011). After the fall of Mubarak, the attitude of the leadership changed, however, as it cautiously supported the soft coup and called upon protesters to leave the square and start negotiations with the SCAF – much to the anger of radical liberals, socialists, and nationalists (see Alexander 2011). The collapse of the NDP left a political vacuum that neither the SCAF nor the existing opposition parties could fill. The Brotherhood leadership was conscious of its potential as a power broker between the generals and the popular masses (Alexander 2011: 536). It desired a small reconfiguration of the neoliberal bloc: the addition of its own capitalist leaders such as Khayrat al-Shater to the dominant stratum within the ruling classes (see Teti and Gervasio 2012). The Brotherhood actively blocked the development of strike movements, proving its value as a counter-revolutionary force to both domestic (especially the military) and foreign (especially the United States) elites (Hanieh 2013: 170–1).

In return for the Brotherhood's loyalty, the SCAF freed Ikhwan activists from prison and recognized the movement's political apparatus: the Freedom and Justice Party (FJP). Furthermore, early elections were to the advantage of the Society since it was the only organized mass opposition force (Wickham 2013: 170–2). However, from its inception the alliance between the SCAF and the Brotherhood was rife with distrust and competition. The generals desired a civil proxy to rule, but they were reluctant to release direct control over the counter-revolutionary process. The SCAF tried to reduce the weight of the Ikhwan in the new political landscape by restricting the number of parliamentary seats reserved for party candidates. Conversely, the Brotherhood did not hesitate to take to the streets to contest certain decisions of the SCAF and display their revolutionary credentials – but always falling short of rejecting military rule altogether.

The Brotherhood's landslide in the parliamentary elections of 2011 and the growing dissatisfaction among the wider population with the SCAF's failing and heavy-handed 'transitional' policies encouraged the Ikhwan to raise the stakes. The Muslim Brotherhood and the Salafists realized that their parliamentary victory was a pyrrhic one, as parliament was still governed by the old constitution that did not even grant them the right to form a cabinet of their own choice. A race began between parliament, which established a committee to write a new constitution that would expand its powers, and the executive – that is, essentially, the SCAF – which began legal proceedings to contest the constitutionality of parliament. Moreover, backtracking on an earlier promise, the Brotherhood decided to nominate a presidential candidate: Khayrat al-Shater. Al-Shater was barred from running for office, however, and the Ikhwan fielded Muhammad Morsi instead. On 14 June 2012, days before the presidential elections, the High Constitutional Court dissolved parliament, and the SCAF took over legislative powers. The SCAF used this momentum to restrict the powers of the future president and reinforce its own position until a new constitution was in place (Pargeter 2013: 231–6).

Rise and Fall of the Muslim Brotherhood

In the first round of the 2012 presidential elections, the 'revolutionary' candidates Hamdeen Sabahi and Abdel Moneim Abul Futuh were beaten by a slim margin into third and fourth place respectively by Muslim Brotherhood contender Muhammad Morsi and regime runner Ahmed Shafiq. In the second round, Egyptians were forced to choose between the lesser of these two evils, each representing a wing of the counter-revolution, respectively Islamist bourgeois democracy and secular military dictatorship. Both candidates portrayed themselves as saviours of the revolution against the counter-revolution. Morsi's victory[2] gave momentum to the 'civil' turn of Caesarism. By June 2012, after a year of military power, internal dissent and the resurgence of street protests revealed the SCAF as a select and self-centred clique that was unable to consolidate its domination over the whole Armed Forces, let alone the other ruling-class factions, or society at large. The victory of Muhammad Morsi was an opportunity for the military to share the burden of governing with a civil ally. Moreover, a growing number of officers were dissatisfied with the leadership of the SCAF. In exchange for the protection of the political and economic interests and privileges of the generals, the Armed Forces would leave the management of the state to the Ikhwan. This would solve the problem of 'dual power' between the Brotherhood presidency and the SCAF. Morsi's constitutional declaration of 12 August 2012 retired old heavyweight SCAF generals such as Hussein Tantawi and Sami Anan. Morsi catapulted Brotherhood sympathizer Abdel Fattah al-Sisi into the position of defence minister and chief of staff of the Armed Forces (Springborg 2012). The Ikhwan president was able to lift the restrictions that the SCAF had put on the powers of the presidency, ending the era of direct military governance. Nonetheless, instead of a demilitarization and democratization of the state, this measure signalled a pragmatic compromise between the Brotherhood and junior leaders of the Armed Forces. The constitution of 26 December 2012, which shielded the defence budget from parliamentary oversight and asserted that the minister of defence was to be chosen from the ranks of the military, affirmed this alliance.

From a passive-revolutionary perspective, Morsi deflected popular initiative by presenting himself as the prime mover of popular revolutionary demands, without, at the same time, endangering the essential interests of the military and the Brotherhood. He resigned from the FJP in order to appear independent from the Brotherhood and function as the president of all Egyptians. As the majority of the population did not accept the Ikhwan as a national, Egyptian organization capable of defending the common good, Morsi tried to channel hegemony directly through means of the Caesarist persona of the president, who, like the Armed Forces, stood above the classes. He sought to develop a hegemonic project by rearticulating revolutionary goals into the Islamist myth of *al-Nahda* (Renaissance) (see Malfait 2015) and trapping the popular will in the institutional framework of a strong presidential, liberal-democratic state. He tried to draw subaltern groups into his project by offering material concessions, such as wage and pension increases for public-sector workers and debt relief and subsidies for peasants. Militant political and social movements whose demands exceeded the limits of bourgeois democracy or social relief were excluded as *fi'awi* from the category of revolutionary people. Morsi reinterpreted revolution as the mechanism that would bring forward an Egyptian Renaissance; its immanent goals of bread, freedom, and social justice were translated into more ambiguous slogans about prosperity, dignity, and stability – which could easily be appropriated in a neoliberal manner.

Whereas the SCAF's blundering rescue and reconfiguration of the ruling bloc after the 25 January uprising constituted a defensive counter-attack against the powerful yet disorganized popular initiative, Morsi's presidency represented a more confident 'counter-revolution in democratic form'. The transformation of the form of state power from more or less outright dictatorship to bourgeois democracy and the governance of what was basically another faction of the Egyptian capitalist class concealed the simple fact that the neoliberal accumulation process continued in full force (Gamal 2012). Despite important differences, the political competition between the Brotherhood, the generals, and other capitalist factions was not about implementing a new strategy of accumulation and transforming Egypt's economic base, but about who would reap the most rentier benefits of neoliberal accumulation.

After the initial enthusiasm among the subaltern classes about Egypt's first 'democratically elected' and civil president, the autumn of 2012 brought growing discontent with the Brotherhood's inability and unwillingness to forge a national consensus, to dismantle and democratize state structures such as the Interior Ministry, to solve the economic crisis, etc. Morsi had to balance the interests of the Ikhwan capitalists with those of the generals, the Salafists – who pressured him from the right – and the masses who had put him into power. Instead of transforming the structures of dictatorship into institutions of bourgeois democracy, the Brotherhood tried to capture positions in the cabinet, ministries, state unions, and professional associations for its own personnel (Pioppi 2013: 63–4). The Brotherhood had not learned the essential lesson of the Paris Commune that it 'cannot simply lay hold of the ready-made State machinery, and wield it for its own purposes' (see Chapter 4). On the economic front Morsi cooperated with businessmen from the Mubarak era, continuing neoliberal reforms that aggravated enduring problems in relation to unemployment, purchasing power, and an unjust tax system (Paciello 2013: 8–15). Labour protests faced heavy-handed state repression. Morsi also accepted a widely contested IMF loan, the implementation of which was stalled in the face of popular protests (Hanieh 2013: 170). Finally, in order to become hegemonic *within* the Sunni Islamist camp, Morsi remained largely silent on sectarian attacks against Shia and Coptic minorities.

These policies undermined Morsi's attempt to present himself as a non-partisan defender of the national interest. Morsi's constitutional declaration on 22 November 2012, which temporarily granted him absolute executive and legislative powers, seemed to confirm the worst fears among secular opposition forces about a 'Brotherhoodization' of political and civil society. In Caesarist fashion, Morsi did not deny that he concentrated state power in the hands of the presidency, but he claimed that this was necessary to defend the 'democratic transition' against the forces of the counter-revolution. The presence of so-called *feloul* elements – supporters of the previous regime – in the ranks of the anti-Brotherhood opposition lent credence to Morsi's claim. The National Salvation Front (NSF) united rightists such as Amr Moussa, liberal democrats such as Muhammed al-Baradei, leftist Nasserists such as Hamdeen Sabahi, and Mubarakists under one broad umbrella against the Brotherhood. While both the Muslim Brotherhood and the NSF claimed to represent the revolutionary path against dictatorship, they contained a mix of revolutionary and counter-revolutionary forces, which were dominated by two factions of the counter-revolution: the Ikhwan and the generals. The deep political dichotomy showed that Morsi had failed to transcend the contradictions in society as a civil Caesar. It also illustrated the success of both counter-revolutionary camps to fracture and absorb popular initiative. The fight between the Brotherhood and oppositional elites over state power was articulated within the revolutionary movement, splitting it into hostile camps, each genuinely believing it was the true representative of the revolutionary people. Vertical relations of hegemony between fractions of capital and subaltern clients cut through still-developing horizontal ties between workers, peasants, and the revolutionary youth.

Morsi leaned heavily on his legitimacy as elected president, which ironically sanctioned the use of street politics as a means to depose him. The struggle between factions of the ruling class over state power remobilized the masses in the streets. The next few months saw an escalation of violent protests between pro-Morsi and anti-Brotherhood demonstrators. The president had to declare a state of emergency in the cities of the Suez Canal Zone. At the end of April 2013 the petition campaign Tamarod (Rebel) was established, which collected signatures calling on President Morsi to step down. The campaign became a huge mass movement, which gathered numbers in the streets comparable only with those of the January 25 uprising. A wide range of leftist and rightist opposition forces participated in the door-to-door campaign, reconnecting national politics to the popular spaces of the streets and workplaces. Popular layers that had remained passive throughout the 2011 insurrection were galvanized into action. In this regard, Tamarod represented a new revolutionary wave of popular initiative 'from below'.

However, unlike January and February 2011, the popular movement was immediately appropriated by the anti-Brotherhood factions of the ruling-class and state apparatus. Seeing that the Ikhwan were incapable of securing political and economic stability and frustrated by the president's inaction against Sinai insurgents (Abul-Magd 2013: 4), the military leaders opened negotiations with Tamarod and the NSF. Tamarod became infiltrated by elements of the Ministry of Interior (al-Sharif and Saleh 2013), sponsored by Coptic billionaire Naguib Sawiris, advised by Mubarakist judge Tahani al-Gebali (Gresh 2013), and widely supported by the mainstream media.

After collecting millions of signatures from ordinary Egyptians, Tamarod launched the 30 June Front to organize protests against the president on the day that commemorated his first year in power. Preparatory demonstrations on 28 and 29 June had already turned violent when they clashed with pro-Morsi supporters. Massive demonstrations and strikes mobilizing millions of Egyptians in the streets erupted on 30 June, demanding nothing less than the resignation of the president. In an echo of 28 January 2011, Tahrir Square reached its maximum capacity of demonstrators. However, Morsi, stressing his legitimacy as democratically elected president, refused to give in.

When the mass protests entered their second day on 1 July, Abdel Fattah al-Sisi, head of the Armed Forces, issued an ultimatum to both camps to solve the crisis within 48 hours or else the military would intervene. After two more days of deadly clashes between pro and anti-Morsi protesters, the 30 June Front met the military leaders, and shortly afterwards al-Sisi declared that the president had been removed from his position and that chief Justice Adli Mansour would head a transitional government as interim president. Morsi was arrested and the army occupied key political and economic sites in the country, cheered by the anti-Morsi masses. Mirroring February 2011, a popular uprising was again 'crowned' with a military coup.

The Timrod insurrection could be perceived as a new high point in the revolutionary process, remobilizing and repoliticizing broad layers of the population through grassroots committees that arranged the collection of signatures and organized demonstrations and strikes (see Elyachar 2014). Yet the character of the movement was from its inception marred by the presence and intervention of *feloul*, opportunist political forces, and members of the security apparatus, able to guide the anger of the masses along a designated path. Whereas the security apparatus had tried to repress and divide the 2011 movement, now its leaders and goals were co-opted in a transformist manner (see Chapter 3). Furthermore, this time the dominant group within the mass movement was the secular middle class, which saturated the protests with its reactionary slogans, flags, and aims, calling for the military leadership to substitute its own agency for that of the masses (Naguib 2014). For these petty-bourgeois layers, the failure of the SCAF to impose its rule in 2011 and 2012 had not tainted the Armed Forces as a national institution; they viewed it as retaining its aura of national impartiality, capable of bringing order and prosperity to the country. The infiltration of the security apparatus, combined with the dominant position of the middle class in the mass movement and the lack of a viable 'third camp' between the Brotherhood and the military, allowed Sisi to intervene successfully. Neither a completely genuine uprising from below, nor a simple top-down military coup, Tamarod was turned into a counter-revolutionary mass movement of which the agency, leadership, and goals were successfully appropriated by the generals and their rightist allies.

Reactionary Caesarism

Initially, Western powers had hoped that the Egyptian Revolution could be absorbed into a neoliberal agenda. They thought that the demands of the protesters could be deflected towards a purely 'democratic transition', replacing the open dictatorship with a 'light' bourgeois-democratic state that was compatible with the imperatives of the neoliberal offensive (Hanieh 2013: 165). The Brotherhood's demise illustrated that the road to bourgeois democracy was blocked, as the military and security apparatus could never accept a legislative and executive power that went too much beyond their direct control. But maybe there was another progressive alternative left under military tutelage? The Caesarist interventions of the SCAF in January 2011 and of Sisi in June 2013 evoked the historical antecedent of the Free Officers' coup of 1952. In that episode, the Armed Forces had also presented themselves as a national 'third party' that forcefully solved the societal stalemate to the advantage of the popular forces. Pulling the past back towards the present, Sisi presented himself as a new Nasser: 'a charismatic, fierce general around whom a country in crisis could unite; and a benevolent tyrant who will stop at nothing to crush dangerous dissent in order to grant his people security and prosperity' (Abdelrahman 2014: 136). However, the Caesarism of Sisi – like those of the SCAF and Morsi before him – was essentially reactionary and quantitative. Unlike the Free Officers, with their programme of anti-imperialism and nationalism, the generals did not advance a political project that transcended their own narrow interests (Kandil 2012: 233). The SCAF and Sisi did not organize their coups on the waves of popular revolution in order to destroy the old society, as in 1952, but to save it. From a world-historical perspective, Nasser's Caesarism was progressive, for it pushed back feudalism and imperialism, developing the productive forces within the boundaries of state-led 'national' capitalism. Conversely, the SCAF was not interested in reinforcing the public sector and opposed court rulings in favour of the renationalization of privatized companies. When the 'transitional government' granted material benefits to workers, this represented an ad hoc tactic of neutralizing strikes, not a systematic popular policy. The intervention of the SCAF merely reconfigured the relations of power between the ruling factions, leaving the main state institutions and the economic base of the neoliberal bloc intact. Whereas Nasser grounded his Bonapartist position increasingly in a popular class base, the SCAF remained essentially chemically connected to (their faction of) the bourgeoisie.

Nevertheless, Kandil has suggested that the institution of the Armed Forces is still capable of transforming Egypt's society, but that the attitude of the military and revolutionary leadership made such 'a real partnership with the officers' impossible in practice (Kandil 2012: 233). Is there still a possibility for a progressive Caesarism in Egypt? Perhaps the fact that Sisi enjoys massive popular support and was easily elected president in 2014 points to such a popular Bonapartist development? The problem with such a perspective is twofold. Firstly, despite Sisi's broad *social* base of support, his *class* base remains essentially bourgeois. In addition to the military apparatus, Nasser had to lean on workers, farmers, and petty-bourgeois intellectuals to constitute a new state that substituted itself for the absent bourgeoisie. Sisi successfully mobilized the popular masses as a social force against a competitor *within* the bourgeois class: the Brotherhood. On the basis of this struggle he was also able to unite under his leadership the quarrelling factions within the Armed Forces (Alexander and Bassiouny 2014: 208), together with the Ministry of Interior, the Mubarakist oligarchs, and opposition businessmen such as Sawiris. The regional alliance of Sisi's regime with the reactionary Saudi monarchy and his fealty to the United States demonstrated that the new dictatorship represented historical continuity rather than rupture (Naguib 2014).

Tamarod created a social base for Sisi's leadership and the subsequent violent repression of the Ikhwan in the streets, by both the security apparatus and Sisi's popular supporters, consolidated his hegemony. Before the autumn of 2012 the revolution had known many violent episodes, often pitting revolutionary protesters against the state apparatus. Nevertheless protesters had conceived of violence on their part as a necessary evil and a means of defence against state power. The clash between Brotherhood supporters and opposition forces brought violence into the ranks of the revolutionaries themselves. Brotherhood sit-ins at Rabea al-Adawiya and al-Nahda squares were dispersed with extreme violence. According to some sources the massacre of Rabea al-Adawiya alone cost the lives of 904 people, of whom 897 were civilians (Schielke 2015). Moreover, after June 2013 violence became endemic to mass mobilization, acquiring an anti-emancipatory logic of its own. Sisi was able to ground popular consent in the state's violent repression of the Ikhwan. His hegemony was not rooted in the masses' utopian desire for liberation from oppression, but on their dystopian drives of fear and uncertainty, which were channelled into an authoritarian project of hysterical hyper-nationalism that revolved around the liquidation of the 'enemy within' and 'a promise of reaching clarity, purity and truth through a decisive battle' (Schielke 2015). If anything, the combination of a popular social base, a bourgeois class base, the forging of consent through street violence, and a hyper-nationalist project of restoration indicated a chemical movement towards a Fascistic state instead of 'progressive' Caesarism.

Secondly, the historical path of progressive Caesarism has been closed off with Egypt's integration into the neoliberal order (see Abdelrahman 2014: 136–7). Nasserist state capitalism had belatedly completed the classical process of bourgeois transformation – the formation of an 'autonomous centre of capital accumulation' – in a particular Caesarist way that was only rendered possible by unique geopolitical and economic circumstances (see Chapter 6). Seeing that Nasserism was already severely limited in its transformative capacities, the willing subjugation of twenty-first century domestic capital to transnational monopoly and finance capital in return for rentier profits does not allow for any 'popular consumption policy' at all (see Hanieh 2013: 73). Sisi's regime became part and parcel of the global neoliberal offensive that served to strengthen the class power of capital against labour through the reconfiguration of the economic base and the superstructures of the post-war Fordist and developmentalist historical blocs. Even if Sisi were to move to the left under pressure from the masses, all he could do would be to distribute rent income in a more equitable way. The military elites could not transform the economic structure itself, for they had become themselves the main beneficiaries of neoliberal accumulation. Material concessions to the popular classes necessarily have had a temporary and superficial character, only lasting until the next fiscal crisis or until the stream of loans from the IMF, Gulf countries, and the United States dried up (Maher 2011).

The fact that the military coup of June 2013 was carried out on the waves of mass protest created a historical debt to these forces. However, in the long run Sisi's dictatorship cannot satisfy the needs and expectations of the subaltern masses. Despite Sisi's strong hegemonic position, both with regard to subaltern groups and elite factions, within the context of global neoliberalism national state power is insufficiently grounded in a stable economic structure, and, consequently, a new organic crisis is on the horizon (Naguib 2014). However, even though a crisis of hegemony may create opportunities for a new revolutionary movement, popular dissatisfaction, desire, and even mobilization are by themselves insufficient to transform society. What is needed is the organization of a counter-hegemony and a political apparatus.

A Question of Hegemony

In the previous chapter, I discussed the limits of the Republic of Tahrir to function as a stable, organized, and centralized hegemonic apparatus for the whole revolution. After February 2011 the revolutionary movement was decomposed into its constituent parts, the civil-democratic and the social movements, which largely withdrew to their proper spheres of activism. The civil-democratic movement was dispersed and rendered powerless as a mass force through the 'counter-revolution in democratic form'. When the people voted for the most conservative political forces in the referenda and elections between 2011 and 2014, in the eyes of many activists the offspring of the revolution seemed monstrous. However, it was not the 'inherent' conservatism of the 'silent majority' that was the main obstacle – this had already been overcome in the praxis of the 18 Days and therefore it could be overcome again – but the practical divide between 'the masses' and 'the vanguard'. The only way of continuing the process of permanent revolution was to find a concrete solution to the problem of hegemony after the fall of Mubarak. The soft coup had cut off the vanguard from its mass base. Civil-democratic activists had to rebuild the disintegrating national–popular subject by reconnecting the vanguard to its mass basis. In the wake of the 18 Days there were still many instances of political emancipation from below. People organized themselves spontaneously in their workplaces and neighbourhoods, but these experiments lacked an institutional form that could consolidate and develop their activity into forms of self-governance (Alexander and Bassiouny 2014: 325). Nonetheless, only a small fraction of the civil-democratic movement realized that if the vanguard could not mobilize the masses it would have to bring the 'spirit of Tahrir' to the popular neighbourhoods and workplaces, where it had to start the difficult, molecular work of building a counter-hegemonic alternative.

Since 2000, the political and social movements against the neoliberal offensive had subsumed each other as moments within a broad process of developing popular revolt. The year 2005 represented the high point of the civil-democratic 'political' moment (and its subsequent collapse). Conversely, the Mahalla uprising of 2008 expressed the culmination of the social struggle (and its ensuing fragmentation). With the 25 January uprising, the dominant moment shifted back to the political – until the departure of Mubarak. While popular initiative in the political sphere was gradually displaced by the pseudo-democratic transition, social movements were able to expand and develop their activity. They advanced roughly the same demands as in the decade before the revolution, focusing on employment, livelihoods, public services, and the right to organize, but now in a mass form. Farmers continued to demonstrate for their rights and to occupy lands; a massive number of them (700,000) joined one of the four independent umbrella organizations that emerged after the uprising (El-Nour 2015: 203–4). Workers returning to their workplaces transposed their revolutionary experience to their social condition as wage labourers. Feeling empowered by the mass strikes and the popular uprising, they began to set up their own trade unions vis-à-vis the factory management and the structures of the GFETU (personal communication with K.A. Eita, 20 March 2011). Moreover, their social struggle acquired a political dimension with the demand of *tathir*, the 'cleansing' of the public sector and the state apparatus in general from corrupt Mubarakists (Alexander and Bassiouny 2014: 211–2). In the months and years following the uprising, almost every section of the Egyptian working class rose in protest against bad working conditions, low wages, and the petty dictatorships of the 'little Mubaraks' presiding over public and private companies (see Alexander 2012).

The September 2011 strike wave represented a growing generalization of workers' coordination and consciousness. In contradistinction to the unplanned and ad hoc worker protests from February until March 2011, these strikes were organized by the new independent trade unions. Conversely, the September strikes taught other workers to coordinate their protests and form trade unionist organizations themselves (Alexander 2012). Trade unionism also reached out to subaltern actors who hitherto had remained relatively passive: 'Hospital doctors, mosque imams, fishermen, Tuk-Tuk drivers, skilled craftsmen, intellectual property rights consultants, daily-paid labourers and the operators of the "scarab boats" that take tourists on Nile river trips' (Alexander 2012: 114–5). Trade unions began to overcome the local and sectorial fragmentation of the proletarian subject. However, at the level of national leadership, independent trade unionism became divided between the radical EFITU of Kamal Abu Eita and the more moderate and cautious Egyptian Democratic Labour Congress (EDLC) of Kamal Abbas (Beinin 2013a). Furthermore, as both Gramsci and Luxemburg emphasized, trade unions defend workers' interests within the framework of capitalism, but they are not political organs, nor do they constitute a transitional form to socialism (see Morton 2007: 82; Thatcher 2007: 32). As Abdelrahman stressed: 'Creating independent unions is one thing. Coalescing workers' efforts into a movement that could play a leadership role in Egypt's revolutionary process is quite another' (Abdelrahman 2014: 87). In order to become a political force, the workers' movement needed a structure that generalized and centralized its fragmented experiences: a 'party' in Gramsci's broad sense.

However, despite initiatives from leftist groups such as the RS and the Socialist Popular Alliance Party, a workers' party that was organically connected to the trade union movement did not materialize.[3] The power of the workers' movement remained fragmented and could not be concentrated into an instrument to resolve the hegemonic crises of the SCAF and Morsi (Alexander and Bassiouny 2014: 194, 217–8). On the other hand, the state could not displace proletarian initiative as easily as it had done with the civil-democratic movement. The Nasserist wing of the workers' movement would prove instrumental in enabling the regime to regain the initiative in the social sphere. Firstly, apart from political leaders such as Hamdeen Sabahi, Nasserist worker leaders were absorbed in the regime apparatus – the most famous example being Kamal Abu Eita, the EFITU leader who became Minister of Manpower in 2012. The 'transformism' of worker leaders such as Abu Eita was the coup de grâce for the EFITU, which was already weakened by internal strife (De Smet and Malfait 2015). Secondly, the military interpellated the deep-seated hostility towards the Muslim Brotherhood in the workers' movement. Thus the political campaign against Morsi also became a means of subsuming the workers' movement under the leadership of the military. Thirdly, despite the debacle of the SCAF, the military's promise of social concessions, which echoed Nasserist redistributive policies, was often accepted by the workers (see Alexander and Bassiouny 2014: 313; De Smet and Malfait 2015).

However, despite promises made since 2011, the regime has not fulfilled the key demands of the workers' movement, which were reformulated ahead of 1 May 2015: the full right of workers to establish completely independent trade unions; protection of trade union activists from severance; the implementation of a system of collective bargaining at all levels; workers' participation in the drafting of the Labour Law, Social Security Law, and Law of Civil Service and the reorganization of the public sector; and the extension of labour rights to temporary workers and labourers in the informal sector (source: CTUWS). Although neoliberal accumulation requires an increase of absolute surplus extraction and an expansion of precarious informal systems, the dictatorship is attacking the workers' movement in a gradual and cautious manner, trying to weaken independent trade unions and to create divisions between public and private workers, different sectors, etc. This offers the Egyptian working class a little breathing space to organize itself. In the face of the triumphant counter-revolution in the political sphere, civil-democratic activists and, of course, leftists especially, would be wise to support the formation of trade unions and their social struggle as an investment in the project of political emancipation. In the future, a new round of political mobilization backed by a powerful trade unionist movement might have a chance of defeating the dictatorship.

9. Conclusions

In the 'Preface', Marx wrote that at a certain point property relations turn 'from forms of development of the productive forces ... into their fetters. Then begins an era of social revolution' (Marx 1987: 263). With regard to capitalist relations, their sublation required the development of the proletarianized masses from a class-in-itself into a class-for-itself. Marx saw this abstract formula rendered concrete in the experiences of the 1848 proletarian uprising and the Paris Commune, which showed the growth of social emancipation from the conditions of the political struggle for democracy, popular sovereignty, and civil rights. Trotsky connected this ever present possibility for 'permanent revolution' with the uneven and combined development of capitalism, which allowed the Russian popular masses to wage an uninterrupted revolution of their own. Lenin's 'April Theses' (1917) outlined the conditions for proletarian hegemony, offering a concrete form for the abstract theory of permanent revolution in the context of the unfolding revolution. Gramsci, for his part, rearticulated these conditions for the Western, post-war working class and the historical circumstances of a 'war of position'.

Moreover, faced with the stubborn survival of capitalism despite its returning crises, Gramsci developed the concept of passive revolution to function as a criterion for the interpretation of the *absence* of permanent revolution and the *failure* of proletarian hegemony, underlining the agility of ruling classes, the flexibility of capitalism, and the leading role of state power in displacing popular initiative. As a concept, passive revolution signifies not a type of capitalist transition or a 'middle road' between revolution and counter-revolution, but a way of understanding successful, stable, and lasting restorations of dominant class power. This political outcome is rendered possible by modifications to a nation's superstructures and economic base, which push crises further into the future. The elastic reconfiguration of national historical blocs is both stimulated and limited by the global development of capitalism and the contemporary geopolitical order.

When neither the ruling nor the subaltern groups is able to assert its domination in a situation of crisis, a 'third party' may substitute its agency for that of the classes involved. Although Bonapartism/ Caesarism appears as the intervention of an independent person or stratum, it is always grounded in a specific class base. With regard to bourgeois Bonapartism, its intervention does not constitute a fundamentally new relation between state and class, but it merely reveals the 'chemical' content of bourgeois hegemony as the political representation of capital or even of a specific fraction of capital. Popular or proletarian Bonapartism, on the other hand, constructs an artificial chemical state on top of a subaltern class base, displacing the *content* of subaltern hegemony (self-emancipation), while becoming popular in *form* – for example through public-sector-led accumulation, redistribution of wealth, a discourse of national liberation, etc. From a world-historical perspective, Gramsci distinguished between progressive forms of Caesarism that moved society forward and reactionary forms that fettered its development. However, in the age of developed capitalism progressive Bonapartism becomes impossible, because its substitution of class power prevents the formation of proletarian hegemony, which is a necessary political condition for overcoming the capitalist mode of production.

Taking into account uneven and combined development things get more complex. In the Global South, imperialism constituted capitalism in a necessarily incomplete way. Hence Trotsky's perspective of permanent revolution was based on the absolute incapacity of domestic ruling classes to pursue the path of political emancipation and establish a proper bourgeois society. The proletariat would have to substitute its class agency for that of the absent bourgeoisie. However, it would not content itself with merely political emancipation from dictatorship, but would immediately struggle for social emancipation as well, turning the national-democratic revolution into a socialist world revolution. Yet conditions of Fordist development and superpower rivalry created opportunities to displace such a process. In some cases the national bourgeoisie was able to overcome its (semi-)colonial predicament and develop the productive forces within a capitalist framework (for example India, South Korea, Turkey). In other cases the incapacity of both the colonial proletariat and the bourgeoisie to become a hegemonic force necessitated the intervention of a 'third party' in order to solve the predicament of imperialist domination and exploitation in a roundabout way. Permanent revolution in the Global South was deflected, in the sense that state power was able to develop capitalism in a popular form. From a world-historical perspective, this type of Caesarism was 'progressive', because it completed the development of capitalism; but from an emancipatory point of view it remained reactionary, because it displaced the movement to socialism from below. Furthermore, popular

Bonapartist regimes were transitional social formations, because they did not only establish new states, but also created a new bourgeoisie, often through a fusion of private elites and fractions of state capital. Finally, their lifespan was dictated by global developments: through the mechanism of debt, domestic private and state capital were subjugated to the interests of international and transnational finance capital.

Neoliberalism represented a global counter-revolution of capital against the relatively strong position of labour in Fordist and developmentalist historical blocs. From a passive-revolutionary perspective, the reconfiguration of Egypt's historical bloc by the Mubarak state, especially from the 1990s onwards, was a failure, as it stimulated popular initiative instead of displacing it, and as its modifications of state and economy created new instabilities instead of a novel equilibrium. From the viewpoint of capital, Sisi's Caesarism was much more promising, as it successfully displaced a revolutionary wave, opening up a national space for transformations from above that could rejuvenate capitalism, following, for example, the Turkish or Brazilian model of an export-led economy dominated by industrial capital. But this national space is immediately restricted by the global neoliberal framework, which nourishes the rentier state and its parasitic domestic and international money-capitalist clients (Achcar 2013: 279, 281). Just like Italian Fascism, Sisi's authoritarian project won't be able to solve the problem of unproductive money capital in a non-revolutionary manner. Egypt's dependent 'crony capitalism' is not the opposite of the Western neoliberal myth, but it's broken mirror, reflecting 'lean' production as deindustrialization and unemployment and flexibility as informality and precariousness. The essence of neoliberalism shines through the broken reflection of its Egyptian appearance.

Similarly, the dictatorship of Sisi reflects a trend towards authoritarianism in the West, in which national constituencies lose their grip over the states that were 'democratized' after the Second World War. Popular sovereignty succumbs to concerns of anti-terror 'security' and fiscal 'stability'. The superficial and short-lived 'democratic' phase of the Egyptian revolution demonstrates that there is little superstructural elasticity in neoliberal times. It also indicates that the basic tasks of political emancipation cannot be accomplished on a neoliberal economic base, which, in turn, points towards the crisis of the neoliberal project in general. Although it is difficult to distinguish conjunctural from organic crises, it seems reasonable to conclude that the financial crisis of 2008, the slow growth rates in core Western capitalist nations, the 'Arab Spring', Latin American and South-European leftist populism, and OWS and similar political and social protest movements are signs of the organic crisis of neoliberal capitalism. As usual, the crisis of capitalism can be resolved in three ways: socialism, barbarism, or revolution–restoration. With regard to socialism the Egyptian revolution clearly reaffirmed the possibility of permanent revolution in the twenty-first century (Choonara 2011). Although Davidson (2010) argued that the theory of permanent revolution has become redundant, seeing that the generalization of the capitalist mode of production has made the tasks for the revolution immediately socialist, the concept remains relevant today (see Zeilig 2010). Firstly, unfortunately, despite the actuality of capitalism, stage theory remains a powerful force among the left (Callinicos 2013). For example, throughout the Egyptian revolution the Stalinist left argued for a coalition between all 'democratic' forces against the dictatorship, including sections of the 'national' bourgeoisie, and subsequently for an alliance with the military against the danger of 'Islamic Fascism' (De Smet 2015). Hence, permanent revolution has an important discursive value as it connects the tasks of political emancipation with those of social emancipation in the era of developed capitalism.

Secondly, whereas uneven and combined development represented the articulation of capitalist and precapitalist forms into a capitalist ensemble during the constitution of the capitalist mode of production, proper capitalist development still presumes an unevenness and combination of 'advanced' and 'backward' forms. The process of differentiation and unity is no longer between historical forms that are external and internal to the logic of capital, but between particular forms of capitalism (see Morton 2013: 59). With every reconstitution of capitalism its previous forms are dragged into new configurations in which they perform new functions. In Egypt, the neoliberal offensive did not destroy state capitalism, but transformed some fractions of state capital into private capital, and partly reincorporated other fractions as subordinate forms (see Alexander and Bassiouny 2014: 95–6). In the context of capitalist uneven and combined development, bourgeois democracy remains either fragile or non-existent. The working class in many nations of the Global South continues to face the task of political emancipation in conjunction with social emancipation. But the task of the democratization of the state is not limited to these countries. The global neoliberal undermining of bourgeois democracy also poses a threat to the rights and freedoms of the organized workers' movement, which has to combine a fight for its political rights in order to wage its social struggle. The bourgeoisie's failure to fulfil its promise of an organic passage opens up a hegemonic opportunity for the proletariat to rally other subaltern forces to the cause of democracy. Furthermore, the development of modern means of communication, in its social as well as its technical sense, renders the almost immediate geographical expansion of revolution much more likely. Hence the core meaning of Marx's original conception of permanent revolution remains valid today (Zeilig 2010).

Although the promise of permanent revolution was saliently projected from the Middle East in 2011, a few years later the region seems buried beneath the weight of counter-revolution. The success of the uninterrupted revolution of 2011, from Tahrir, to Wall Street, to Gezi, has been overshadowed by permanent counter-revolution. Enduring civil war, violence, and the 'collapse of civilization' in Iraq, Libya, Palestine, and Yemen illustrate 'barbarism' as another outcome of organic crisis. But the term 'barbarism' may be a misnomer for the actual process going on; although it seems madness, there is method in it. It is not so much civilizational barbarism as imperialist barbarism, sponsored and (often vainly) directed by regional powers such as Iran, Israel, Saudi Arabia, and Turkey and international powers such as the United States, the European Union, and Russia. The fragmented mechanical state that operates in these collapsed countries – mercenary bands operating as state power protecting the interests of specific capitals – is quite appropriate for the profitable short-term strategy of accumulation by dispossession.

However, in the long run regional instability infects the whole system, and a more stable solution has to be found. And despite the huge problems facing capitalism, we should take its persistent capacity to survive crises seriously. From a passive-revolutionary viewpoint the bourgeois class may be able to deflect a new wave of permanent revolution by reinventing capitalism and pursuing a new accumulation strategy that is grounded in a broad consensus. For example, the ecological question may be appropriated as a means of forging a bourgeois hegemony around new forms of morality, production, consumption, and international relations that unite the need for austerity with the demand for sustainability. The reformulation of the common good on ecological lines may perversely strengthen bourgeois class power; for 'sacrifices' have to be made and consumption and waste have to be reduced. Cosmopolitan petty-bourgeois layers may be easily absorbed in such a class project. Hence state coercion of 'wasteful' and 'demanding' subaltern groups or nations becomes rooted in popular consent.

In any case, until a reconfiguration of the global neoliberal order takes place, the material base for hegemony will remain limited in Egypt. Sisi's populist authoritarianism and regional and US aid have temporarily displaced the revolutionary wave, but popular consent will inevitably break down when the dictatorship is unable to fulfil the basic needs of the population. At the moment of writing, the Fascistic mass enthusiasm for Sisi's leadership is already evaporating, making way for political fear, cynicism, and passivity. Either the organized workers' movement must show the collapsed civil-democratic movement a way out of the mire, or the nation faces a protracted period of counter-revolutionary state terror.

Notes

Chapter 1

1. This was 'a direct import from Tunisia' (Khalil 2012: 144), where a similar uprising between 17 December 2010 and 14 January 2011 had forced dictator Zine El Abidine Ben Ali to resign from the presidency. During the Tunisian revolt protesters had chanted the famous slogan at the Avenue Habib Bourguiba until Ben Ali stepped down. The phrase 'the people want' referred to a popular poem of the Tunisian poet Abu al-Qasim al-Shabbi (1909–34), whose final two lines had been incorporated into the national anthem: 'If the people want life someday, fate will surely grant their wish. Their shackles will surely be shattered and their night surely vanish' (Achcar 2013: 13).
2. As Draper (2011a: 131) points out, the term 'proletariat' has a long history, originally denoting the poor, propertyless class. Here the term is used in its precise sense of a modern labour population that has been dispossessed from its means of production, is forced to sell its labour force in order to make a living, and produces surplus value in the course of commodity production. The basic unit of the proletariat is the 'collective worker': 'the ensemble of workers whose labour taken together is necessary to produce a given commodity' (Draper 2011b: 35), which includes workers that do not produce surplus value 'on their own', but as part of the collective. The proletariat is the core of the modern working class, which is the wage-labour population in its broad sense. Apart from modern wage workers there are also layers of the petty bourgeoisie that constitute a 'working class', in the sense that they depend on self-employed labour and/or small-property ownership: artisans, shopkeepers, doctors, small farmers, etc.
3. In the original broad Gramscian sense of social groups that are subordinated to the ruling classes.
4. See also: 'Upon the different forms of property, upon the social conditions of existence, rises an entire superstructure of different and distinctly formed sentiments, illusions, modes of thought and views of life. The entire class creates and forms them out of its material foundations and out of the corresponding social relations' (Marx 1979a: 128).

Chapter 2

1. Ellen Meiksins Wood criticizes the historical conflation of 'bourgeois' with 'capitalist', asserting that 'the word was once conventionally used to mean nothing more than someone of non-noble status who, while he worked for a living, did not generally dirty his hands and used his mind more than his

body in his work. That old usage tells us nothing about capitalism, and is likely to refer to a professional, an office-holder, or an intellectual, no less than to a merchant' (Wood 2012: 42). However, when deployed critically, the notion serves to distinguish the traditional nobility from those non-aristocratic groups that were able to strengthen their class power based on private property. The original bourgeoisie is the 'monied' class, although its class character changes fundamentally in the transition from commercial society to industrial capitalism. The commercial bourgeoisie of the Ancien Régime differs as much from the industrial bourgeoisie of capitalist modernity as the waged craftsmen from the urban proletariat.

2. The emphasis on the role of transformations in the relations of production – and property rights as their superstructural form – in the origin of capitalism loosely follows the 'social property relations' approach of Robert Brenner (1977, 1985a, 1985b) and E.M. Wood (2012). Unlike Blaut (1993) I think it is possible to stress the crucial role of the 'periphery' in the rise of commercial society and the concentration of money capital in the 'core', while maintaining that this development was a necessary but insufficient factor in the emergence of a capitalist *mode of production*, which was only possible in conditions of modern private property relations, a proletarianized labour population, and, eventually, industrialization.

3. Only, however, from the perspective of developed capitalism. Arguably, there is no historical necessity involved in the transition from late or modern feudalism to proper capitalism (see Versieren and De Smet 2014; Wood 1991).

4. An accumulation strategy is a concept of the specific ensemble of structural and superstructural elements that is suited for capital accumulation in a certain historical context (see Jessop 1990: 198). In other words, an accumulation strategy is the *design* of a capitalist historical bloc.

5. In Chapter 4 I connect this different form of governance to Hegel's concepts of mechanism and chemism.

6. Coutinho (2012: 151) remarks that for Marx civil society represented the sphere of the relations of production (thus part of the 'economic structure'), whereas Gramsci placed it in the domain of the superstructures. This opposition may be misleading, as the superstructures are simply the 'form' of the economic 'content' (see Gramsci 1971: 377; Q7§21).

7. They wore trousers instead of the knee-breeches (*culottes*) that were traditionally worn by the nobility and the bourgeoisie.

8. This notion of sovereignty does not simply turn absolutism into its popular opposite, but, as Wood remarks, Rousseau 'travels that route not past, but through, the concerns of constitutionalism and the tradition of popular resistance' (Wood 2012: 168).

9. Although it is correct that Gramsci develops 'a more textured and complex notion of politics and the state', he did not move away from Marx's and Lenin's concept of the 'dictatorship of the proletariat', as Fontana claims (2004: 192–4). Gramsci developed Lenin's concept of hegemony, which defined the relation between the Russian proletariat and the peasantry in

their alliance against czarism as one where workers played a leading role, adapting it to the national context of Italy and Western Europe in general (Morton 2007: 88; Townshend 1996: 245). In doing so Gramsci leaned on Croce's concept of 'ethico-political history', which emphasized the role of culture and morality; on Machiavelli's idea of the Prince, which connected political leadership to a materialist dynamic; and on his language studies at the University of Turin, which made him aware of the power of discourse (Roccu 2012: 43–5).

10. In itself, the notion of non-violent methods of class rule was not a novelty, for Marx and Engels had already discussed 'the inculcation of inertia and apathy; moral subjugation; falsification of information; concessions and reforms; division of the ruled into more and less favoured groups; from Janissaries to scapegoats; cooptation-winning over or buying out potential opposition leadership, including assimilation into the ruling class; direct and indirect corruption; and nationalism' (Draper 2001: 264). Arguably, Gramsci's contribution to a Marxist theory of the state was a systematization of such notions – within the limits set by the fragmentary nature of the *Prison Notebooks*.

11. The essential relation that is lost in the schematic and typological representation of political and civil hegemony by Perry Anderson (1976; see also Roccu 2012: 48–9).

12. For Gramsci 'intellectuals' played a crucial role in the development and consolidation of a ruling group's hegemony. Although every human is an intellectual and a philosopher (Gramsci 1971: 347; Q10ii§52), in the general sense that every human activity involves a degree of intellect, society assigns to some of its members the social function of intellectual. The development of the technical and social division of labour implies that throughout history each class produces its own 'specialists' who fulfil specific functions in the realm of production, culture, and politics.

13. A reference to the Gironde department, from which the original group of representatives hailed.

14. A reference to their seats at the high end of the hall (*montagne* = mountain).

15. Finance capital differed from precapitalist money capital in the sense that it was an advanced form of money capital embedded within (and not external to or in opposition to) a developing capitalist mode of production: 'bankers, stock-exchange kings, railway kings, owners of coal and iron mines and forests, a part of the landed proprietors associated with them' (Marx 1978: 48).

16. The nature of this 'Caesarist' regime will be explored in Chapter 4.

17. In the 'Eighteenth Brumaire' (1852) Marx quipped that: 'The French bourgeoisie had long ago found the solution to Napoleon's dilemma: "Dans cinquante ans, l'Europe sera républicaine ou cosaque." It had found the solution to it in the "république cosaque"' (Marx 1979a: 182).

18. The permanent revolution is 'the class dictatorship of the proletariat as the necessary transit point to the abolition of class distinctions generally, to the abolition of all the relations of production on which they rest, to

the abolition of all the social relations that correspond to these relations of production, to the revolutionising of all the ideas that result from these social relations' (Marx 1978: 127).

Chapter 3

1. Gramsci appropriated this term from the French historian Edgar Quinet (1803–75).
2. A Commune was a self-governing medieval town, which provided the resident burghers with its own forms of legal and military organization. In northern Italy the development of the Communes led to the rise of strong and independent city states, which blocked the formation of a national territory.
3. Gramsci complicated this binary picture with a distinction between: '1. The Northern urban force; 2. the Southern rural force; 3. the Northern–Central rural force; 4. the rural force of Sicily; 5. that of Sardinia', but remarked that '[t]he first of these forces retains its function of "locomotive"' (Gramsci 1971: 98; Q19§26).
4. The idea of such a process of class co-optation goes back to Marx and Engels, as Draper (2011a: 268) asserted.
5. Gramsci appropriated the concept of 'myth' from Georges Sorel (1847–1922) as 'a political ideology expressed neither in the form of a cold utopia nor as learned theorizing, but rather by a creation of concrete phantasy which acts on a dispersed and shattered people to arouse and organise its collective will' (Gramsci 1971: 126; Q13§1). The myth functions as an ideological instrument that constructs hegemony, and as such it is embodied by the political party or 'Modern Prince' (Gramsci 1971: 128–9; Q13§1).
6. A 'continuous organic and dialogic exchange between leaders and the masses; between revolutionary theory and "good sense"; and between workers and their subaltern allies' (De Smet 2015: 87; see Thomas 2009: 437–8).
7. This highlighted a more complex relation between universal suffrage and political emancipation than Marx originally put forward in his critique of Hegel's philosophy of right (see Draper 2011a: 93).
8. 'The monopoly of capital becomes a fetter upon the mode of production which has flourished alongside and under it. The centralization of the means of production and the socialization of labour reach a point at which they become incompatible with their capitalist integument. This integument is burst asunder. The knell of capitalist private property sounds. The expropriators are expropriated' (Marx 1990: 929).
9. Until 1870 'monopoly is in the barely discernible, embryonic stage' (Lenin 1964a: 202). After the economic crisis of 1873, cartels began to emerge, but they remain a 'transitory phenomenon', until after the boom and slump cycle around the turn of the century '[c]artels become one of the foundations of the whole of economic life' (Lenin 1964a: 202). The concentration of capital was not merely a concentration of capitalist property, as it went hand in

hand with ... the universal substitution of mechanical for manual labour' (Lenin 1964a: 204).

10. 'One of the special features of imperialism connected with the facts I am describing, is the decline in emigration from imperialist countries and the increase in immigration into these countries from the more backward countries where lower wages are paid' (Lenin 1964a: 282).

11. Marx had referred to 'the United States of North America, where, though classes already exist, they have not yet become fixed, but continually change and interchange their component elements in constant flux, where the modern means of production, instead of coinciding with a stagnant surplus population, rather compensate for the relative deficiency of heads and hands, and where, finally, the feverish, youthful movement of material production, which has to make a new world its own, has left neither time nor opportunity for abolishing the old spirit world' (Marx 1979a: 111). However, America's progressive semblance veiled a process of industrialization through the exploitation and domination of weakly unionized immigrant workers (Clarke 1990: 16).

12. As Clarke emphasised, 'Fordism' in the narrow, abstract sense of 'the decomposition and recomposition of the labour process as the basis for the generalisation of industrial production methods and the internalization of the sources of technological dynamism' (Clarke 1990: 13) was simply the general process of capitalist extended reproduction. Conversely, 'Fordism' in its pure sense of the specific production methods used by Henry Ford was never generalized throughout the capitalist world (Smith 2000: 1), and in fact lacked, by the 1930s, many of the elements of 'Fordism', such as high wages. Here the term is deployed in its broad meaning of a particular capitalist ensemble – i.e. as a historical bloc. This is an intermediate category that allows for an analysis that is situated 'between the general logic of capital and individual case studies' (Smith 2000: 2).

13. Gramsci's concept of Fordism travelled through Italian Autonomism to the Regulation School (see Aglietta 1979; Lipietz 1982) and neo-Gramscian approaches to international relations (see Cox 1983; Gill 1988; Van der Pijl 1998).

14. In practice, policies of the post-war period were never completely Keynesian (Kiely 2005: 49) and when Keynesian theory was applied most vigorously in the 1970s, it exacerbated Fordism's unfolding crisis (Clarke 1990: 32–3).

15. Although, in a strict sense, the New Deal represented a negation of Ford's *personal* labour controlling schemes (Clarke 1990: 28), it was the vindication of the Fordist *system*.

16. 'Once the mechanised systems of production had been introduced to those sectors that could be reorganised on Fordist lines, productivity rates were bound to slow down. Increased productivity could then only occur through the reorganisation of mechanised assembly lines, the intensification of management pressure on labour and the speeding up of already established work practices. Attempts to intensify productivity also gave rise to resistance by labour, which was confident in the face of more or less full employment.

The result was a gap between wage and productivity growth, which further fuelled inflation' (Kiely 2005: 62).

17. Note that the organizational decentralization of capital and the expansion of subcontracting do not preclude capital's further concentration and monopolization. What happens is that the form of monopolization becomes much more differentiated and sophisticated, as hierarchical relations between dominant and subordinate fractions of capital and units of the production and distribution process are now often enforced through the 'dull compulsion of economic relations' instead of by the direct, vertical supervision and control of the core company. Just like Fordism, neoliberalism represents a qualitatively new phase in the development of monopoly capital, rather than its negation.

18. '[L]aissez-faire too is a form of state "regulation", introduced and maintained by legislative and coercive means. It is a deliberate policy, conscious of its own ends, and not the spontaneous, automatic expression of economic facts. Consequently, laissez-faire liberalism is a political programme, designed to change – in so far as it is victorious – a State's leading personnel, and to change the economic programme of the State itself – in other words the distribution of the national income' (Gramsci 1971: 160; Q13§18).

19. During the 1980s American monetarist policies that sought to control inflation through high interest rates were combined with a 'military Keynesianism', which sustained demand through military deficit spending (Kiely 2005: 65). The heightened Cold War tensions legitimized a channelling of public resources into the military–industrial complex.

20. However, neoliberal thought was already influencing governments, even social-democratic ones, in the first half of the 1970s (Cahill 2015).

21. I follow Tony Smith's critique of the post-industrialism thesis: the existence of the expanding service sector remains directly dependent on manufacturing (Smith 2000: 9). I am also subscribing to his view that the current reconfiguration is not merely a form of 'neo-Fordism' but a qualitatively different accumulation strategy (Smith 2000: 19–23).

22. 'Neo-liberalism with its proclamation of the end of conformism and its attack on the "nanny state" can in this context be understood as a policy designed to absorb the agility of the emerging subject for the new potential of a more flexible mode of production, while at the same time keeping this new subject from gaining the necessary experience to challenge the old positions of individual profits and leadership' (Barfuss 2008: 846).

23. Which, in turn, only comes to the surface in its immediate 'conjunctural' form (see above).

24. For a discussion of the concepts of 'war of manoeuvre' and 'war of position', see Chapter 4.

Chapter 4

1. Achcar solves this conundrum by distinguishing between a 'revolutionary dynamic' as the process of revolution and 'revolution' as its proper outcome (Achcar 2013: 15). The difference with my approach is semantic, not logical.

2. This argument has been put forward earlier, however (see Ginsborg 2014).

3. Marx and Engels never discussed the concept of bourgeois revolution in a systematic way (Ginsborg 2014: 32).

4. Louis Auguste Blanqui (1805–81) was a French socialist who believed that the conquest of power was the matter of a small group of enlightened and battle-hardened revolutionaries, which would prepare society for the rule of the popular masses.

5. '[T]he emancipation of the workers contains universal human emancipation – and it contains this, because the whole of human servitude is involved in the relation of the worker to production, and all relations of servitude are but modifications and consequences of this relation' (Marx 1975b: 280).

6. In his discussion of Trotsky's concept of permanent revolution, Thomas claims that Trotsky understood 'the emergence of a qualitatively new type of revolution in the early twentieth century, irreducible to the sum of its supposed historical parts, which placed the division between civil and political societies itself in question' (2015: 288). However, I argue that instead of describing a specific type of revolution, proper to a particular capitalist era – in Trotsky's time, imperialism – permanent revolution highlights a possibility for working-class independence and hegemony relevant to capitalist society in general – as Thomas acknowledges in his investigation of Marx's notion of the revolution in permanence (2015: 300). Marx's discussion of the social and political soul of revolution concurs with this interpretation since they are neither synchronic 'types' of revolution nor predetermined diachronic 'phases', but moments that have to be 'worked out' in ways relevant to the individual social formation and particular era of capitalism.

7. '[L]arge landed property, despite its feudal coquetry and pride of race, has been rendered thoroughly bourgeois by the development of modern society. Thus the Tories in England long imagined that they were enthusiastic about monarchy, the church and the beauties of the old English Constitution, until the day of danger wrung from them the confession that they are enthusiastic only about rent' (Marx 1979a: 128).

8. Luxemburg, for example, highlighted the role of the spontaneous, offensive strike as a collective learning process, preparing the German proletariat for its conquest and exertion of power *before* the moment of a general insurrection. Conversely, Lenin emphasized the need for organization and education of the Russian working class in preparation of an uprising (Higgins 1967). We could understand their different emphasis on, respectively, spontaneous activity and careful organization of the working class as necessary tactical corrections of the 'pure' German war of position and Russian war of movement.

9. This undermines Callinicos's claim that Gramsci confused the modalities of bourgeois and proletarian revolution (Callinicos 2010: 499). However, it could be argued that, because of the Jacobin experience, Gramsci overestimated the bourgeoisie's capacity to effectively organize an organic passage from the masses to the state.

10. A historical reference to the role of imperial guards and their commanders in the late Roman Empire in forcefully solving political crises: 'The army is no longer to maintain the rule of one part of the people over another part of the people. The army is to maintain its own rule, personated by its own dynasty' (Marx 1986b: 465).

11. The revolutionary division of feudal landed property among the petty peasantry had become a financial burden for small-plot holders, whose private property was subjugated to capital and the state through mortgages, loans, and taxes (Marx 1979a: 191).

12. Draper argued that Marx entertained the possibility of a Bonapartist state achieving full autonomization from its constituent class (Draper 2011a: 460–3).

13. In fact, Lenin himself understood the Russian 'institutions of the Bonapartist monarchy' as the terrain of a higher stage of the class struggle, because of the connection between czarist Bonapartism and imperialist capital (Lenin 1963b: 338; 1964b: 305).

14. With regard to the English revolution of the seventeenth century, Engels commented that 'Cromwell is Robespierre and Napoleon rolled into one' (Engels 1975a: 473; see above). The moment of Jacobinism and progressive Caesarism were united in the figure of Cromwell.

15. Note that Gramsci stressed that even in its 'pure' military form, Caesarism remained essentially political: '[T]he soldiers saw in Caesar not only a great military leader but especially their political leader, the leader of democracy' (Gramsci 1971: 88; Q19§28).

16. Draper pointed out that Marx himself had made analogies with Caesarism and that 'the main point is not that Caesar was a Bonaparte or Bonaparte a Caesar, but that both exemplified a more inclusive phenomenon: state autonomization resting on a class equilibrium' (Draper 2011a: 466–7f).

17. Arguably, before 1924 the Russian Communist Party already functioned as a more or less 'benign' substitute for proletarian hegemony, rather than its organic mediation, because of the small size and cultural level of the proletariat, the adverse conditions of civil war, and the absence of a supportive socialist revolution in the advanced capitalist nations. These tendencies reinforced the relative autonomy of the political apparatus and the bureaucratic stratum towards its constituent class.

Chapter 5

1. A military caste of slaves, used by the Ottoman Empire to populate its armies and control its provinces.

2. A reference to the access gate (*porte*) of the governmental palace of the Ottoman Sultan in Istanbul.

3. The urban workforce was classified and organized according to the specific handicraft, commercial activity, service, or trade in which the labourers were employed. Analogous to Western feudal guilds, their organization was the *ta'ifa* (plural: *tawa'if*), which 'vertically' gathered the productive forces relevant to a particular profession (Lockman 1994: 78).

4. On the other hand, the cultivation of long-staple cotton, introduced in 1821, was labour-intensive, required new production methods, and was successful only on large plots. Still, such changes in the countryside did not lead to new property relations that were governed by market imperatives and the subsumption of labour under capital. The relation between the global market and local production units was strictly organized by the command economy of the state and remained isolated from the Egyptian home market.

5. 'You cannot maintain a net of railways over an immense country without introducing all those industrial processes necessary to meet the immediate and current wants of railway locomotion, and out of which there must grow the application of machinery to those branches of industry not immediately connected with railways. The railway-system will therefore become, in India, truly the forerunner of modern industry' (Marx 1979b: 220).

6. '[A] land-tenure system that combines a small number of owners holding very large estates with a large number of owners holding very small farms' (Richards and Waterbury 2008: 177).

7. This is not a normative judgment from a 'pro-Western' standpoint of history, but the material reality of, on the one hand, previously peripheral European nations able to subjugate old empires and rich civilizations because of their industrial, technological, and scientific advances – and, on the other, non-capitalist countries hurrying to 'catch up' with the West in order to compete for power.

8. This recalls Marx's remark with regard to the 1848 revolutions: 'In France, the petty bourgeois does what normally the industrial bourgeois would have to do; the worker does what normally would be the task of the petty bourgeois; and the task of the worker, who accomplishes that? No one.' (Marx 1978: 117).

9. Thomas, however, suggests that Trotsky's concept of permanent revolution is at its core a political theory of revolution 'because it necessarily points towards a theory of organisation of the revolutionary forces that would be able to coordinate relations between revolutionary struggles in the history of a specific national formation, and their insertion in and overdetermination by an international mode of production and state system' (Thomas 2015: 284).

10. 'There were only 15 modern European style factories employing 30–35,000 workers in Egypt in 1916' (Beinin 1981: 15).

11. Only commonly known as Iran in the Western world since 1935.

12. For example, Russia and Britain obstructed the building of railways, as both powers feared that this strategic infrastructure would fall into the hands of their opponents (Keddie 1981: 37–9).

13. Shiite clerics (sing. *alim*).

Chapter 6

1. Arguably, Nasser's real capacity to mobilize the masses as the result of a personal political relation only developed during the Suez War in 1956 (Kandil 2012: 49).

2. One feddan is 1.038 acres or 0.42 hectares (Bush 2007: 1601).
3. Other leaders such as Max Schachtman (1904–72) had already broken with the party line before the Second World War, rejecting Trotsky's continued unconditional critical defence of the USSR in the wake of the Hitler–Stalin pact and the coordinated German and Soviet invasion of Poland in 1939.
4. Unfortunately I do not have the room to engage in detail with the debate on the nature of the Soviet Union here. From a political perspective, I do think that any analysis of 'really existing socialism' has to take into account the fact that political and social emancipation of the working class is impossible if the working class does not govern. Unlike the bourgeoisie, the proletariat can *only* rule by governing.
5. Later, in 1964, he acknowledged that 'capitalism succeeded in stabilizing itself for an entire epoch' (Grant 1989: 311).
6. See Grant in 1978: 'But all history shows that where, for one reason or another, the new progressive class is incapable of carrying out its functions of transforming society, this is often done (in a reactionary way, perhaps) by other classes or castes' (Grant 1989: 350–1). He continues by giving the examples of the *Junkers*, and of Bismarck carrying out the bourgeois revolution and unification of Germany.
7. I won't dwell on the nature of state capitalism (for a typological discussion see Cooper 1983). Here I offer a simple working definition: the state functions as a capitalist *economic* entity, not only regulating, but directly organizing capital accumulation through public instead of private property. State capital as a whole may contain different fractions of statified capital, such as industrial, military, and commercial sectors (see Alexander and Bassiouny 2014: 9). State capitalism is a mode of capital accumulation that has in itself nothing to do with socialism: during the 1960s the share of public investment in almost all Arab states, republican or monarchical, conservative or socialistic, was 50 per cent or more (Ayubi 1992: 90–1). State capitalism represents a fusion of state and class power, which may in form be similar to precapitalist tributary or bureaucratic systems (see Draper 2011a), but its content is determined by the process of capital accumulation.
8. Cliff considered China and Cuba as classic forms of deflected permanent revolution, whereas other colonial revolutions such as those in Ghana, India, Egypt, Indonesia, and Algeria were 'deviations from the norm' or 'bastard forms'. However, the purely proletarian Bonapartist trajectories of China and Cuba, which Cliff took as models of deflected permanent revolution, were exceptional compared to the 'bastard forms': the majority of radical nationalist regimes, where the national bourgeoisie was often suppressed but not entirely liquidated. In Egypt the old elites were bereft of formal political power and direct control over the state apparatus, but the military clique had not completely destroyed the economic base of their class power. Private capital withdrew itself in the economic domains of landed property, real estate, internal trade, and construction. Their grip over the countryside, as well as new alliances with high-ranking officers and bureaucrats, enabled

the old ruling classes to influence the political decision-making process through informal networks and channels.

9. However, Grant saw proletarian Bonapartism as based, not on a social relationship between an independent stratum and the working class, but on the material outcome of the Russian or Chinese revolutions: 'the nationalised economy' (Grant 1989: 308). Arguably, this perspective confused the concept of Bonapartism (Caesarism), which expresses a *political* relation between intellectuals, state, and class, with that of 'statification', which expresses a *legal* relation between state and property rights. The nationalized economy was a necessary material precondition for the Caesarist relation between the bureaucracy and the working class – the economic dimension of Stalinist hegemony.

10. Renamed the State Security Investigation Sector (SSIS) in 1971 (Kandil 2012: 19).

11. During the 1970s the public sector failed to absorb the increasing number of graduates, who were turned into a group of frustrated unemployed with university degrees.

12. Paul Volcker, chairman of the US Federal Reserve, decided to raise interest rates in early 1979 in order to attract capital, combat inflation, reverse the declining credibility of the American dollar, and restore the Federal Reserve's control over monetary policy. The interest rate rose from an average of 8 per cent in 1978 to a staggering 20 per cent in 1981. As most nations in the Global South borrowed at variable rates, the 'Volcker Shock' became a huge financial burden, initiating the so-called Third World debt crisis, which, in turn, represented the main economic mechanism for introducing neoliberal reform on a global scale (Schatan 1987).

Chapter 7

1. Ironically, the introduction of market-oriented production and price formation in the countryside reinforced the dominating rentier logic, strengthening low productivity and increasing the prices of agricultural goods.

2. During the 1993 Cairo Book Fair, President Mubarak claimed that he aimed 'to spare Egypt the fate of Algeria', where a civil war raged between the secular military forces and militants of the *Front Islamique du Salut* (FIS) (in Abdalla 1993: 29).

3. In the late 1990s, farmers were one of the first subaltern groups to begin protesting against the effects of neoliberal accumulation. Their demonstrations, sit-ins, and land occupations were violently repressed by the state and largely ignored by urban middle-class political activists (El-Nour 2015: 202).

4. Such virtual networks were not actors in themselves, but tools and expressions of physical spaces, connections, and actors 'on the ground' (Sassen 2011: 578). Paul Amar keenly observed that '[t]he so-called "Facebook revolution" is not about people mobilizing in virtual space; it is about Egyptian internet cafes and the youth and women they represent, in

real social spaces and communities, utilizing the cyberspace bases they have built and developed to serve their revolt' (Amar 2011).

5. Suleiman had been the regime's favoured candidate for the position of vice-president for two years. He headed the General Intelligence Services, which were directly dependent on foreign funding and worked closely with the United States and Israel, and which were distrusted by the general public (Hajjar 2011). Ahmed Shafiq, for his part, had been a chief of staff of the Air Force, which together with the Republican Guard constituted the two elite branches of the armed forces and those sections of the military that were closest to Mubarak.

6. Later, many of the pro-Mubarak forces were shown to be plainclothes Central Security police or rank-and-file NDP members (Sallam, Stacher and Toensing 2011). Nonetheless, some popular layers of the counter-revolution consisted of protesters who had switched sides after the president's speech on Tuesday night, arguing that the people's demands were met and that life should now return to normal.

7. Paul Amar, however, claims that '[t]he military were trying as best they could to battle the police/thugs, but Suleiman had taken away their bullets for fear the military would side with the protesters and use the ammunition to overthrow him' (Amar 2011).

8. 'This is a gigantic, many-colored picture of a general arrangement of labour and capital which reflects all the complexity of social organization and of the political consciousness of every section and of every district; and the whole long scale runs from the regular trade-union struggle of a picked and tested troop of the proletariat drawn from large-scale industry, to the formless protest of a handful of rural proletarians, and to the first slight stirrings of an agitated military garrison, from the well-educated and elegant revolt in cuffs and white collars in the counting house of a bank to the shy-bold murmurings of a clumsy meeting of dissatisfied policemen in a smoke-grimed dark and dirty guardroom' (Luxemburg 1970: 170).

Chapter 8

1. Workers, for their part, were reluctant to engage in 'politics' and *hizbiyya*, 'partyism'. Labour leaders often displayed a pragmatic and gradual view on the development of the workers' movement.

2. Although there were allegations that Ahmed Shafiq had, in fact, won the elections but the military chose to reverse the results in order not to provoke the streets (Beilin 2013). True or not, it was clear that in the Spring of 2012 the generals were at least hesitant to enforce their own governance in the face of renewed protests (Alexander and Bassiouny 2014: 205).

3. For a discussion of possible causes see Alexander and Bassiouny 2014 and De Smet 2015.

Bibliography

References to LCW and MECW denote respectively the collected works of Lenin and the collected works of Marx and Engels, published by Progress Publishers. Websites were last accessed on 4 September 2015.

Abdalla, Ahmed. 1993. 'Egypt's Islamists and the State'. *Middle East Research and Information Project* 183: 28–31.

Abdelrahman, Maha. 2009. '"With the Islamists? – Sometimes. With the State? – Never!" Cooperation between the Left and Islamists in Egypt'. *British Journal of Middle Eastern Studies* 36(1): 37–54.

—— 2014. *Egypt's Long Revolution: Protest Movements and Uprisings*. London and New York: Routledge.

Abul-Magd, Zeinab. 2013. 'The Egyptian Military in Politics and the Economy: Recent History and Current Transition Status'. *CMI Insight* 2 (October). Available at www.cmi.no/publications/file/4935-the-egyptian-military-in-politics-and-the-economy.pdf

Achcar, Gilbert. 2013. *The People Want: A Radical Exploration of the Arab Uprising*. London: Saqi Books.

Aglietta, Michel 1979. *Theory of Capitalist Regulation: The US Experience*. London and New York: New Left Books.

Akhavi, Shahrough. 1975. 'Egypt's Socialism and Marxist Thought: Some Preliminary Observations on Social Theory and Metaphysics'. *Comparative Studies in Society and History* 17(2): 190–211.

Alexander, Anne. 2011. 'Brothers-in-Arms? The Egyptian Military, the Ikhwan and the Revolutions of 1952 and 2011'. *Journal of North African Studies* 16(4): 533–4.

—— 2012. 'The Egyptian Workers' Movement and the 25 January Revolution'. *International Socialism* 133. January 9. Available at www.isj.org.uk/index.php4?id=778andissue=133

Alexander, Anne, and Mostafa Bassiouny. 2014. *Bread, Freedom, Social Justice: Workers and the Egyptian Revolution*. London: Zed Books.

Allinson, Jamie, and Alexander Anievas. 2010. 'The Uneven and Combined Development of the Meiji Restoration: A Passive Revolutionary Road to Capitalist Modernity'. *Capital & Class* 43(3): 469–90.

Amar, Paul. 2011. 'Why Egypt's Progressives Win'. *Jadaliyya*, 8 February. Available at www.jadaliyya.com/pages/index/586/why-egypts-progressives-win

—— 2012. 'Why Mubarak Is Out'. In Bassam Haddad, Rosie Bsheer, and Ziad Abu-Rish (eds). *The Dawn of the Arab Uprisings: End of an Old Order?* pp. 83–90. London: Pluto Press.

Amin, Samir. 2011. '2011: An Arab Springtime'. *Monthly Review* 63(5). Available at http://monthlyreview.org/2011/10/01/an-arab-springtime/

Anderson, Betty S. 2011. 'The Student Movement in 1968'. *Jadaliyya*, 9 March. Available at www.jadaliyya.com/pages/index/838/the-student-movement-in-1968

Anderson, Perry. 1976. 'The Antinomies of Antonio Gramsci'. *New Left Review* (1)100: 5–78.

Angus, Ian. 2014. 'The Origin of Rosa Luxemburg's Slogan "Socialism or Barbarism"'. http://johnriddell.wordpress.com/2014/10/21/the-origin-of-rosa-luxemburgs-slogan-socialism-or-barbarism/

Antoon, Sinan. 2011. 'Singing for the Revolution'. *Jadaliyya*, 31 January. Available at www.jadaliyya.com/pages/index/508/singing-for-the-revolution

Aoude, Ibrahim G. 1994. 'From National Bourgeois Development to Infitah: Egypt 1952–1992'. *Arab Studies Quarterly* 16(1): 1–23.

Armbrust, Walter. 2012. 'The Revolution against Neoliberalism'. In Bassam Haddad, Rosie Bsheer, and Ziad Abu-Rish (eds). *The Dawn of the Arab Uprisings: End of an Old Order?* pp. 113–23. London: Pluto Press.

Ates, Davut. 2005. 'Economic Liberalization and Changes in Fundamentalism: The Case of Egypt'. *Middle East Policy* 12(4): 133–44.

Ayubi, Nazih N. 1991. *The State and Public Policies in Egypt since Sadat*. London: Ithaca Press.

—— 1992. 'Withered Socialism or Whether Socialism? The Radical Arab States as Populist–Corporatist Regimes'. *Third World Quarterly* 13(1): 89–105.

Bair, Jennifer, and Marion Werner. 2011. 'Commodity Chains and the Uneven Geographies of Global Capitalism: A Disarticulations Perspective'. *Environment and Planning A* 43(5): 988–97.

Bamyeh, Muhammad. 2011. 'The Egyptian Revolution: First Impressions from the Field [Updated]'. *Jadaliyya*, 11 February. Available at www.jadaliyya.com/pages/index/561/the-egyptian-revolution_first-impressions-from-the

Barfuss, Thomas. 2008. 'Active Subjects, Passive Revolution'. *Cultural Studies* 22(6): 837–49.

Bassiouny, Mustafa, and Saud Omar. 2008. 'A New Workers' Movement: The Strike Wave of 2007'. *International Socialism* 118, 31 March. Available at www.isj.org.uk/index.php4?id=429&issue=118

Bayat, Asef. 1993. 'Populism, Liberalization and Popular Participation: Industrial Democracy in Egypt'. *Economic and Industrial Democracy* 14: 65–87.

—— 2011. 'Egypt, and the Post-Islamist Middle East'. *Jadaliyya*, 10 February. Available at www.jadaliyya.com/pages/index/603/egypt-and-the-post-islamist-middle-east-

Beattie, Kirk J. 2000. *Egypt during the Sadat Years*. New York: Palgrave.

Behrooz, Maziar. 1999. *Rebels with a Cause: The Failure of the Left in Iran*. New York: I.B. Tauris.

Beilin, Yossi. 2013. 'Morsi didn't win the elections'. *Israel Hayom*, August 18. Available at www.israelhayom.com/site/newsletter_opinion.php?id=5395

Beinin, Joel. 1981. 'Formation of the Egyptian Working Class'. *Middle East Research and Information Project Reports* 94: 14–23.

—— 1989. 'Labor, Capital, and the State in Nasserist Egypt, 1952–1961'. *International Journal of Middle East Studies* 21(1): 71–90.

—— 1996. 'Will the Real Egyptian Working Class Please Stand Up?' In *Workers and Working Class in the Middle East: Struggles, Histories and Historiographies*, edited by Zachary Lockman, 247–70. Albany: New York State University Press.

—— 1999. 'The Working Class and Peasantry in the Middle East: From Economic Nationalism to Neoliberalism'. *Middle East Report* 210: 18–22.

—— 2001. *Workers and Peasants in the Modern Middle East*. Cambridge: Cambridge University Press.

—— 2005a. 'Political Islam and the New Global Economy'. *The New Centennial Review* 5(1): 111–39.

—— 2005b. 'Popular Social Movements and the Future of Egyptian Politics'. *Middle East Research and Information Project Online*, 10 March. Available at www.merip.org/mero/mero031005

—— 2009. 'Neo-liberal Structural Adjustment, Political Demobilization, and Neo-authoritarianism in Egypt'. In Laura Guazzone and Daniela Pioppi (eds). *The Arab State and Neo-Liberal Globalization: The Restructuring of State Power in the Middle East*, edited by Laura Guazzone and Daniela Pioppi, pp. 19–46. Reading: Ithaca Press.

—— 2011. 'A Workers' Social Movement on the Margin of the Global Neoliberal Order, Egypt 2004–2009'. In Joel Beinin and Frédéric Vairel (eds). *Social Movements, Mobilization, and Contestation in the Middle East and North Africa*, pp. 181–201. Stanford, CA: Stanford University Press.

—— 2013a. 'Workers, Trade Unions and Egypt's Political Future'. *Middle East Research and Information Project*. 18 January 2013. Available at www.merip.org/mero/mero011813

—— 2013b. 'Was There A January 25 Revolution?' *Jadaliyya*. 25 January. Available at www.jadaliyya.com/pages/index/9766/was-there-a-january-25-revolution

—— 2014a. 'History and Consequences'. *Jadaliyya*. 19 March. Available at www.jadaliyya.com/pages/index/16966/history-and-consequences

—— 2014b. 'On Revolutions and Defeated Revolutionary Movements: A Reply to Brecht De Smet'. *Jadaliyya*. 11 June. Available at www.jadaliyya.com/pages/index/18109/on-revolutions-and-defeated-revolutionary-movement

Beinin, Joel, and Zachary Lockman. 1987. *Workers on the Nile: Nationalism, Communism, Islam, and the Egyptian Working Class, 1882–1954*. Princeton: Princeton University Press.

Beinin, Joel, and Hossam al-Hamalawy. 2007. 'Strikes in Egypt Spread from Center of Gravity'. *Middle East Research and Information Project Online*, 9 May. Available at www.merip.org/mero/mero050907

al-Bendary, Amina. 2011. 'Making History in Tahrir'. *Jadaliyya*, February 7. Available at www.jadaliyya.com/pages/index/578/making-history-in-tahrir

Blaut, James. M. 1993. *The Colonizer's Model of the World: Geographical Diffusionism and Eurocentric History*. New York: Guilford Press.

—— 1999. 'Marxism and Eurocentric Diffusionism'. In R. Chilcote (ed.). *The Political Economy of Imperialism: Critical Appraisals*, pp. 127–40. Boston, MA: Kluwer Academic Publishers.

Brenner, Robert. 1977. 'The Origins of Capitalist Development: A Critique of Neo-Smithian Marxism'. *New Left Review* 104: 25–92.

—— 1985a. 'Agrarian Class Structure and Economic Development in Pre-Industrial Europe'. In T.H. Aston and C.H.E. Philpin (eds). *The Brenner Debate: Agrarian Class Structure and Economic Development in Pre-Industrial Europe.* Cambridge: Cambridge University Press.

—— 1985b. 'The Agrarian Roots of European Capitalism'. In T.H. Aston and C.H.E. Philpin (eds). *The Brenner Debate: Agrarian Class Structure and Economic Development in Pre-Industrial Europe.* Cambridge: Cambridge University Press.

Bruff, Ian. 2010. 'Germany's Agenda 2010 Reforms: Passive Revolution at the Crossroads'. *Capital & Class* 34(3): 409–428.

Buci-Glucksmann, Christine. 1979. 'State, Transition and Passive Revolution'. In C. Mouffe (ed.). *Gramsci and Marxist Theory.* London: Routledge.

—— 1980. *Gramsci and the State.* London: Lawrence & Wishart.

Burawoy, Michael. 1989. 'Two Methods in Search of Science: Skocpol versus Trotsky'. *Theory and Society* 18(6): 759–805.

Bush, Ray. 2000. 'An Agricultural Strategy without Farmers: Egypt's Countryside in the New Millennium'. *Review of African Political Economy* 27(84): 235–49.

—— 2007. 'Politics, Power and Poverty: Twenty Years of Agricultural Reform and Market Liberalisation in Egypt'. *Third World Quarterly* 26(8): 1599–615.

—— 2009. 'When "Enough" is not Enough: Resistance during Accumulation by Dispossession'. *Cairo Papers in Social Science: Political and Social Protest in Egypt* 29(2–3): 85–99.

Cahill, Damien. 2015. 'Labour and Neoliberalism: Victim or Vanguard?' *Progress in Political Economy* [website]. http://ppesydney.net/labour-and-neoliberalism-victim-or-vanguard/

Callinicos, Alex. 1982. 'Trotsky's Theory of "Permanent Revolution" and its Relevance to the Third World Today'. *International Socialism* 16. Available at www.marxists.org/history/etol/writers/callinicos/1982/xx/tprtoday.html

—— 1989. 'Bourgeois Revolutions and Historical Materialism'. *International Socialism* 43 (Summer). Available at www.marxists.org/history/etol/writers/callinicos/1989/xx/bourrev.html

—— 2010. 'The Limits of Passive Revolution'. *Capital & Class* 34(3): 491–507.

—— 2011. 'The Return of the Arab Revolution'. *International Socialism* 130. Available at www.isj.org.uk/index.php4?id=717andissue=130

—— 2013. 'The Dynamics of Revolution'. *International Socialism* 137. Available at www.isj.org.uk/index.php4?id=869

Carver, Terrell. 2004. 'Marx's Eighteenth Brumaire of Louis Bonaparte,' pp. 103–27 in P. Baehr and M. Richter (eds). *Dictatorship in History and Theory: Bonapartism, Caesarism, and Totalitarianism.* Cambridge: Cambridge University Press.

Chaichian, Muhammad A. 1988. 'The Effects of World Capitalist Economy on Urbanization in Egypt, 1800–1970'. *International Journal of Middle East Studies* 20(1): 23–43.

Chalcraft, John T. 2001. 'The Coal Heavers of Port Sa'id: State-Making and Worker Protest, 1869-1914.' *International Labor and Working-Class History* 60: 110–24.

Choonara, Joseph. 2011. 'The Relevance of Permanent Revolution: A Reply to Neil Davidson'. *International Socialism* 131. Available at www.isj.org.uk/?id=745

Clarke, Simon. 1990. 'The Crisis of Fordism and the Crisis of Capitalism'. Available at https://homepages.warwick.ac.uk/~syrbe/pubs/telos.pdf (shorter version published as 'The Crisis of Fordism or the Crisis of Social Democracy'). *Telos* 83: 71–98.

Clawson, Patrick. 1978. 'Egyptian Industrialization: A Critique of Dependency Theory'. *Middle East Research and Information Project Reports* 72: 17–23.

Clément, Françoise. 2009. 'Worker Protests under Economic Liberalization in Egypt'. *Cairo Papers in Social Science: Political and Social Protest in Egypt* 29(2/3): 100–16.

—— 2011. 'Le rôle des mobilisations des travailleurs et du mouvement syndical dans la chute de Moubarak'. *Mouvements* 66(2): 69–78.

Cliff, Tony. 1963. 'Permanent Revolution'. *International Socialism* (1st series) 12 (Spring).

—— 1984 [1950]. 'The Class Nature of the People's Democracies', in *Neither Washington nor Moscow: Essays on Revolutionary Socialism*. London: Bookmarks. Available at www.marxists.org/archive/cliff/works/1950/07/index.htm

—— 2000. *Marxism at the Millennium*. London: Bookmarks.

Colla, Elliott. 2011. 'State Culture, State Anarchy'. *Jadaliyya*, 5 February. Available at www.jadaliyya.com/pages/index/558/state-culture-state-anarchy

Cook, Steven. 2007. *Ruling But Not Governing: The Military and Political Development in Egypt, Algeria, and Turkey*. Baltimore, MD: The Johns Hopkins University Press.

Cooper, Mark. 1979. 'Egyptian State Capitalism in Crisis: Economic Policies and Political Interests, 1967–1971'. *International Journal of Middle East Studies* 10(4): 481–516.

—— 1983. 'State Capitalism, Class Structure, and Social Transformation in the Third World: The Case of Egypt'. *International Journal of Middle East Studies* 15(4): 451–69.

Coutinho, Carlos N. 2012. *Gramsci's Political Thought*. Leiden: Brill.

Cox, Robert W. 1983. 'Gramsci, Hegemony and International Relations: An Essay in Method'. *Millennium* 12(2): 162–175.

—— 1987. *Production, Power, and World Order: Social Forces in the Making of History*. New York and Chichester: Columbia University Press.

Davidson, Neil. 2005. 'How Revolutionary Were the Bourgeois Revolutions? (contd.)'. *Historical Materialism* 13(4): 3–54.

—— 2010. 'From Deflected Permanent Revolution to the Law Of Uneven and Combined Development'. *International Socialism* 128 Available at www.isj.org.uk/?id=686

—— 2012. *How Revolutionary Were the Bourgeois Revolutions?* Chicago: Haymarket Press.

Deeb, Marius. 1976. 'Bank Misr and the Emergence of the Local Bourgeoisie in Egypt'. *Middle Eastern Studies* 12(3): 69–86.

De Smet, Brecht. 2012. 'Egyptian Workers and "Their" Intellectuals: The Dialectical Pedagogy of the Mahalla Strike movement'. *Mind, Culture, and Activity* 19(2): 139–55.

—— 2014a. 'Revolution and Counter-Revolution in Egypt'. *Science & Society* 78(1): 11–40.

—— 2014b. 'Theory and Its Consequences: A Reply to Joel Beinin'. *Jadaliyya*. Available at www.jadaliyya.com/pages/index/18004/theory-and-its-consequences_a-reply-to-joel-beinin

—— 2014c. 'Once Again on Caesarism: Continuing the Debate with Joel Beinin'. *Jadaliyya*. Available at www.jadaliyya.com/pages/index/18719/once-again-on-caesarism_continuing-the-debate-with

—— 2014d. 'Tahrir: A Project(ion) of Revolutionary Change'. In Andy Blunden (ed.). *Collaborative Projects: An Interdisciplinary Study*, pp. 282–307. Leiden: Brill.

—— 2015. *A Dialectical Pedagogy of Revolt: Gramsci, Vygotsky, and the Egyptian Revolution*. Leiden: Brill.

De Smet, Brecht and Seppe Malfait. 2015. 'Trade Unions and Dictatorship in Egypt'. *Jadaliyya*. Available at www.jadaliyya.com/pages/index/22526/trade-unions-and-dictatorship-in-egypt

Dobb, Maurice. 1976. *Studies in the Development of Capitalism*. New York: International Publishers.

Draper, Hal. 1971. 'The Principle of Self-Emancipation in Marx and Engels'. *Socialist Register* 8:81–109.

—— 2011a [1977]. *Karl Marx's Theory of Revolution, i: State and Bureaucracy*. New York: Monthly Review Press; Delhi: Aakar Books.

—— 2011b [1972]. *Karl Marx's Theory of Revolution, ii: The Politics of Social Classes*. London: Monthly Review Press; Delhi: Aakar Books.

El-Nour, Saker. 2015. 'Small Farmers and the Revolution in Egypt: The Forgotten Actors'. *Contemporary Arab Affairs* 8(2): 198–211.

Elyachar, Julia. 2014. 'Upending Infrastructure: Tamarod, Resistance, and Agency after the January 25th Revolution in Egypt'. *History and Anthropology* 25(4): 452–71.

Engels, Friedrich. 1975a [1844] 'The Condition of England, i: The Eighteenth Century'. MECW 3: 469–88

—— 1975b [1844]. 'The Condition of England, ii: The English Constitution'. MECW 3: 489–513.

—— 1976 [1845]. 'The Festival of Nations in London'. MECW 6: 3–14.

—— 1985 [1867]. 'Review of Volume One of *Capital* for the Beobachter'. MECW 20: 224–27.

—— 1987 [1878]. 'Anti-Dühring (Herr Eugen Dühring's Revolution in Science)'. MECW 25: 1–310.

—— 1988 [1873]. 'The Republic in Spain'. MECW 23: 417–21.

—— 1989a [1878]. 'The Workingmen of Europe in 1877'. MECW 24: 207–30.

—— 1989b [1880]. 'Socialism: Utopian and Scientific'. MECW 24: 281–326.

—— 1989c [1883]. 'Refugee Literature, v: On Social Relations in Russia'. MECW 24: 39–50.

—— 1990a [1894]. 'Afterword [to "On Social Relations in Russia"]'. MECW 27: 421–33.

—— 1990b [1895]. 'Introduction [to Karl Marx's "The Class Struggles in France: 1848 to 1850"]'. MECW 27: 506–24.

Farag, Fatemah. 1999. 'Cleansing the Party'. *Al-Ahram Weekly* 440 (July–August). Available at http://weekly.ahram.org.eg/1999/440/eg10.htm

—— 2007. 'Chronicles of an Uprising'. *Al-Ahram Weekly* 828 (January). Available at http://weekly.ahram.org.eg/2007/828/special.htm

Farah, Nadia R. 1986. *Religious Strife in Egypt: Crisis and Ideological Conflict in the Seventies*. New York: Gordon & Breach Science Publishers.

—— 2009. *Egypt's Political Economy: Power Relations in Development*. Cairo: American University in Cairo Press.

Fontana, Benedetto. 2004. 'The Concept of Caesarism in Gramsci'. In P. Baehr and M. Richter (eds). *Dictatorship in History and Theory: Bonapartism, Caesarism, and Totalitarianism*, pp. 175–95. Cambridge: Cambridge University Press.

Foucault, Michel. 1980. *Power/Knowledge: Selected Interviews and Other Writings, 1972–1977*. Brighton: Harvester Press.

Gaddis, John L. 1997. *We Now Know: Rethinking Cold War History*. New York: Oxford University Press.

Gamal, Wael. 2012. 'The Brotherhood's One Percent'. *Jadaliyya*. Available at www.jadaliyya.com/pages/index/9765/brothers-and-officers_a-history-of-pacts

al-Ghobashy, Mona. 2005. 'The Metamorphosis of the Egyptian Muslim Brothers'. *International Journal of Middle East Studies* 37 (3): 373–95.

Gill, Stephen. 1988. *The Global Political Economy: Perspectives, Problems and Policies*. Baltimore, MD: Johns Hopkins University Press.

Ginsborg, Paul. 2014 [1979]. 'Gramsci and the Era of the Bourgeois Revolution in Italy'. In J.A. Davis (ed.). *Gramsci and Italy's Passive Revolution*, pp. 31–66. Abingdon and New York: Routledge.

Goldstone, Jack. 2001. 'Toward a Fourth Generation of Revolutionary Theory'. *Annual Review of Political Science* 4: 139–87.

Gramsci, Antonio. 1971. *Selections from the Prison Notebooks of Antonio Gramsci*, edited and translated by Quintin Hoare and Geoffrey Nowell-Smith. New York: International Publishers.

—— 2005 [1926]. *The Southern Question*. Toronto: University of Toronto Press.

—— 2011a. *Prison Notebooks*, vol.i. Edited with an Introduction by Joseph A. Buttigieg. New York: Columbia University Press.

—— 2011b. *Prison Notebooks*, vol.ii. Edited with an Introduction by Joseph A. Buttigieg. New York: Columbia University Press.

—— 2011c. *Prison Notebooks*, vol.iii. Edited with an Introduction by Joseph A. Buttigieg. New York: Columbia University Press.

Grant, Ted. 1989. *The Unbroken Thread: The Development of Trotskyism over 40 Years*. London: Fortress Books.

Gresh, Alain. 2013. 'Don't exclude the Muslim Brotherhood: Shadow of the army over Egypt's revolution'. *Le Monde Diplomatique* (English edition). 9 December 2014. Available at http://mondediplo.com/2012/ 08/02Egypt

Gribbon, Laura, and Sarah Hawas. 2012. 'Signs and Signifiers: Visual Translations of Revolt'. In Samia Mehrez (ed.). *Translating Egypt's Revolution: The Language of Tahrir*, pp. 103–42. Cairo: American University in Cairo Press.

Haddad, Bassam. 2011. 'English Translation of Interview with Hossam El-Hamalawy on the Role of Labor/Unions in the Egyptian Revolution'. *Jadaliyya*, 30 April. Available at www.jadaliyya.com/pages/index/1387/english-translation-of-interview-with-hossam-el-ha

Hajjar, Lisa. 2011. 'Omar Suleiman, the CIA's Man in Cairo and Egypt's Torturer-in-Chief'. *Jadaliyya*, 30 January. Available at www.jadaliyya.com/pages/index/503/omar-suleiman-the-cias-man-in-cairo-and-egypts-tor

Halpern, Manfred. 1963. *The Politics of Social Change in the Middle East and North Africa*. Princeton: Princeton University Press.

al-Hamalawy, Hossam. 2011. 'Jan 25: The workers, middle class, military junta and the permanent revolution'. *Arabawy*. 12 February. Available at www.arabawy.org/2011/02/12/permanent-revolution.

Hampton, Paul. 2009. 'Who Will Win Green Socialism: Workers, or a Vague Alliance?' *Workers Liberty*. Available at www.workersliberty.org/story/2009/09/09/who-will-win-green-socialism-workers-or-vague-alliance

Hanieh, Adam. 2013. *Lineages of Revolt: Issues of Contemporary Capitalism in the Middle East*. Chicago: Haymarket Books.

Harvey, David. 2004. 'The "New" Imperialism: Accumulation by Dispossession'. *Socialist Register* 40: 63–87.

Hashim, Ahmed. 2011. 'The Egyptian Military, Part Two: From Mubarak Onward'. *Middle East Policy* 18(4): 106–28.

Hassan, Bassem. 2011. 'Egypt: The Continuing Legacy of the Mubarak–Sadat Regime'. *Al Jazeera Centre for Studies*. www.aljazeera.net/mritems/streams/2011/6/8/1_1066868_1_51.pdf

Hegel, G.W.F. 1975 [1830]. *Hegel's Logic: Being Part One of the Encyclopaedia of the Philosophical Sciences*, translated by William Wallace. Oxford: Clarendon Press.

—— 2010 [1812]. *The Science of Logic*, translated and edited by George Di Giovanni. Cambridge: Cambridge University Press.

Hesketh, Chris. 2010. 'From Passive Revolution to Silent Revolution: Class Forces and the Production of State, Space and Scale in modern Mexico'. *Capital & Class* 43(3): 383–407.

Higgins, Jim. 1967. 'Luxemburg and Lenin'. *International Socialism* 27 (Winter). Available at https://www.marxists.org/archive/higgins/1966/xx/luxlen.htm

Hirschkind, Charles. 2011. 'The Road to Tahrir'. *Economic and Political Weekly* 46(7): 13–15.

Howeidy, Amira. 2005. 'A Chronology of Dissent'. *Al-Ahram Weekly* 748 (June). Available at http://weekly.ahram.org.eg/2005/748/eg10.htm

—— 2006. 'What's Left of the Left?' *Al-Ahram Weekly* 778 (January). Available at http://weekly.ahram.org.eg/2006/778/eg8.htm

Huntington, Samuel P. 2006. *Political Order in Changing Societies*. New Haven: Yale University Press.

Hurewitz, Jacob C. 1969. *Middle Eastern Politics: The Military Dimension*. New York: Praeger.

Ismael, Tareq Y., and Rifa'at al-Sa'id. 1990. *The Communist Movement in Egypt 1920–1988*. Syracuse: Syracuse University Press.

Jameson, Frederic. 2003. 'Future City'. *New Left Review* 21 (May–June): 65–79.

Jessop, Bob. 1990. *State Theory: Putting the Capitalist State in Its Place*. University Park, PA: Pennsylvania State University Press.

Joya, Angela. 2011. 'The Egyptian Revolution: Crisis of Neoliberalism and the Potential for Democratic Politics'. *Review of African Political Economy* 38(129): 367–86.

Johnson, Peter. 1973. 'Retreat of the Revolution in Egypt'. *Middle East Research and Information Project Reports* 17 (May): 3–6.

Kandil, Hazem. 2011. 'Hazem Kandil: Revolt in Egypt (interview)'. *New Left Review* 68 (March–April). Available at www.newleftreview.org/?view=2884

—— 2012. *Soldiers, Spies, and Statesmen: Egypt's Road to Revolt*. London and New York: Verso.

Kautsky, Karl. 1910 [1892]. *The Class Struggle (Erfurt Program)*. https://www.marxists.org/archive/kautsky/1892/erfurt/index.htm

Keddie, Nikki R. 1981. *Roots of Revolution: An Interpretive History of Modern Iran*. Binghamton, NY: Yale University Press.

Keraitim, Sahar, and Samia Mehrez. 2012. 'Mulid al-Tahrir: Semiotics of a Revolution'. In Samia Mehrez (ed.). *Translating Egypt's Revolution: The Language of Tahrir*, pp. 25–68. Cairo: American University in Cairo Press.

al-Khafaji, Isam. 2004. *Tormented Births: Passages to Modernity in Europe and the Middle East*. New York: IB Tauris.

Khalil, Ashraf. 2012. *Liberation Square: Inside the Egyptian Revolution and the Rebirth of a Nation*. New York: St. Martin's Press.

Kiely, Ray. 2005. *The Clash of Globalisations: Neo-Liberalism, the Third Way and Anti-Globalization*. Leiden: Brill.

Koptiuch, Kristin. 1996. 'Other Workers: A Critical Reading of Representations of Egyptian Petty Commodity Production at the Turn of the Twentieth Century'. In Zachary Lockman (ed.). *Workers and the Working Classes in the Middle East: Struggles, Histories, Historiographies*, pp. 41–70. Albany, NY: State University of New York Press.

Lachine, Nadim. 1977. 'Class Roots of the Sadat Regime: Reflections of an Egyptian Leftist'. *Middle East Research and Information Project* 56 (April): 3–7.

Le Blanc, Paul (ed.). 1996. *From Marx to Gramsci: A Reader in Revolutionary Marxist Politics*. New York: Humanity Books.

Lenin, Vladimir I.U. 1962 [1905]. 'Two Tactics of Social Democracy in the Democratic Revolution'. LCW 9: 15–140.

—— 1963a [1908]. 'The Assessment of the Present Situation'. *Proletary* 38. November 1(14). LCW 15: 267–80.

—— 1963b [1909]. 'How the Socialist-Revolutionaries Sum Up the Revolution and How the Revolution has Summed Them Up'. LCW 15: 330–44.

—— 1963c [1912]. 'Concerning the Workers' Deputies to the Duma and Their Declaration'. LCW 18: 420–3.

—— 1964a [1916]. 'Imperialism, the Highest Stage of Capitalism: A Popular Outline'. LCW 22: 185–304.

—— 1964b [1917]. 'Letters from Afar'. LCW 23: 295–342.

—— 1964c [1917]. 'The State and Revolution: The Marxist Theory of the State and the Tasks of the Proletariat in the Revolution'. LCW 25: 385–540.

Levant, Alex. 2012. 'Rethinking Spontaneity beyond Classical Marxism: Re-reading Luxemburg through Benjamin, Gramsci and Thompson'. *Critique* 40(3): 367–87.

Lia, Brynjar. 1998. *The Society of the Muslim Brothers in Egypt: The Rise of an Islamic Mass Movement 1928–1942*. Reading: Garnet.

Lipietz, Alain. 1982. 'Towards Global Fordism?' *New Left Review* 132 (March–April): 33–47.

Lockman, Zachary (ed.). 1994. *Workers and Working Classes in the Middle East: Struggles, Histories, Historiographies*. Albany, NY: State University of New York Press.

Losurdo, Domenico. 2015. *War and Revolution: Rethinking the Twentieth Century*. London and New York: Verso.

Löwy, Michael. 1981. *The Politics of Combined and Uneven Development: The Theory of Permanent Revolution*. London: New Left Books.

Luxemburg, Rosa. 1916. 'The Junius Pamphlet: The Crisis of German Social Democracy', translated by Dave Hollis. Available at https://www.marxists.org/archive/luxemburg/1915/junius/index.htm

—— 1970. *Rosa Luxemburg Speaks*, edited by Mary-Alice Waters. New York: Pathfinder Press.

Mackel, Austin. 2012. 'Weaving Revolution: Harassment by the Egyptian Regime'. *Interface: Journal for and about Social Movements* 4(1): 17–19.

Maher, Stephen. 2011. 'The Political Economy of the Egyptian Uprising'. *Monthly Review* 63(6). Available at http://monthlyreview.org/2011/11/01/the-political-economy-of-the-egyptian-uprising

Malfait, Seppe. 2015. 'An Islamist Caesar in Egypt's Passive Revolution? A Discourse Theoretical Analysis of Morsi's Hegemonic Project'. MA thesis, Ghent University. Available at http://lib.ugent.be/fulltxt/RUG01/002/060/112/RUG01-002060112_2013_0001_AC.pdf

Mandel, Ernest 1976. *Late Capitalism*. New York: Monthly Review Press.

Marfleet, Philip. 2011. 'Act One of the Egyptian Revolution'. *International Socialism* 130, 4 April. Available at www.isj.org.uk/index.php4?id=721

Marshall, Shana, and Joshua Stacher. 2012. 'Egypt's Generals and Transnational Capital'. *Middle East Report* 42(262): 12–18.

Marx, Karl. 1975a [1844]. 'Critical Marginal Notes on the Article: "The King of Prussia and Social Reform: By a Prussian"'. MECW 3: 189–207.

—— 1975b [1844]. 'Economic and Philosophic Manuscripts of 1844'. MECW 3: 229–347.

—— 1976 [1847]. 'The Poverty of Philosophy'. MECW 6: 105–212.

—— 1977 [1848]. 'The Bourgeoisie and the Counter-Revolution'. MECW 8: 154–78.

—— 1978 [1850]. 'The Class Struggles in France: 1848 to 1850'. MECW 10: 45–146.

—— 1979a [1852]. 'The Eighteenth Brumaire of Louis Bonaparte'. MECW 11: 99–197.

—— 1979b [1853]. 'The Future Results of British Rule in India'. MECW 12: 217–22.

—— 1981 [1860]. '[Garibaldi in Sicily:] Affairs in Prussia'. MECW 17: 381–5.

—— 1985a [1867]. 'Rules and Administrative Regulations of the International Working Men's Association'. MECW 20: 441–7.

—— 1985b [1869]. 'Preface [to the second edition of "The Eighteenth Brumaire of Louis Bonaparte"]'. MECW 21: 56–8.

—— 1986a [1857–58]. 'Economic Manuscripts'. MECW 28: 3–430.

—— 1986b [1858]. 'The Rule of the Pretorians'. MECW 15: 464–7.

—— 1986c [1871]. 'The Civil War in France: Address of the General Council of the International Working Men's Association'. MECW 22: 307–56.

—— 1987 [1859]. 'A Contribution to the Critique of Political Economy: Part One'. MECW 29: 257–418.

—— 1990 [1867]. *Capital*, vol.i. London: Penguin Books.

—— 1991 [1894]. *Capital*, vol.iii. London: Penguin Books.

—— 1992a. *Early Writings*. London: Penguin Books.

Marx, Karl, and Friedrich Engels. 1975a [1844–45] 'The Holy Family or Critique of Critical Criticism Against Bruno Bauer and Company'. MECW 4: 1–212.

—— 1975b [1845–46]. 'The German Ideology: Critique of Modern German Philosophy according to its Representatives Feuerbach, B. Bauer and Stirner, and of German Socialism according to its Various Prophets'. MECW 5: 19–538.

—— 1976 [1848]. 'Manifesto of the Communist Party'. MECW 6: 477–520.

—— 1989 [1879]. 'Circular Letter: August Bebel, Wilhelm Liebknecht, Wilhelm Bracke and Others'. MECW 24: 253–70.

McGreal, Chris. 2011. 'Egypt's army "involved in detentions and torture"'. *The Guardian*, February 15. Available at www.guardian.co.uk/world/2011/feb/09/egypt-army-detentions-torture-accused

Mitchell, Richard P. 1993. *The Society of the Muslim Brothers*. New York: Oxford University Press.

Mitchell, Timothy. 1999. 'No Factories, No Problems: The Logic of Neo-Liberalism in Egypt'. *Review of African Political Economy* 26(82): 455–68.

—— 2002. *Rule of Experts: Egypt, Techno-Politics, Modernity*. Berkeley: University of California Press.

Morton, Adam David. 2007. *Unravelling Gramsci: Hegemony and Passive Revolution in the Global Economy*. London: Pluto Press.

—— 2010. 'The Continuum of Passive Revolution'. *Capital & Class* 34(3): 315–42.

—— 2013. 'Traveling with Gramsci,' in Michael Ekers, Gillian Hart, Stefan Kipfer, and Alex Loftus (eds). *Gramsci: Space, Nature, Politics*, pp. 47–65. Chichester: Wiley-Blackwell.

Naguib, Sameh. 2009. 'The Muslim Brotherhood: Contradictions and Transformations'. *Cairo Papers in Social Science: Political and Social Protest in Egypt* 29(2–3): 155–74.

—— 2011. 'Egypt's Unfinished Revolution'. *International Socialist Review* 79 (September–October). Available at http://isreview.org/issues/79/feature-egyptianrevolution.shtml

—— 2014. 'From the End of One Revolutionary Wave to Preparing for Another'. openDemocracy [website]. Available at https://www.opendemocracy.net/

arab-awakening/sameh-naguib/from-end-of-one-revolutionary-wave-to-preparing-for-another

Negri, Antonio. 1982. 'Archaeology and Project: The Mass Worker and the Social Worker'. In *Revolution Retrieved: Writings on Marx, Keynes, Capitalist Crisis and New Social Subjects (1976–83)*, pp. 199–228. London: Red Notes.

Owen, Roger. 2005 [1972]. 'Egypt and Europe: From French Expedition to British Occupation'. In Albert H. Hourani, Philip S. Khoury, and Mary C. Wilson (eds). *The Modern Middle East: A Reader*, pp. 111–24. New York: I.B. Tauris.

Paciello, Maria C. 2013. 'Delivering the Revolution? Post-Uprising Socio-Economics in Tunisia and Egypt'. *International Spectator* 48(4): 7–29.

Pargeter, Alison. 2013. *The Muslim Brotherhood: From Opposition to Power.* London: Saqi Books.

Perlmutter, Amos. 1974. *Egypt: The Praetorian State.* New Brunswick, NJ: Transaction Books.

Picard, Elizabeth. 1990. 'Arab Military in Politics: From Revolutionary Plot to Authoritarian State'. In Giacomo Luciani (ed.). *The Arab State*, pp. 189–219. London: Routledge.

Pioppi, Daniela. 2013. 'Playing with Fire: The Muslim Brotherhood and the Egyptian Leviathan'. *International Spectator* 48(4): 51–68.

Posusney, Marsha P. 1996: 'Collective Action and Workers' Consciousness in Contemporary Egypt'. In Zachary Lockman (ed.). *Workers and Working Classes in the Middle East: Struggles, Histories, Historiographies*, pp. 211–46. Albany, NY: New York State University Press.

Poulantzas, Nicos. 1973. *Political Power and Social Classes*. London: New Left Books.

Rashed, Muhammad A. 2011. 'The Egyptian Revolution: A Participant's Account from Tahrir Square, January and February 2011'. *Anthropology Today* 27(2): 22–7.

Richards, Alan, and John Waterbury. 2008. *A Political Economy of the Middle East.* Boulder, CO: Westview Press.

Roccu, Roberto. 2012. 'Gramsci in Cairo: Neoliberal Authoritarianism, Passive Revolution and Failed Hegemony in Egypt under Mubarak, 1991–2010'. D.Phil. thesis submitted to the Department of International Relations of the London School of Economics.

Rosengarten, Frank. 2009. 'The Contemporary Relevance of Gramsci's Views on Italy's "Southern Question"'. In J. Francese (ed.). *Perspectives on Gramsci: Politics, Culture and Social Theory*, pp. 134–44. Abingdon and New York: Routledge.

Sallam, Hesham. 2011a. 'Reflections on Egypt after March 19', *Jadaliyya*, 31 May 31. Available at www.jadaliyya.com/pages/index/1728/reflections-on-egypt-after-march-19

—— 2011b. 'Striking Back at Egyptian Workers'. *Middle East Research and Information Project* 259. Available at www.merip.org/mer/mer259/striking-back-egyptian-workers

Sallam, Hesham, Joshua Stacher, and Chris Toensing. 2011. 'Into Egypt's Uncharted Territory'. *Jadaliyya*, 3 February. Available at www.jadaliyya.com/pages/index/523/into-egypts-uncharted-territory

Sassen, Saskia. 2011. 'The Global Street: Making the Political'. *Globalizations* 8(5): 573–9.

Sassoon, Anne S. 1987. *Gramsci's Politics*. Minneapolis: University of Minnesota Press.

Schatan, Jacobo (in collaboration with Gilda Schatan). 1987. *World Debt: Who Is to Pay?* London: Zed Books.

Schielke, Samuli. 2011. '"You'll Be Late for the Revolution!" An Anthropologist's Diary of the Egyptian Revolution'. *Jadaliyya*, 8 February. Available at www.jadaliyya.com/pages/index/580/youll-be-late-for-the-revolution-an-anthropologist

—— 2015. 'There Will Be Blood: Expecting Violence in Egypt, 2011–2013'. *Kings Review*, 3 February. Available at http://kingsreview.co.uk/magazine/blog/2015/02/03/there-will-be-blood-expecting-violence-in-egypt-2011–2013/

Schwedler, Jillian, and Janine A. Clark. 2006. 'Islamist–Leftist Cooperation in the Arab World'. *ISIM Review* 18: 10–11.

al-Shakry, Omnia. 2012. 'Egypt's Three Revolutions: The Force of History behind the Popular Uprising'. In Bassam Haddad, Rosie Bsheer, and Ziad Abu-Rish (eds). *The Dawn of the Arab Uprisings: End of an Old Order?* pp. 97–103. London: Pluto Press.

al-Sharif, Asma, and Yasmine Saleh. 2013. 'Special Report: The Real Force behind Egypt's 'Revolution of the State'. *Reuters*, 10 October. Available at www.reuters.com/article/2013/10/10/us-egypt-interior-specialreport-idUSBRE99908D20131010

Shenker, Jack 2011a. 'Egypt braced for "day of revolution" protests: Youth activists, Islamists, workers and football fans to hold rallies and marches against Mubarak government'. *The Guardian*, 24 January. Available at www.guardian.co.uk/world/2011/jan/24/egypt-day-revolution-protests

—— 2011b. 'Muhammad ElBaradei lands in Cairo: "There's no going back"'. *The Guardian*, January 27. Available at www.guardian.co.uk/world/2011/jan/27/elbaradei-return-cairo-egypt

Shokr, Ahmed. 2012. 'The Eighteen Days of Tahrir'. In Jeannie Sowers and Chris C. Toensing (eds). *The Journey to Tahrir: Revolution, Protest, and Social Change in Egypt*, pp. 41–6. New York: Verso.

Simon, Rick. 2010. 'Passive Revolution, Perestroika, and the Emergence of the New Russia'. *Capital & Class* 34(3): 429–48.

Skocpol, Theda. 1979. *States and Social Revolutions: A Comparative Analysis of France, Russia, and China*. Cambridge: Cambridge University Press.

Smith, Tony. 2000. *Technology and Capital in the Age of Lean Production: A Marxian Critique of the 'New Economy'*. Albany, NY: State University of New York Press.

Solidarity Center. 2010. *Justice for All: The Struggle for Worker Rights in Egypt*. Washington: Solidarity Center.

Sowers, Jeannie. 2012. 'Egypt in Transformation'. In Jeannie Sowers and Chris C. Toensing (eds). *The Journey to Tahrir: Revolution, Protest, and Social Change in Egypt*, pp. 1–20. London and New York: Verso.

Springborg, Robert, 2009. 'Protest against a Hybrid State: Words without Meaning?' *Cairo Papers in Social Science: Political and Social Protest in Egypt* 29(2–3): 6–18.

—— 2012. 'The View from the Officers' Club'. *Egypt Independent*. Available at www.egyptindependent.com/opinion/view-officers-club

Stacher, Joshua. 2011a. 'Egypt's Democratic Mirage'. *Foreign Affairs*, 7 February. Available at www.foreignaffairs.com/articles/67351/joshua-stacher/egypts-democratic-mirage?page=2

—— 2011b. 'Egypt without Mubarak'. *Middle East Report Online*, 7 April. Available at www.merip.org/mero/mero040711?utm_source=twitterfeedandutm_medium=twitter

Taha, Amira, and Christopher Combs. 2012. 'Of Drama and Performance: Transformative Discourses of the Revolution'. In Samia Mehrez (ed.). *Translating Egypt's Revolution: The Language of Tahrir*, pp. 69–102. Cairo: American University in Cairo Press.

Thatcher, Ian. D. 2007. 'Left-Communism: Rosa Luxemburg and Leon Trotsky Compared'. In Daryl Glaser and David M. Walker (eds). *Twentieth-Century Marxism: A Global Introduction*, pp. 30–45. Abingdon and New York: Routledge.

Teti, Andrea, and Gennaro Gervasio. 2012. 'After Mubarak, before Transition: The Challenges for Egypt's Democratic Opposition (interview and event analysis)'. *Interface: Journal for and about Social Movements* 4(1): 102–12.

Thomas, Peter. 2006. 'Modernity as "passive revolution": Gramsci and the Fundamental Concepts of Historical Materialism'. *Journal of the Canadian Historical Association / Revue de la Société historique du Canada* 17(2): 61–78.

—— 2009. *The Gramscian Moment*. Leiden: Brill.

—— 2015. 'Uneven Developments, Combined: The First World War and Marxist Theories of Revolutions'. In Alexander Anievas (ed.). *Cataclysm 1914: The First World War and the Making of Modern World Politics*, pp. 280–301. Leiden: Brill.

Townshend, Jules. 1996. *The Politics of Marxism: The Critical Debates*. London: Leicester University Press.

Trotsky, Leon. 1956 [1935]. 'The Workers' State, Thermidor and Bonapartism [The Soviet Union Today]'. *International Socialist Review* 17(3): 93–101, 105.

—— 1972 [1936]. *The Revolution Betrayed*. New York: Pathfinder Press.

—— 2001 [1930]. *History of the Russian Revolution*. New York: Pathfinder Press.

—— 2005 [1919]. *The Permanent Revolution and Results and Prospects*. New Delhi: Aakar Books. Available at www.marxists.org/archive/trotsky/1931/tpr/pr-index.htm

Tucker, Judith. 1978. 'While Sadat Shuffles: Economic Decay, Political Ferment in Egypt'. *Middle East Research and Information Project Reports* 65 (March): 3–9, 26.

—— 2005 [1979]. 'Decline of the Family Economy in Mid-Nineteenth-Century Egypt'. In Albert H. Hourani, Philip S. Khoury, and Mary C. Wilson (eds). *The Modern Middle East: A Reader*, pp. 229–54. New York: I.B. Tauris.

Van der Pijl, Kees. 1998. *Transnational Classes and International Relations*. London: Routledge.

van de Sande, Mathijs. 2013. 'The Prefigurative Politics of Tahrir Square – An Alternative Perspective on the 2011 Revolutions'. *Res Publica* 19(3): 223–39.

Vatikiotis, Panayiotis J. 1972. *Revolutions in the Middle East and Other Case Studies*. London: Allen & Unwin.

Versieren, Jelle, and Brecht De Smet. 2014. 'Urban Culture as Passive Revolution: A Gramscian Sketch of the Uneven and Combined Transitional Development of Rural and Urban Modern Culture in Europe and Egypt'. In B. Fraser (ed.). *Marxism and Urban Culture*, pp. 191–212. Lanham, MD: Lexington Books.

Versieren, Jelle, and Brecht De Smet. 2015. 'The Passive Revolution of Spiritual Politics: Gramsci and Foucault on Modernity, Transition and Religion'. In D. Kreps (ed.). *Gramsci and Foucault: A Reassessment*, pp. 111–30. Farnham: Ashgate Publishing.

al-Werdani, Mahmoud. 2011. 'The Ultras and the Egyptian Revolution'. *Jadaliyya*, 25 December. Available at www.jadaliyya.com/pages/index/3759/the-ultras-and-the-egyptian-revolution.

Wickham, Carrie R. 2013. *The Muslim Brotherhood: Evolution of an Islamist Movement*. Princeton: Princeton University Press.

Williams, Raymond. 1991. 'Base and Superstructure in Marxist Cultural Theory'. In C. Mukerji and M. Schudson (eds). *Rethinking Popular Culture: Contemporary Perspectives in Cultural Studies*, pp. 407–23. Berkeley, Los Angeles and London: University of California Press.

Wood, Ellen Meiksins. 1991. *The Pristine Culture of Capitalism: A Historical Essay on Old Regimes and Modern States*. London: Verso.

—— 2007. 'A Reply to Critics'. *Historical Materialism* 15: 143–70.

—— 2012. *The Ellen Meiksins Wood Reader*, edited by Larry Patriquin. Leiden: Brill.

Zeilig, Leo. 2010. 'Tony Cliff: Deflected Permanent Revolution in Africa'. *International Socialism* 126. Available at www.isj.org.uk/?id=641

Zemni, Sami, Brecht De Smet, and Koen Bogaert. 2013. 'Luxemburg on Tahrir Square: Reading the Arab Revolutions with Rosa Luxemburg's "The Mass Strike"'. *Antipode* 45(4): 888–907.

Žižek, Slavoj. 1999. 'Human Rights and Its Discontents'. 16 November, Bard College. Available at www.egs.edu/faculty/slavoj-zizek/articles/human-rights-and-its-discontents/

Index